Sgyrsiau Noson Dda
DYFED EVANS

Sgyrsiau Noson Dda

Dyfed Evans

Cyflwyno'r Gŵr Gwadd

Gol. Gwenno Elin Griffith

Argraffiad cyntaf: 2013

ⓗ Dyfed Evans/Gwasg Carreg Gwalch

Rhif rhyngwladol: 978-1-84527-428-3

Mae'r cyhoeddwr yn cydnabod cefnogaeth ariannol
Cyngor Llyfrau Cymru

Cynllun clawr: Olwen Fowler

Cyhoeddwyd gan Wasg Carreg Gwalch,
12 Iard yr Orsaf, Llanrwst, Conwy, LL26 0EH.
Ffôn: 01492 642031 Ffacs: 01492 641502
e-bost: llyfrau@carreg-gwalch.com
lle ar y we: www.carreg-gwalch.com

Cyflwynedig .

i Doris

Cynnwys

Cyflwyno'r Gŵr Gwadd

Yn ôl Dyfed Evans, neu Os, i'w ffrindiau bore oes, 'ma' pob dim ym Mynytho,' ac yno, yn ei nefoedd y cafodd ei eni a'i fagu. Lle 'diddorol anghyffredin' ydyw yn ôl ei hen ffrind, y Parch. Emlyn Richards: 'Toedd 'na ddim tafarn na chapel Methodist yno, ac yr oedd hynny'n gaffaeliad mawr. O ganlyniad roeddynt yn methu â chrwydro ac ni ddaeth piwritaniaeth gul y Methodist i'w cystwyo nhw i'w rhych, ac felly, yr oeddynt yn bobl wreiddiol iawn.' Yn sicr, mae iddo rhyw falchder o fod yn 'un o'r hen betha' Mynytho 'na,' ac fel y dywed Emlyn Richards: 'pobl ddigon busneslyd, yn wir, yn arbenigwyr ar fusnesu oeddynt, ac roedd Dyfed wedi'i fagu ynghanol y rhain.' Pa ryfedd felly, rhwng y gwreiddioldeb a'r busnesu, i Dyfed Evans ddod yn newyddiadurwr a 'chymeriad amlwg, ryfeddol' yn ei gymdeithas?

Bu'n rhaid iddo ymuno â'r Llynges yn ystod y rhyfel, ac ar ôl dychwelyd aeth i Goleg Harlech i wneud cwrs Cymraeg a chael swydd gyda'r *Cymro* ar 13 Ebrill, 1949. Fe gafodd gar ar ôl ymuno â'r *Cymro* fel yr eglura Laura Goodman, gweddw un o'i ffrindiau pennaf, Dic Goodman: 'Fe grwydrodd Gymru benbaladr ar ôl gwahanol straeon ac yn cyfweld â gwahanol bobl,' a chrwydro a wnaeth byth ers hynny. Aeth mor bell â Phatagonia, yn rhan o daith *Cwmni Drama Llwyndyrys*. Nid cariwr clecs mohono chwaith, 'Dydi o byth yn cario straeon ac eto mae o isio'r straeon i gyd!' meddai Wil Lodge am y 'dyn drws nesa 'cw'.

Ymhyfryda mewn straeon nodwedd ac 'roedd ei ffeithiau fo bob amser yn gywir, yn drylwyr, ac roedd o'n gydwybodol iawn – dim byd ffwrdd-a-hi,' yn ôl newyddiadurwr arall *Y Cymro*, Ioan Roberts. Dywed: 'Yr hyn mae pobl yn ei gofio amdano fo ydi fod 'na gymaint o raen ar bob dim o'dd o'n 'neud, ar ei 'sgrifen o... dwi'm yn meddwl ei fod o erioed wedi teipio, ond doedd dim gwahaniaeth.

9

Roedd pob dim mor ddealladwy, ac yn sicr mae'i iaith o'n berffaith!'

Ar y 27 Mawrth, 1953 fe briododd â Doris, merch Hafod Lon, Y Ffôr a thros amser cawsant dri o feibion, tri o wyrion, dwy wyres a dau orwyr.

Gadawodd *Y Cymro* yn 1968 pan sylweddolodd ei fod yn ysgrifennu'r un stori am y trydydd tro, a'r ffaith fod swyddfa'r *Cymro* wedi symud o Gaernarfon i Fangor. Aeth ymlaen i wneud cwrs athro yn y Coleg Normal a chafodd swydd athro ym Mhenygroes, ac yna ym Mhwllheli lle bu hyd ei ymddeoliad.

Bu'n Drefnydd y Wasg yn yr Eisteddfod Genedlaethol am flynyddoedd hyd ei ymddeoliad yn 2006 yn Eisteddfod Abertawe, ac un cymwynasgar iawn oedd o. Meddai y ddiweddar Hafina Clwyd yn ei dyddiadur eisteddfodol yn *Y Wawr* y flwyddyn honno: 'Cyfarfod amser cinio i ddiolch i Dyfed Evans am ei wasanaeth dros ugain mlynedd fel Swyddog y Wasg. Mae hwn yn fonheddwr arbennig iawn a deuthum ar ei draws gyntaf pan oedd yn gweithio i'r *Cymro* erstalwm. Nid oedd ball ar ei gymorth a'i hynawsedd ac fe fydd hi'n chwith iawn hebddo fo.'

'Dwi'n meddwl ei fod o'n arwyddocaol iawn, ar ôl iddo 'neud ei bŵl fel athro, ac ymddeol, ei fod o'n dal hyd heddiw yn g'neud pethau i'r *Ffynnon*. Mae'n amlwg fod newyddiaduraeth yn ei waed o go iawn,' meddai Ioan Roberts. Nid newyddiadura'n unig a wna fel y

Ar gefn ei geffyl ym Mhatagonia

pwysleisia Wil Lodge: 'Mae o'n gweithio yn ddi-ddiwadd. Os nad ydy o ar *Y Ffynnon* mae o ar rwbath arall – adolygu neu rwbath. Ac os nad 'di hynny – trwy'r ha' mae o'n chwynnu, yn garddio, yn peintio.

"Wil ydi'r ystol yn ei lle?"

"Yndi."

"O, ga'i fynd i'w nôl hi?"

"Ddo'i fyny hefo chi rŵan."

Ac i fyny i Gae Newydd i'w nôl hi. Peintio'r hen landeri 'na, golchi'r ffenestri... Arglwydd, mae o'n 87!!'

Mae'i ffyddlondeb a'i ddeddfgarwch i'w weld hyd yn oed yn ei arddio fo! Sicrha fod ganddo hyn a hyn o datws ymhob rhes bob blwyddyn, a gwna'n siŵr fod

11

ganddo fo ddigon o gennin ar gyfer swpar y gymdeithas ar ŵyl Dewi. Fe wna bopeth o fewn y gymdeithas honno – o actio, i olygu, i arwain Eisteddfod y Groglith a oedd 'yn hwyl ynddo'i hun, yn deud rhai da am bobl, yn pryfocio, ond fydda fo byth yn troseddu wrth ddeud,' eglura Gwilym Plas. 'Mae o'n ganwr tenor da hefyd os geith o rywun wrth ei ochr o!'

Fe ŵyr pawb am ei sgyrsiau bywiog, gwybodus am Bob Owen Croesor, am Fynytho, ac am Lŷn a llawer, llawer mwy. Cofia Gwilym Plas un trip yn arbennig, arafodd y bws o flaen ei gartref ym Mhencaenewydd a phwyntiodd at y tŷ a chyhoeddi: 'Dyna chi, fyny fanna ma' Doris yn byw!'

Ond yn ôl Wil Lodge: 'Dydi o ddim yn godwr bora, ar wahân i pan mae o'n chwara golff. Os ydi hi'n fora dydd Iau mae o fel ceiliog! Ond boreua erill, *lie-in* ydi hi.'

Ac felly, dim ond yn y prynhawniau y gwelwch chi o, ar gefn ei feic yn yr haf, yn danfon tudalennau'r *Ffynnon* i'r Ffôr yn barod i'w teipio!

'Gŵr tawel, gwybodus, di-ymhongar, cymwynaswr bro, ac ardal' ydyw, meddai Laura Goodman. Ni ellir methu'r wên lydan honno sy'n eich croesawu bob tro, a'i fawredd yw fod ei ddiddordebau yr un mor eang, fel y dywed Wil Lodge: 'Mae ganddo fo ddiddordab ymhob dim, ac yn bawb – ffwtbol, rygbi, golff, a'r wybodaeth sydd ganddo fo ac yn cofio bob peth – gofyn am bennill ac mae o'n gwbod yn union lle i'w gael o.'

Yng ngeiriau Rhian Lodge: 'sbesh o ddyn!'

1. Atgofion am Fynytho

'Gan imi fod yn ohebydd i'r *Cymro* am bron ugain mlynedd ac yn ohebydd i'r *Ffynnon*, ein papur bro yn Eifionydd, am 36 mlynedd arall – hyd yma – bu geiriau a straeon o gryn ddiddordeb i mi o safbwynt bywoliaeth a difyrrwch. Ond roedd gennyf beth diddordeb cyn hynny hefyd.

Pobl ddyfeisgar iawn oedd ein hynafiaid mae'n rhaid. Y tebygrwydd yw mai geiriau am rannau o'r corff a ddaeth yn gyntaf i'w rhan, ond meddyliwch mor ddeheuig y buont wedyn i'w mabwysiadu i roi enwau ar rannau o'r tirwedd a phethau o'u cwmpas. Mae gan bob mynydd ei ben, ei ysgwydd, ei gesail, ei fol a'i draed. Ceg sydd i'r afon, llygad i'r ffynnon ac ael i'r bryn. Os edrychwch ar fap fe welwch Drwyn Cilan a Braich y Pwll. Dan y ddaear wedyn, ceir gwythïen o lo neu aur.

Beth ddywedwch chwi am ddarn o oren – yr hyn a elwir yn Saesneg yn *segment*? Cwch efallai, neu botel neu fochyn. I mi rhan eto o'r corff, sef ewin. Y mae peth mwdredd o bethau cyfarwydd yn dwyn enwau corfforol – ffroen gwn, talcen tŷ, coes brws, troed rhaw, tafod esgid, dwrn drws, gwadn aradr, bys cloc, clust jwg, gwddw potel, perfedd wats, dannedd cribin, cefn nionod a thin clawdd. Hwyrach y medrwch chi feddwl am ychwaneg.

Gair na chlywais mohono er pan oeddwn yn ifanc iawn yw *meilwng*. Gyda fy nain y magwyd fi, a hi yw'r unig un a glywais yn ei ddefnyddio yn ei gyswllt naturiol. 'Sgidiau hoelion, cefn uchel a wisgem ni'n blant, a phan oeddent yn newydd, doedden nhw ddim yn esmwyth iawn, yn tueddu i grafu'r croen uwchben y sawdl. Un ffordd o liniaru'r boen oedd torri rhiciau yn nghefn yr esgid fel bod y lledr caled yn plygu. Cyngor arall gan Nain oedd: 'Paid â'i chau yn rhy dynn ar dy feilwng'. A'r meilwng, meddai'r geiriadur yw 'y rhan fain o'r goes rhwng y ffêr a chroth y goes.'

'Bachgen bach o Lŷn wyf fi,' a diddorol iawn yw fel y mae pobl sy'n byw mewn gwahanol ardaloedd wedi cael enwau torfol. Pam tybed mai moch sy'n sir Fôn, cŵn yn Ninbych, a chathod yn Rhuthun? Un o'r 'lloiau' wyf fi er imi fyw yn Eifionydd yn nes at stondars Llanystumdwy ers blynyddoedd meithion. Ond yn ogystal â bod yn llo rwyf hefyd yn un o filgwn Mynytho yn ôl y llyfr

Llysenwau a olygwyd gan Myrddin ap Dafydd. Mae'n rhaid mai ar ôl i mi ymfudo oddi yno y mabwysiadwyd yr enw oherwydd ni chlywswn mohono cynt. Ond mae gen i syniad o ble y tarddodd.

Yn ei gyfrol *Crwydro Llŷn ac Eifionydd* y mae Gruffudd Parry yn manylu am y mathau o gŵn a welid yn Llanbedrog, ac yna, wedi dringo allt Cerrig Bychain i Fynytho, fe ddywed: 'Ni fu gan ardal Mynytho erioed y fath amrywiaeth o gŵn ag sydd yn Llanbedrog ond bu ganddi gymaint nifer o filgwn ag unrhyw ardal arall pan oedd cwningod yn bla yn Llŷn.'

Ond ai milgwn fyddai lluosog milgi i ni, ynteu milgwns fel y clywais gan un o drigolion Caernarfon? Roeddwn yn gweithio ar *Y Cymro* pan ddaeth *Chwedlau Pendeits*, cyfrol William Owen, Southport o'r wasg yn 1961. Mae'r gyfrol yn cynnwys rhai o eiriau ac ymadroddion unigryw y Cofis – fel 'swallow' am dynnu mwg sigaret, 'jinipedars' am Gennin Pedr a 'strew' am aderyn to. I gael stori, penderfynias fynd oddi amgylch un o'r ystadau tai i holi a fyddai'r deiliaid yn defnyddio'r geiriau hyn.

Yn y tŷ cyntaf bûm yn aflwyddiannus. Er curo a churo ni ddaeth neb i'r drws, er y buaswn yn taeru'r du yn wyn imi weld y llenni yn ysgwyd. 'Waeth ichi heb na churo yn fan'na heddiw,' meddai rhyw ddyn a âi heibio. 'Mae'n ddydd Llun. Diwrnod rhent.' Felly dyma drio'r drws nesa.' Eglurai William Owen mai 'ar lab' a ddywedai'r Cofis am brynu rhywbeth ar goel. Gofynnais innau: 'Fyddwch chi'n deud *ar lab*?' a daeth yr ateb yn gryno a swta iawn: 'Ches i ddim byd 'rioed ar lab, yli co.' I wraig arall mentrais ofyn: 'Fyddwch chi'n deud *'mwnciciat*?' Ac meddai hithau: 'A be' sy rong yn hynny, mab?'

Doeddwn i fawr nes i'r lan a dweud y gwir nes daeth dyn bychan bach i lawr y stryd yn tywys dau filgi mawr, un ymhob llaw. Honnai William Owen y defnyddid *cŵns* am ragor nag un ci. Gofynnais innau yn ddigon diniwed: 'Fyddwch chi'n deud cŵns?' Edrychodd y dyn bach yn gegrwth arnaf, ac meddai toc: 'Milgwns, ia. Cŵns, nefar.' A diflannodd rownd y tro heb yngan un gair yn ychwaneg.

Efallai y dylwn sôn yn fan hyn fod gennym ninnau ein lebal hefyd oni fodolai Milgwn Mynytho cyn cyhoeddi *Crwydro Llŷn ac Eifionydd* yn 1960. Megis y mae pobl Uwchaled yn cyfeirio at 'Rhywun o Bentrefoelas' a 'Rwbath o Ysbyty Ifan', bu graddio yn Llŷn hefyd: 'Byddigions Abersoch', 'pobl Llanbedrog' a 'hen betha Mynytho 'na'.

Un o Nebo oedd fy nain. Roedd hi'n dechrau gweini yn naw oed ar fferm Chatham, Llanwnda a thrwy i fy nhaid fynd yno'n was, maes o law, y cyfarfu'r ddau. Roedd nain yn hoff iawn o adrodd penillion ac un a ddaethai efo hi o du hwnt i'r Eifl oedd tua'r cyntaf i mi i'w ddysgu:

Siôn Huw Elis a aeth ar ei hynt,
Yn ymyl bwlch 'Stumllech fe welodd y gwynt,
Siôn Huw Elis a deimlodd yn ffôl,
A Siôn Huw Elis a drodd yn ei ôl.

Yn yr oes ddi-deledu – a di-radio hefyd yn tŷ ni – yr oedd llawer o'n difyrrwch yn ymwneud â geiriau; megis adrodd llyfrithen, llyfrithen saith gwaith ar un gwynt a cheisio ymestyn y gamp o saith i ddeg neu ddwsin a mwy. Dyfalu wedyn ym mha dŷ to sglaets y trigai Wil y gŵr, a Catrin y wraig a John y mab a cheisio ateb cwetiynau heb ddweud *ie* a *nage* wrth smalio mynd ar daith i'r dre'. Ffefrynnau i'w darllen, a'u dysgu hefyd, oedd cerddi fel 'Dowch i America', 'Sesiwn yng Nghymru' a 'Gelert Ci Llywelyn'. Pan oeddwn yn wyth oed cefais *Lyfr Mawr y Plant* yn anrheg Nadolig. Nid canmol yr ydwyf ond dwedyd y gwir, chwedl yr hen bennill, pan ddywedaf y medrwn ar un adeg adrodd pob un o'r cerddi sydd ynddo a chlytiau helaeth o'r straeon hefyd. Dadleua rhai pobl mai cyhoeddi *Beibl Bach*, 1630 neu *Cannwyll y Cymru* fu'r chwyldro mwyaf yn hanes darllen Cymraeg. Yn yr ugeinfed ganrif â'r anrhydedd, ddalia i, i *Lyfr Mawr y Plant*. Mae'r hen drysor gennyf yn ddiogel iawn o hyd.

Yr oedd yna hefyd benillion mwy lleol am bobl yr ardal. Y Parch J. Hawen Rees – ein gweinidog – yn un.

Roedd rhywun wedi llunio pennill amdano ef a'r teulu:

Mae twll bach bach yng nghrys
Y Parchedig Hawen Rees,
Mrs Rees yn mynd o'i cho',
Ac Alaw Non yn ei drwsio fo.

Un o waelod Sir Aberteifi oedd ef yn enedigol, bardd
da a ffrind bore oes i feibion hynaf y Cilie. Ac Alaw Non
y ferch oedd yr un y datguddiwyd ymhen blynyddoedd
ei bod yn ysbïwraig yn cadw llygad ar y datblygiadau ym
Mhenyberth cyn y paratoadau i roi'r gwersyll ar dân.

Gydag odl, neu weithiau led-odl, roedd y pethau hyn
yn apelio ac yn hawdd i'w cofio. Manteisiodd Robert
Roberts Caergybi ar hynny wrth broffwydo'r tywydd yn
ei almanaciau: 'Gwynt a glaw/ Yma a thraw: Twrf
taranau/ Mewn rhai mannau.' Hawdd i'w cofio debyg
iawn ond, pwysicach fyth, fe fyddai'r broffwydoliaeth
yn siŵr o fod yn gywir – yn rhywle. Oni cheid glaw ym
Mhenrhyn Llŷn fyddai neb ddim callach nad oedd hi'n
tresio bwrw ym Mhenrhyn Gŵyr.

Gyda chymorth yr odl y mae rhywun yn cofio'r
pethau rhyfeddaf a mwyaf dibwys o ddyddiau ieuenctid.
Mewn cystadleuaeth llinell goll yng nghapel Carmel, y
Wesleaid, rhyw flwyddyn fel hyn y terfynai un pennill:

Beth a welais ar gae Crugan?
Daniel Ellis ar ôl hogan.

Oni bai am yr odl byddai wedi hen fynd i ebargofiant, wrth gwrs. Y Daniel Ellis hwnnw, gyda llaw, oedd y gŵr y daethpwyd i'w adnabod wedyn fel Dan Dean. Dyna ei enw barddol ran hwyl, a byddai'n 'sgwennu'n aml i'r *Herald* i ateb rhai o gerddi Wil Parsal ac Annie Rhydau. Roedd Dan yn llawiach garw efo Dic Goodman ac mae stori am y ddau ar y stryd ym Mhwllheli un tro pan ddaeth cydnabod i Dic heibio:

'Dach chi'n nabod Dan, mae'n siŵr,' meddai Dic.

'Hwn ydi Dan Dean.'

'Na, wir, 'dwaenwn i mono fo,' atebodd y dyn. 'Ond dwi'n gybyddus iawn â'i fab o – Twll.'

Mae stori fel yna yn dueddol o hel traed. Unwaith y daw o'r cwd, mae'n cerdded wedyn o le i le a'i thadogi i wahanol bobl. Ysgrifennodd rhyw Americanwr lyfr am y ffenomena. Ei deitl yw *The Vanishing Hitchiker* ac mae ynddo un stori o Gymru. Edrydd hanes gŵr a gwraig ifanc o Fedlinog yn darganfod fod eu car wedi'i ladrata. Ar y ffordd i hysbysu'r heddlu, fodd bynnag, fe'i gwelsant ar ochr y stryd ac ynddo nodyn yn egluro fel y trawyd rhywun yn wael ac iddynt fenthyca'r car i ddwyn y claf i ysbyty. Tu mewn hefyd yr oedd dau docyn i fynd i theatr yn y dre ac ynghlwm wrth hynny, fwrdd i ddau wedi ei neilltuo mewn bwyty crand. Dyna'r ad-daliad am beri'r boen a'r drafferth. Mwynhaodd y pâr ieuanc eu noson yn fawr, ond pan ddychwelasant adref cafwyd fod rhywun wedi torri i mewn i'r tŷ a lladrata oddi yno bron bopeth o bwys. Digwyddodd hynny ym Medlinog, ond o fewn dim yr oedd yr un stori, air am air, am barau ieuanc yn Ystrad Mynach, Tonyrefail a Phenrhiwceiber.

Digwyddodd yr un peth yn hanes William Roberts, Pencarth yn Eifionydd. Aethai ef at y Parch. L. G. Roberts, gweinidog yr Annibynwyr yn Chwilog gyda chais iddo ei gladdu. 'Pan fydda i farw,' medda fo, 'dwi isio fy llosgi. Wedyn ewch â'r llwch i le'r incwm tacs ym Mhorthmadog ac mi fyddan nhw wedi cael y blydi lot wedyn.' Clywais y stori yna ddwywaith ar y radio – unwaith am ddyn o Lannerch-y-medd, a thro arall am rywun o sir Ddinbych.

Ond sôn am odli yr oeddwn i cyn dechrau mynd i grwydro. Gyda chymorth mesur ac odl y trosglwyddwyd cynghorion yr hen benillion o genhedlaeth i genhedlaeth:

Dwedai hen ŵr llwyd o gornel,
'Gan fy nhad mi glywais chwedel,
A chan ei daid y clywsai yntau
Ac ar ei ôl mi gofiais innau.'

Yn y canu caeth y mae'r gynghanedd hefyd yn gymorth i gofio. Yn ddeg oed, roeddwn i yng nghyfarfod agoriadol neuadd Mynytho yn 1935 pan adroddodd R. Williams Parry ei englyn o'r llwyfan. Buan iawn y dysgasom hwnnw, ond yr oedd o leiaf ddau englyn yn gybyddus inni cynt. Roedd un i'r Foel Gron y safai'r ysgol yn ei chysgod:

Arsyllfa haf braf ein bro – ydyw hon
　Od o hardd a chryno:
　Gwellt a grug yw gwallt y gro
　Ym mhen eithaf Mynytho.

William Williams, Pandy oedd awdur hwnna, ond hyd y gwn does neb a ŵyr pwy a luniodd y llall. Pan aem i'r siop i 'mofyn chwarter o de byddai John Morris y Post yn ei godi'n rhydd o gist fawr gron, ei dywallt ar ddarn o bapur petryal, ei lapio a'i glymu'n dwt â darn o linyn. Ar du allan y papur roedd llun bwch gafr yn sefyll yn dalsyth ar graig ac o dan y llun, yr englyn hwn:

O! londer hen ddail India – bâr asbri
　I ysbryd y gwanna',
　A gwaeddwn oll fel gwydda'
　Hwre! Wel, dyma de da.

Dyna'r englyn cyntaf i mi ei ddysgu – a hynny wrth gerdded adref o'r siop ac heb wybod hefyd mai englyn ydoedd. Ymhen blynyddoedd fe ddangoswyd imi fod fy enw fy hun yn cynganeddu. Wnaeth hynny mohonof yn fardd, ysywaeth, ond deuthum i werthfawrogi peth ar gamp pobl eraill. Mae enw Johann Sabastian Bach hefyd yn cynganeddu ac mor gelfydd y defnyddiwyd ef gan T. Llew Jones wrth lunio englyn i'r Deryn Du:

Ba artist â chân bertach? – hwyr denor
    Du ei ŵn fel mynach:
  Dyma gerddor rhagorach
  Na Johann Sebastian Bach.

Doedd dim llawer o lyfrau yn tŷ ni ond roeddwn i wedi clywed am rai pwysig iawn yn bur fychan, sef *Llyfr Du Caerfyrddin, Llyfr Coch Hergest* a *Llyfr Gwyn Rhydderch*. I egluro sut y clywswn amdanynt mae'n rhaid imi fynd yn ôl eto at Nain. Ar ddyddiau Llun byddai hi yn mynd i Dremfan yn Llanbedrog i olchi. Gŵr y tŷ oedd yr ysgolhaig Dr John Gwenogfryn Evans. Fel y mae'i enw'n awgrymu, fe hanai o Lanwenog yn sir Aberteifi. Bu'n weinidog gyda'r Undodiaid ond fe gollodd ei lais o ganlyniad i'r teiffoid. Aeth wedyn i Rydychen ac ymddiddori yn yr hen lawysgrifau Cymraeg dan ddylanwad Syr John Rhys. Fel roedd ei iechyd yn dirywio, fe'i cynghorwyd i gartrefu yn rhywle lle roedd yr hin yn dyner. Felly y daeth i Lŷn a chodi tŷ newydd yn Llanbedrog. Sefydlodd yno wasg law fechan i argraffu'r hen destunau ac felly y gwelodd fy nain hwy.

Roedd Gwenogfryn yn ŵr boneddigaidd a chlên, meddai Nain, ac o glywed hynny fe ddeuthum i yn bur hoff ohono rhywsut. Fe'i claddwyd mewn craig mewn cae gerllaw Tremfan ac ar y bedd gosodwyd carreg yn pwyso dwy dunnell o draeth Llanbedrog – carreg a brynasai ymlaen llaw gan Solomon Andrews, y gŵr busnes o Gaerdydd, am swllt. Pan euthum i gario allan mewn siop yn Llanbedrog ar ôl gadael yr ysgol, byddwn yn rhyw led-gyfarch y Doctor bob dydd wrth fynd i lawr y lôn heibio i'w fedd.

Mae'n rhyfeddol fel y gall un gair, o'i ddefnyddio mewn cyswllt annisgwyl, wneud stori'n gofiadwy. Ar derfyn y rhyfel daeth nifer o academyddion i Lŷn i wneud arolwg cyffredinol ar y penrhyn dan gyfarwyddyd Peter Scott, gŵr a gyflawnodd lawer i gynorthwyo'r diwaith ym Mryn-mawr yn Ne Cymru. Cafodd ychydig ohonom ninnau, bobl leol, waith i fynd o gwmpas yn casglu gwybodaeth i'r arbenigwyr. Dewis rhyw unigolyn ym mhob ardal a chael manylion ganddo/ganddi am bob tŷ. Doedd dim eisiau enwau'r trigolion nac unrhyw sylwadau, dim ond ystadegau moel. A oedd yno ŵr, gwraig, plant? Pa ricyn oed? Eu gwaith, iaith, enwad? A oedd radio? Pa bapurau a ddarllenid? A manylion tebyg.

Morris Roberts, a adwaenai ei ardal fel cefn ei law, oedd un o'r rhai yr euthum ato i'w holi: 'Oes yno ŵr, Morris Roberts?'

'Gŵr ddeudist ti? Wnaeth o ddim cnoc erioed.

Dyna iti'r creadur dioca' yn y plwy 'ma.'

Doedd arnaf ddim eisiau gwybod dim o'r fath, wrth

gwrs, ond felly yr aeth hi.

'Oes yno wraig, Morris Roberts?'

'Gwraig ddeudist ti? Oes, a hen slebog fudur ydi hi hefyd.'

'Oes yna blant?'

'Plant? Mae yno blant y greadigaeth. Isio coltario eu hen betha nhw sydd.'

Mae enghraifft arall o'r gair annisgwyl mewn stori o Langian, lle roedd William Owen wedi bod yn glochydd ers blynyddoedd. Doedd y person, a gyfenwid Tobi oherwydd ei goler, ddim yn enwog iawn am ei brydlondeb. Roedd o'n ddiarhebol o hirymarhous a dweud y gwir. A dyna lle roedd William Owen wedi bod yn canu'r gloch ers meityn iawn a dim hanes o'r person yn unman. Yn wir, roedd y clochydd wedi hen ddiffygio ac wedi rhoi'r rhaff dros ei ysgwydd a gwyro i fyny ac i lawr i arbed tipyn ar ei freichiau. Ac meddai Lewis Jones, un o'i gymdogion a gerddai ar hyd y pentref â'i ddwy law ar ei din: 'Os na ddaw Tobi yn o handi, mi fydd Wil Ŵan wedi tynnu'r blydi Synagog ar ei gefn.'

Straeon a berodd dipyn o benbleth i mi fu rhai am ysbrydion. Cawswn fy magu yn sŵn sibrydion am fwgan Pant-y-Wennol. Nid rhyw gysgod tocyn eithin neu rhywun efo cynfas wen dros ei ben mo hwn, ond bwgan go iawn yn cyflawni gorchestion syfrdanol. Hogan ifanc bedair ar ddeg oed, wedi ei geni ar 21 Medi, 1851 oedd Elin Evans, pan gyhuddwyd hi o godi bwganod. Fe'i herlidwyd i garchar gan yr awdurdodau ac fe'i hysgymunwyd gan gymdeithas. Bu farw ar 12 Ebrill, 1919 – chwe blynedd cyn fy ngeni i – ond gellwch fentro fod y straeon amdani yn parhau. Adroddai Nain rai ohonynt. Un tro, meddid, yr oedd cynhebrwng ym Mhant-y-Wennol ar ddiwrnod crasboeth yng Ngorffennaf. Tŷ bychan ydoedd, llawr, siambr a thaflod, ac o ddiffyg lle yn y tŷ safai'r bobl ar lechwedd gerllaw. Oherwydd y gwres cadwodd y dynion eu hetiau am eu pennau, ond yn sydyn ar ganol y gwasanaeth chwipiwyd yr hetiau i'r llawr yn un rhes. Cerydd oedd hynny, meddai rhai, am beidio â dangos parch at y marw.

Dro arall, yn ôl Nain, yr oedd pedwar o ddynion wedi gwirfoddoli i geisio dal y bwgan a dyma nhw'n cuddio dan y gwely a chadw'n effro drwy'r nos. Welson nhw ddim byd, chlywson nhw ddim byd, ond yr hyn sy'n rhyfeddol yw fod twll crwn yn nhin trowsus pob un o'r pedwar pan ddaethant o'u cuddfan yn y bore.

Yn ystod fy mlynyddoedd yn ohebydd bûm ar drywydd amryw byd o straeon ysbryd. Yn Ffordd Rhondda yn Abertawe, er enghraifft, lle roedd y llestri wedi'u malu'n degins ac ym Mrynsiencyn lle symudid hen gist drom o un pen yr ystafell i'r llall. Ac wedyn mewn fferm yn Eifionydd. Daethai pâr ieuanc newydd briodi yno'n denantiaid i'r tŷ, ond nid i ffermio. Ni fuont yno ond cyfnod byr iawn. Gyda'r nosau fe glywent rhyw sŵn distaw, wylofus a ddenai'r defaid yn gylch o gwmpas y tŷ. Ymorolai'r wraig am lyfnhau'r dillad wrth wneud y gwely ond pan âi i'r llofft wedyn roedd ôl rhywun yn eistedd arno. Ofer ymhelaethu ac nid enwaf y lle gan i rywrai bryd hynny haeru y gallasai'r stori yn y papur ostwng pris y tŷ ar y farchnad. Nid oedd gennyf le i amau gair yr un o'r bobl a ddaliai fod bwgan yn tarfu arnynt ac eglurodd y Parch. Tom Morris, Pentrefelin yn fanwl imi sut yr aeth ati i fwrw allan yr ysbryd o'r fferm yn Eifionydd. Ac eto, er gwaethaf hyn oll, rwy'n dal mewn tipyn o benbleth...

Gan imi ddechrau drwy sôn am ddyfeisgarwch ein hynafiaid wrth drin geiriau, dof â'r llith i ben gyda thystiolaeth bendant sut y daethom ninnau i fabwysiadu un gair a ddefnyddiwn bellach yn ddigwestiwn. Eisteddai Twm Titsiar ar ei stôl wrth y bar yng nghlwb golff Nefyn pan ofynnodd rhyw Sais: '*What would you say for 'no problem' in Welsh?*' Pan atebodd Twm 'dim problem' aeth y Sais yn bur ymosodol ac uchel ei gloch. '*There you go, all you do is borrowing English words*,' meddai. Ac meddai Twm yntau yn hollol ddigyffro: '*We have to in this case because the word was not in our vocabulary until you lot came.*'

Nid y gwir i gyd, efallai – ond effeithiol iawn i roi caead ar y piser.

2. Papurau Pwllheli

O safbwynt y Wasg Gymraeg, Caernarfon debyg iawn, biau'r hawl i'w galw ei hun yn Brifddinas yr Inc. Yn ôl rhyw gyfrif fe gyhoeddwyd 26 o bapurau newydd yn y dref honno rhwng 1836 a 1903, a 40 o gylchgronau rhwng 1800 a 1922.

Ond nid Caernarfon biau'r clod i gyd. Bu gan Bwllheli hithau ei phapurau, a mwy ohonynt, mae'n debyg, na threfi eraill o'r un maint. *Yr Eifion* oedd y cyntaf o'r rhain, y papur Cymraeg cyntaf i'w werthu am ddimai. Fe'i sefydlwyd gan Hugh Hughes – Tegai – gŵr o Landygái yn 1856. Ni chafodd ef erioed ddiwrnod o ysgol. Gweithiai yn chwarel Cae Braich y Cafn – chwarel y Penrhyn – a manteisio i'w ddiwyllio ei hun ar yr Ysgol Sul a Chymdeithas Cymreigyddion Bethesda. Yn y man daeth yn weinidog gyda'r Annibynwyr. Cafodd alwad i eglwysi Llanystumdwy a Rhoslan. Treuliodd dair blynedd wedyn ym Manceinion lle dyblodd nifer yr aelodau yn Jackson Street, ac wedi cyfnod byr yn Llanrug, lle'r aeth ei wraig yn wael, dychwelodd eilwaith i Eifionydd yn weinidog Capel Helyg a Chwilog.

Dyna pryd y prynodd Wasg William Edwards ym Mhwllheli ar ôl i'r gŵr hwnnw ymfudo i'r America. Cyhoeddodd saith ar hugain o lyfrau gan gynnwys rhai o'i waith ei hun. Rhoes Dr Lewis Edwards eirda i'w ramadeg, canmolai J. R. Llanbrynmair a Gwilym Hiraethog ei ryddiaith. Ac meddai Dr D. Tecwyn Evans amdano yn ddiweddarach: 'Gellir ei ystyried yn enghraifft bur nodedig o werinwr difanteision wedi ei ddiwyllio ei hun nes cyrraedd safle anrhydeddus ymhlith ei gyfoeswyr.'

Dyna Tegai. Ar 3 Ionawr, 1856 yr ymddangosodd y rhifyn cyntaf o'r *Eifion*. Dewisiodd yr enw oherwydd mai yng nghwmwd Eifionydd yr oedd yn weinidog a mabwysiadodd linell gan Dewi Wyn yn arwyddair. Dwy ddihareb oedd gan *Yr Herald Cymraeg* o dan y pennawd, sef 'Cas gŵr na charo'r wlad a'i maco', a 'Rhydd i bawb ei farn ac i bob barn ei llafar'. 'Fy arwyddair fo rhyddid' a welid uwch pennawd *Yr Eifion*.

Roedd yn y papur fanion bach diddorol o'r cychwyn. Cawn brawf, er enghraifft, fod rhai merched yn ddigon croendenau ynglŷn â'u hoed yr adeg honno. Yn y trydydd rhifyn y mae'r cywiriad annisgwyl hwn: 'Bu ychydig gamsyniad yn ein rhifyn diwethaf ynghylch oed Mrs Mary Jones, Llanystumdwy. Pump a deugain y dylsai fod, nid chwech a deugain fel y cofnodwyd gennym.'

Un o'r colofnwyr oedd rhywun a'i galwai ei hun *Y Bwch*. Disgrifia ffair newydd Pwllheli fel lle ofnadwy, yn un uwd o feddwi a maeddu ac anlladrwydd. Dyma ei gyngor i ieuenctid y dref: 'Na fynychwch y gwibiadau ffeiriol. Os am gariad, mynnwch gael golwg arni gartref unwaith y mis – a hynny cyn cinio.'

Nid ym Mhwllheli yn unig y trigai drwgweithredwyr ychwaith. Roedd haid o ladron wedi dwyn pedwar swllt ar ddeg oddi ar wraig yng Nghynwyd, y cwbl a feddai ar ôl cynilo i brynu mochyn.

Un o ryfeddodau'r *Eifion* yw sut y llwyddai i gael newyddion o bell. Roedd hyn yng nghanol Rhyfel y Crimea, ond nid dibynnu ar fanylion ail-law trwy gyfieithu o'r Saesneg a wnâi Tegai ond manteisio ar lygad-dystion. Roedd Capten John Jones o'r brigantîn *Elizabeth Bowen* yn sgwennu'n rheolaidd at ei gyfaill Francis Evans yn y dref, a throsglwyddai yntau yr hanes i Tegai i'w gynnwys yn y papur. Ar 26 Chwefror, 1856 mae John Jones yn sôn fel yr oedd ef a Capten Hughes o'r *Royal William*, llong o Gaernarfon, yn cychwyn o Sebastapol i weld bedd Capten Richard Lloyd Edwards, Nanhoron a laddwyd ym mrwydr fawr Cathcart Hill. Dyma a ddywed: 'Gwelais gryn lawer ar fy nheithiau erioed, ond dim i'w gymharu â Sebastapol. Y mae y lle wedi ei berffaith ddinistrio. Nid oes un tŷ yn y dref braidd nad yw wedi ei ddryllio. Y mae cannoedd o belenau i'w gweld wedi suddo i'r muriau.' A galliodd dynoliaeth? Go brin.

Ar ôl cyrraedd pen y daith dywed John Jones: 'Pan welais yr argraff ar y maen teimlwn fel pe buasai rhyw berthynas agos i mi wedi ei gladdu yno. Er nad oeddwn yn gybyddus â'r bonheddwr, eto roeddwn yn teimlo fel buaswn wedi colli cyfaill annwyl.'

I goffáu ei fab, a oedd yn 22 oed ac yn aelod o Gatrawd 68 y Gwŷr Traed, cyflwynodd y tad lôn newydd trwy ddyffryn Nanhoron i'r Cyngor Sir. Mae carreg ag arni'r enw Balaclava yn ymyl Rhydgaled hyd heddiw. Yr oedd un arall yn dwyn yr enw Inkerman ar bont Llidiart-y-Dŵr hefyd ond diflannodd honno yn gymharol ddiweddar, ysywaeth.

I haneswyr y mae hen bapurau yn bwysig iawn wrth gwrs, ac yn rhifyn 24 Ebrill, 1856 dywed *Yr Eifion* mai ar y 'Sadwrn, 12 cyfisol' y gosodwyd carreg sylfaen pentref bychan o dai i weithwyr Cloddfa Llanaelhaearn. Dyna ddechrau pentref Trefor.

O 3 Ionawr 1856 hyd 5 Mehefin y flwyddyn honno y parhaodd *Yr Eifion*. Ar ôl hanner blwyddyn dyblwyd ei faint, dyblwyd ei bris a newidiwyd yr enw i'r *Arweinydd*. Cadwodd llinell gynganeddol Dewi Wyn ei lle uwch y pennawd ond rhoddwyd hysbysebion yn lle newyddion ar y dudalen flaen.

Rhoddir lle amlwg yn y rhifyn cyntaf i ddyddiadur a rydd hanes mordaith yr *Hindoo* o Gaernarfon i Boston a manylir cryn dipyn am y tywydd, yn naturiol. Llawn mor ddiddorol i rai efallai fyddai darllen am y ffrae a gododd ar ôl i rywun gael cam gan feirniad y traethodau yn 'steddfod Capel Helyg.

Wedi dyblu'r maint, roedd yn rhaid i'r *Arweinydd* fynd ymhellach oddi cartref i lenwi'r colofnau, mae'n amlwg. Ar 5 Mehefin cawn wybod y bu farw Mr Blanket ym Mryste, gan egluro mai efe oedd y gwehydd cyntaf i gynhyrchu blanced. (Erbyn hyn mae amheuaeth am hynny a sôn fod y gair *blankette* i'w gael mewn hen Ffrangeg.)

Hyd y gwn, does dim dadl na chafodd gwraig o Mount Pleasant, Lerpwl, bisyn grôt mewn ŵy hwyaden fel y cofnodir yn rhifyn 29 Mehefin. Mae yno stori hefyd am wraig gariadus yn wylo uwchben corff ei gŵr, ac meddai hi: 'Onid yw'n drueni fod Siôn bach wedi marw. Mae ei ddannedd o cystal ag erioed.'

Yr hyn sy'n arbennig am *Yr Arweinydd* yw y byddai Ceiriog a Gwilym Cowlyd yn cyfrannu iddo'n gyson. Ysgrifennai Ceiriog dan yr enw 'Syr Meurig Grynswth' gan ddilorni ffug-barchusrwydd y gymdeithas Gymraeg. I ddychanu'r eisteddfod a beirdd eraill nad ystyriai cystal ag ef ei hun, wrth gwrs, mae'n cynnig gwneud arwerthiant ar ei eiddo. Er budd y rheini rhoddai ar werth fyrddiwn a hanner o linellau cynganeddol ar unrhyw bwnc, deunaw mil o englynion ar eu hanner, cywyddau wrth y llath a llawer, llawer mwy.

Tair blynedd fu oes *Yr Arweinydd*. Yn 1859 cafodd Tegai alwad i Fethel, Aberdâr. Fe'i trawyd yw wael ar ganol pregethu yno ar 4 Rhagfyr, 1864. Disgynnodd i freichiau ei ddiaconiaid. Ni ddeallodd neb air a ddywedodd wedi hynny a bu farw o fewn ychydig ddyddiau yn 59 oed.

Trefnwyd tysteb genedlaethol iddo, rhan ohoni i fynd i'w weddw a rhan arall i godi cofeb iddo. Mae tri englyn ar y gofeb, gan Caledfryn, Hiraethog a Dewi Wyn o Esyllt. Caledfryn piau'r gorau, efallai:

Bardd da, athraw da, diwyd – oedd efe
　　Rhydd ei farn a hyfryd;
A chyfaill mor wych hefyd
Â neb o'i ôl sy'n y byd.

Fel mae'n digwydd, gellir mynd â'r cysylltiad newyddiadurol ymhell iawn o Bwllheli. Jane, hogan o Landygái fel yntau, oedd gwraig Tegai. Priodasant pan oedd hi yn ddeunaw ac yntau flwyddyn yn hŷn. Cawsant bedwar ar ddeg o blant. Ymhen ychydig dros flwyddyn wedi marw Tegai, ymfudodd Jane a'r teulu i'r America – i Efrog Newydd i ddechrau; symud wedyn i Bath, Pensylfenia ac yna i Utica. Pan fu hi farw ar 5 Mai

1885 yr oedd saith o'r plant yn fyw yn ôl y *Cenhadwr Americanaidd*, a'r hyn sy'n ddiddorol o gofio am y tad a'i *Eifion* a'i *Arweinydd* a'i wasg ym Mhwllheli, yw i Henry, un o'r hogiau, fynd yn argraffydd yn Utica, canolfan argraffu fwyaf America yn yr iaith Gymraeg yr adeg honno. At hynny, aeth un arall o'r meibion, John Quincy Hughes, yn brentis ar *Y Drych* a gweithio wedyn ar yr *Utica Morning Herald*, a sefydlwyd gyda llaw, gan Ellis Henry Roberts, Cymro o Lanuwchllyn a fu'n drysorydd cyngres America.

Wedi machlud *Yr Arweinydd*, bu Pwllheli heb bapur am naw mlynedd ar hugain. Ar 4 Ionawr, 1888 yr ymddangosodd y rhifyn cyntaf o *Udgorn Rhyddid*, papur pwysig iawn, a hynny yn anad dim, oherwydd y manylion a rydd inni am ddechrau gyrfa Lloyd George. Wrth geisio dadansoddi athrylith y dewin o Lanystumdwy, yn ôl y diweddar Emyr Price, yr awdurdod ar yr hanes, mae'n rhaid priodoli ei lwyddiant i raddau helaeth i'w allu diamheuol i drin y wasg yn gelfydd. Daeth hynny i'r amlwg yn gynnar, cyn iddo ddod yn ffrindiau â barwniaid Stryd y Fflyd.

Yn Ebrill 1890 yr aeth Lloyd George i'r Senedd drwy drechu Ellis Nanney o ddeunaw pleidlais. Ond fu'r siwrnai ddim yn hwylus. Methodd â chael enwebiad y Rhyddfrydwyr i fod yn ymgeisydd ym mwrdeisdrefi Arfon yn 1885 ac ym Meirionydd yn 1886. Yr hyn a wnaeth er sicrhau gwell cyfle oedd troi at bapurau pwerus Caernarfon, gan ysgrifennu erthyglau a llythyrau iddynt dan ei enw ei hun a chael cyfeillion dylanwadol i anfon llythyrau i'w gymeradwyo fel ymgeisydd ifanc disglair â thân yn ei fol.

At hyn, aeth ati wedyn i sefydlu ei bapur ei hun ym Mhwllheli. Yn y pamffled a hysbysebai'r dyddiad cyhoeddi dywedid fod *Udgorn Rhyddid* (*The Trumpet of Freedom*) yn newyddiadur gwerinol Cymreig a ddadleuai dros hawliau amaethwyr, masnachwyr, chwarelwyr a gweithwyr Cymru a bod Mr John Parry, Llanarmon ac amryw o brif gyfeillion rhyddid a hawliau Cymru eisioes wedi addo ysgrifennu iddo.

Ac meddai mewn llythyr at D. R. Daniel, trefnydd Undeb Dirwest Gogledd Cymru ar y pryd, ac a ddaeth wedyn yn ysgrifenydd Undeb y Chwarelwyr: '*It is to be thorough nationalist and sosialist, a regenerator in every aspect.*'

Lloyd George ei hun a fabwysiadodd yr enw i'w bapur. Roedd hyn wrth gwrs, yng nghanol Rhyfel y Degwm pan genid utgorn i rybuddio fod beiliaid ar eu ffordd i atafaelu eiddo. Wrth sôn am enw i'r papur dywed mewn llythyr arall at D. R. Daniel: '*Why not 'Udgorn Rhyddid'. Something stirring. Never mind the bombast if the stuff that is in it is good.*'

Lansiwyd *Udgorn Rhyddid* ar 4 Ionawr, 1888 ac ymhen tair wythnos, ar 24 Ionawr, yr oedd Lloyd George yn priodi yng nghapel Pencaenewydd.

Cyhoeddwyd saith o benillion i'r achlysur yn y papur. Dyma un:

Mi gredwn na chollet byth case mewn un lle,
Ond ha! Serch a'th drechodd yn hollol ynte?'
Judge Cupid ddywedai: '*According to laws*
Verdict for "serch" – *and all costs in the cause*.'

Golygydd *Udgorn Rhyddid* oedd Lewis D. Řoberts ac fe'i argreffid yng ngwasg Richard Jones yn Stryd Penlan. Cymraeg oedd iaith y mwyafrif mawr o'r hysbysebion. Ymysg y rhai difyrraf y mae cyfres o benillion yn canmol 'darpariaeth anffaeledig' William Owen, y fferyllydd, at ddifa cyrn ar y traed a 'Quinine Bitters' Gwilym Evans i iachau anhwylderau o bob math – gwaed amhur, doluriau y frest, gwyntogrwydd. Enwir un ar bymtheg o'r anhwylderau hyn ac ar y diwedd ychwanegir 'ac yn y blaen'.

Y Gwilym Evans hwn, gyda llaw, gŵr o Lanymddyfri oedd y Cymro cyntaf i'w ethol yn aelod o Gymdeithas y Cyffurwyr (MPS).

Gollyngwyd y 'Rhyddid' o'r pennawd ar 19 Hydref, 1898 a newidiodd yr 'Udgorn' wedyn i'r *Utgorn* yn 1949. Bu amrywiaeth ym maint y tudalennau fwy nag unwaith cyn i'r papur ddod i ben yn 1952. Dau sinema y dref oedd y prif hysbysebwyr erbyn hynny.

Yn y cyfasmer, bu o leiaf bump o bapurau eraill yn

cyd-redeg â'r *Udgorn*. *The Pwllheli Chronicle* a ymgorfforai hefyd y *North Wales Gazette and Advertiser* oedd un ohonynt. Papur Saesneg oedd hwn, wrth gwrs, a rhoddai le amlwg i lys ynadon y dref ar y dudalen flaen. Yn Ebrill 1890, dedfrydwyd Mary Jones i bythefnos o garchar am fod yn feddw ar y Stryd Fawr. Er tristed hynny, roedd dedfryd ffyrnicach efallai yn wynebu Elisabeth Jones, barmaid gwesty'r Whitehall. Dygid achos o enllib yn ei herbyn hi gan Capten Owen Lewis am iddi haeru mewn cardiau Ffolant ei fod wedi llofruddio dwy wraig a chadw puteiniad yn y tŷ. I geisio denu rhagor o ddarllenwyr, y mae'r *Chronicle* yn datgan hefyd: *'If we are not mistaken we shall hear another scandal soon.'* O 7 Rhagfyr, 1889 i 16 Medi, 1895 y parhaodd y *Chronicle*. Does dim un copi ohono ar gael yng Nghymru ond y mae set gyflawn yn yr Amgueddfa Brydeinig yn Llundain.

Papur arall a gyhoeddid ym Mhwllheli oedd y *Pwllheli and Abersoch Visitor and South Caernarvonshire Advertiser*. Dyna'r pennawd ar y tu blaen ond *Nevin Visitor* sydd ar y cefn. Ar wahân i fân hysbysebion, y cwbl a geir yn hwn yw enwau'r ymwelwyr a letyai mewn gwahanol westyau a thai. Ar yr wythnos gyntaf o Fedi 1894 yr oedd deugain o ymwelwyr yng ngwesty'r South Beach yn y dref, gan gynnwys chwech o deulu Solomon Andrews o Gaerdydd. Ym Modlondeb, Morfa Nefyn lletyai Mr a

Mrs Alfred Holt, pobl y llongau o Lerpwl, a Mademoiselle Daujeen o Baris.

Dim ond un papur arall tebyg i hwn y clywais i sôn amdano. Mae gan yr Athro Bedwyr Lewis Jones gyfeiriad at *The Amlwch Advertizer and Visitors List* a gyhoeddwyd gyntaf yng Ngorffennaf 1904 ac y dosbarthwyd pum can copi ohono.

Yn ôl ym Mhwllheli ymddangosai'r *Pwllheli News* bob dydd Llun yn nhri degau'r ganrif ddiwethaf. Papur rhad ac am ddim oedd hwn i hysbysebu atyniadau yn y dref a phlas Glyn-y-Weddw, Llanbedrog. Pisyn o'r un brethyn oedd y *Pwllheli Chat* hefyd.

Clywais sôn hefyd am y *Pwllheli Home Messenger* ond ni welais erioed rifyn ohono. Fe'i cyhoeddid yn ddwyieithog rhwng 1899 a 1902 dan nawdd y capel Saesneg.

Y papur olaf i'w argraffu ym Mhwllheli oedd y *Leader – y South Caernarvon and Meirioneth Leader (Yr Arweinydd)* i fod yn fanwl. Ond papur Porthmadog oedd hwn, a'i olygydd a'i berchennog oedd Herbert Thomas, gweithiwr egnïol ryfeddol. Ceid yn y *Leader* golofn Gymraeg yn cofnodi digwyddiadau bro Garndolbenmaen a'r cylchoedd gan J. P. Thomas a cholofn Saesneg yn trafod rhaglenni radio a'r celfyddydau gan John Ellis Williams, y dramodydd. Ond ar wahân i hynny Herbert Thomas a lenwai bob modfedd ohono fwy neu lai. Mynychai bump o gynghorau a dau lys barn, gwyliai ornestau pêl-droed, casglai newyddion lleol, gofalai am yr hysbysebion... Dyn â ŵyr sut y llwyddai i ddod i ben â hi.

Yn 1953, flwyddyn ar ôl *Yr Utgorn*, daeth y *Leader* yntau i ben.

3. Bob Owen

Pan ofynnid i mi ddweud gair am Bob Owen mewn rhyw gymdeithas, byddai'n rhaid imi gydnabod na ddylai hynny, ynddo'i hun, fod yn llawer o broblem, oherwydd yr oedd Bob wedi hyrddio – a dyna'r gair – wedi hyrddio miloedd ar filoedd o eiriau ataf fi i ddweud tipyn o hanes ei fywyd. Roeddwn innau wedyn wedi crynhoi rhyw 80,000 ohonynt yn benodau yn *Y Cymro*.

Bu Bob Owen farw ar y dydd olaf o Ebrill 1962. Rhaid ichi felly fod spel dros eich hanner cant i'w gofio – dyn byr, sydyn ei osgo, llygaid bychan bywiog, cof 'gyda'r mwyaf crafangog yng ngred,' meddai Dr Tom Richards, mwstas cribog, dant bob ochr i'w geg – yn 'foel fantach' ond wiw sôn am ddannedd gosod.

Roedd yn llawn crydcymalau wedi treulio oriau bwygilydd mewn hen selerydd a chrogloffftydd oerion a llaith yn tyrchu ar ôl hen lyfrau a phapurach a'r rheini yn llwydni trostynt yn aml. Llawn crydcymalau, ie – a llawn anghysonderau o bob math. Dyma rai: uchel ei gloch ym mhob man; yn ymosodol o uchel ei gloch ar adegau, ond yn galon feddal ryfeddol, a thu hwnt o garedig.

Yn ôl ei gyfaddefiad ei hun, doedd o'n gwybod fawr ddim am elfennau cerddoriaeth, ond eto fe wrandawai ar fiwsig digon uchel-ael ar y radio trwy'r dydd a reidio beic o Groesor i Landudno i gyngerdd gan gerddorfa. Ei bobl oedd Sibelius, Beethoven, Greig, Vagner a'r rheina, ac yn arbennig Bach. Doedd o ddim yn or-hoff o Handel na Joseph Parry am fod eu cyfansoddiadau, medda fo, yn ailadroddus.

Canmolai arferion bwyta'r oes o'r blaen i'r cymylau. Fedrech chi gael dim byd tebyg i uwd a llymru, picws mali, sucan gwyn, brywes a maidd yr iâr. Ac eto, ei hoff fwyd ef ei hun oedd tun samon a brechdan driog.

Roedd ganddo ddiddordeb anhygoel yn Unol Daleithiau America – a dim i'w ddweud wrth Batagonia na'r Cymry dewr a ymfudodd yno.

Roedd yn grwydwr mawr i bob rhan o'r wlad – a thros y ffin – i annerch mewn cymdeithasau, ond dewisai fyw yng Nghroesor lle nad oedd bws na thrên, 'byw ym mach walbant y greadigaeth,' yn ôl y Parch. Hugh Roberts, Rhyd-y-main.

Dyna rai anghysonderau. Ac wedyn mae dryllio a

chodi delwau. Wrth ddryllio fe dynnodd lawer iawn o bobl yn ei ben.

Wn i ddim beth yw eich barn am Edmwnd Prys. I'r mwyafrif, bid siŵr, dyma Archddiacon parchus, gŵr a fu'n cynorthwyo'r Esgob William Morgan i gyfieithu'r Beibl a'r bardd a roes inni'r Salmau Cân. Ond i Bob Owen, offeiriad hunanol yn ysbeilio tiroedd ac ystadau oddi ar ei gymdogion a chamwyro'r gyfraith i'w fantais ei hun. Dyna Edmwnd Prys.

A dyna Mary Jones hithau a'i thaith o Lanfihangel y Pennant i 'mofyn Beibl yn y Bala, a hynny yn ei dro yn peri sefydlu'r Feibl Gymdeithas. Wel rwtsh! Doedd a wnelo hi un dim â sefydlu'r gymdeithas honno. Ac am gerdded yn droednoeth, onid oedd ugeiniau, gannoedd o genod o'i hoed hi yn cerdded felly yn yr un cyfnod?

A beth am John Elias, y creadur? I'r mwyafrif, pregethwr mwyaf poblogaidd a nerthol ei ddydd. Ef oedd 'Tywysog y Bobl.' Ond i Bob Owen, hen Dori cul, crebachlyd ac os maddeuwch y gair mwys, un yn torri gwell pobl nag ef ei hun o'r seiat.

Oherwydd y safbwyntiau hyn y cyfeirid at Bob Owen fel drylliwr delwau. Daliai yntau ar ei beth mawr na ddrylliodd ond rhyw hanner dwsin ond iddo godi ugeiniau.

Gweini ar ffermydd a wnâi yn ei ddyddiau cynnar. Yn hogyn o'r ysgol, aeth Robin Bach Twll Wenci (fel yr adwaenid Penparc ei gartref yn Llanfrothen ar lafar), yn was bach i Blas Brondanw am £2.10 yr hanner tymor. Bu wedyn yng nghefn Cyffin, Tŷ Newydd y Rhyd a'r Wern cyn mynd yn glerc i chwarel Parc a Chroesor. Treuliodd ddeng mlynedd ar hugain fan honno cyn i'r chwarel gau oherwydd y dirwasgiad ac iddo yntau maes o law gael swydd gyda Chyngor Gwlad sir Gaernarfon ac yna darlithio i ddosbarthiadau Cymdeithas Addysg y Gweithwyr. Dyna droeon yr yrfa.

Fo, yn 47 oed, oedd yr ieuengaf erioed i gael gradd anrhydedd gan Brifysgol Cymru. Fo yn sicr oedd yr unig un i gael y fath radd â'r derbynydd ar y dôl. Roedd hi'n fyd digon main arno ar y pryd, a chwarae teg i'w gyfeillion yng ngholeg Bangor, criw yr Academig Dost a fyddai'n cyfarfod yn ystafell Syr Ifor Williams bob pnawn Llun – Syr Ifor ei hun, R. T. Jenkins, Thomas Richards, Thomas Parry, R. Williams Parry ac R. Alun Roberts – aethant ati ymysg ei gilydd i gasglu digon o arian i logi cap a gŵn iddo a thalu ei dreuliau i'r seremoni anrhydeddu yn Abertawe. Am hynny, bu'n fythol ddiolchgar iddynt.

Fel y clywsoch sawl gwaith mae'n siŵr, ef hefyd oedd yr unig un i gyfarch y Fam Frenhines fel y gwnaeth pan aeth i dderbyn yr OBE. Mae sawl fersiwn o'r stori ar led, rhai wedi magu mwy o gynffonnau na'i gilydd. Sut bynnag, roedd Bob ar sgawt yn rhywle pan gyrhaeddodd y llythyr, a bu cryn drafod ymysg y teulu yn Ael-y-bryn p'run a dderbyniai yr OBE ai peidio. Barnai Nel, y wraig ac Owain Tudur, y mab, y byddai'n gwrthod. Credai Nanw, y ferch hynaf, y byddai'n derbyn ac roedd yn awyddus iddo wneud hynny. Cytunai Sian, y ferch ieungaf â'i chwaer fawr. Roedd hi ar y pryd yn nyrs yn Carsholton yn ne Lloegr a rhagwelai gyfle da i gael dillad newydd.

Yn enw Churchill y daethai'r llythyr yn cynnig iddo yr OBE am ei wasanaeth i hanes a llenyddiaeth Cymru. Roedd ganddo gryn feddwl o Churchill a bu hynny o gryn ddylanwad. Derbyn a wnaeth.

Cyn mynd i Lundain bu mewn tipyn o gyfyng-gyngor sut i ymddwyn o flaen y Frenhines a sut i'w chyfarch petai raid. Aeth i ymarfer efo'r Henadur David Tudor o Drawsfynydd a dderbyniasai yr MBE y flwyddyn cynt. 'Yes, my Majesty' oedd piau hi wedyn.

Pan ddaeth y diwrnod mawr, roedd y Frenhines ar daith yn Seland Newydd a'r Fam Frenhines a gyflwynai'r medalau ym Mhlas Buckingham. '*I believe you take interest in Literature and History Mr Owen*', meddai hi. A dyna hi'n bîg ar Bob. Aeth yr ymarferion i'r gwellt, ac meddai '*Yes, my mother*.' Chwerthin wnaeth hi ond pan glywodd am ei lyfrau ychwanegodd: '*And all those books*.' '*Yes*', meddai Bob '*and the wife buried amongst them*.'

Ar wahân iddo ef ei hun, ei ryfeddod mwyaf oedd ei lyfrgell, mae'n debyg. Llond y tŷ o lyfrau; llyfrau ar ben llyfrau, llyfrau tu ôl i lyfrau, llyfrau bob ochr i'r grisiau, nodiadau mewn tuniau a bocsys creision...

Pan oedd o'n priodi ac yn mudo o Lanfrothen i Groesor symudwyd pedwar llwyth trol o lyfrau a dau geffyl yn tynnu pob llwyth. Daliodd ati i gasglu wedyn nes roedd ganddo yn y diwedd 47,000 o gyfrolau.

Dechreuodd hel llyfrau yn sgil cystadleuaeth rhwng clercod swyddfa'r chwarel. Faint o enwogion a fedrent ddarganfod yn dwyn eu cyfenwau hwy eu hunain ac aeth yn gystadleuaeth dynn iawn, fe ymddengys, rhwng y Wiliamsiaid a'r Oweniaid.

Roedd Bob Owen wedi hel £100 i brynu motobeic. Rhoesai ei fryd ar Indian tanc coch i fynd i'r cyngherddau yn Llandudno ond yn y twymiad fe glywodd fod Ellis William Owen, saer o Lanfrothen wedi marw a bod Idwal ei fab am fynd i America a gwerthu llyfrau ei dad. Aeth Bob yno a gwariodd y £100 bob dimai am y llyfrau. A dyna'r clwy wedi cydio.

Roedd Bob yn 38 oed yn priodi â Nel, merch o Gaeathro, a ddaethai i'r Wern yn forwyn. Fe'u priodwyd ar fore Llun yn Siloam, Llanfrothen a mynd ar eu mis mêl i Aberystwyth. Ben bore ddydd Mawrth aeth Bob ar y trên i Gaerfyrddin i siop llyfrau ail-law Dafydd Williams yn Heol y Brenin, a dyna lle bu mewn storws fan honno yn ymbalfalu yn y llwch a'r baw yn ei siwt nefi blw newydd. Dychwelodd i Aberystwyth am ddeg o'r gloch y nos gyda dau sachiad o lyfrau.

Dyletswydd cyntaf Nel yn wraig briod fu cario un o'r sachau o'r stesion i'r tŷ lojin. Do, dechreuodd Nel ei bywyd priodasol yn un o fil, ac fe barhaodd yn un o filiwn. *Asset* mawr fu cael gwraig fel'na, meddai Bob.

Ond fe gewch yr hanesion yn y gyfrol *Bywyd Bob Owen*, ac yn lle ail-adrodd y peth mwyaf synhwyrol i mi ei wneud efallai fyddai dweud sut yr aed ati i gael yr hanes. Fel y dywedais ar y dechrau, gohebydd ar *Y Cymro* oeddwn i. Roedd y Golygydd, John Roberts Williams, wedi dechrau cyfres yn y papur gan enwogion yn adrodd tipyn o'u hanes – Syr Thomas Parry-Williams, John O. John, Sam Jones BBC, Telynores Maldwyn, Meuryn ac eraill. Ceid ganddynt dair pennod bob un.

Roedd Bob Owen yn yr arfaeth hefyd ond y gamp fyddai ei berswadio i ysgrifennu. Y gwir amdani yw fod Dr Tom Richards wedi bod yn cynio llawer arno i sgwennu ei hanes ac yn sgil yr anogaeth roedd wedi llunio un bennod – wel hanner pennod, ta beth, ac wedyn rhoi'r ffidil yn y to.

Ar faes y Brifwyl yng Nglyn Ebwy, 1958 y gofynnodd y Golygydd am dair pennod ond doedd na thywysu na thagu fe wrthodai Bob Owen yn lân â chytuno. Y canlyniad fu bargeinio, sef fy mod i i gael y deunydd a sgwennu'r stori. Doedd gen i ddim dewis, wrth gwrs. Gwas cyflog – ewch a gwnewch. Ond wedi cael y maen hwnnw i'r wal fe ddywedodd y Golygydd, chwarae teg:

'Go brin y cewch chi bopeth a ddywed Bob Owen i dair pennod, gwnewch nhw'n chwech.'

Pan euthum i Groesor i roi pethau ar y gweill cyn dechrau, pwy oedd yno ond Dr Thomas Richards, llyfrgellydd Coleg Bangor a ffrind mawr Bob. Ym mis Awst bob blwyddyn âi ar ei wyliau i Groesor i lygadu pa drysorau o'r newydd oedd yno, a cheisio bargeinio am ambell lyfr prin.

Dyn main, talsyth a golwg braidd yn sarrug arno oedd Doc Tom. Edrychodd arnaf dros ei sbectol hirgul, estynnodd ei wddf a gwyro ei ben ymlaen, ac meddai: 'Chi sy'n mynd i sgwennu hanes Bob Owen? Ydych chi'n meddwl y medrwch chi sgwennu hanes Bob Owen yn well na Bob Owen ei hun? Ydych chi'n meddwl fod yna rywun yn rhywle ar wyneb daear a fedr sgwennu hanes Bob Owen yn well na Bob Owen ei hun?' Fel yna o un cwestiwn rhethregol i'r llall.

Pan gefais i gyfle, a magu digon o blwc, dyma fi'n ceisio egluro nad oeddwn yn meddwl dim o'r fath beth ond fod gresyn y byddai stori fawr yn mynd i ebargofiant oni wneid rhywbeth yn ei chylch. Yr unig ymateb fu dau air bach syml: 'ia, wel.'

Synhwyrwn erbyn hyn nad oedd yn or-frwdfrydig ynglŷn â'r trefniant, ond yr oeddwn, wrth lwc, yn lled gyfarwydd â'i ffordd ffwr-bwt. Buaswn yn gwrando arno'n traddodi cyfres o ddarlithoedd mewn Ysgol Haf a chofio fel y tynnai ei wats o boced ei wasgod pan gyrhaeddai rhyw druan yn hwyr. Buaswn hefyd yn ei gartref yn ei holi am hen chwaraewyr pêl-droed cydwladol Cymru yr ymddiddorai ynddynt – fel Mills Roberts, Preston North End, R. l. Roose, Lerpwl a Billy Meredith, Manchester City. Tu ôl i'r ymddangosiad sych, di-serch gwyddwn fod llawer o raslonrwydd a direidi hefyd.

Ofn i Bob Owen nogio roeddwn i wrth wrando ar ei gyfaill yn bwrw trwyddi. Ond, o drugaredd wnaeth o ddim. Roedd o'n cynnal Ysgol Haf yn Abersoch ym mhen y mis ac yn aros yng Nghastellmarch. Byddai'n rhydd Ddifiau a dydd Gwener ac felly dyma drefnu imi i'w nôl acw i Bencaenewydd am ddeg fore Iau.

Smociodd Bob ei Wdbeins. (Smociai 24 y dydd, 40 i leddfu ei nerfau ddiwrnod y Cyngor Sir a thair yn ychwanegol pan oedd yn gadeirydd y pwyllgor addysg.) Siaradodd yn ddibaid tan bump ar wahân i doriad byr am ginio – tun samon a brechdan driog – ac i ffwrdd â fo i Abersoch i ddarlithio am ddwyawr (o leiaf) ac i siarad efo Mrs Edmunds yn 'Stellmarch tan ddau y bore. Dilynwyd yr un patrwm drannoeth, Bob yn siarad a minnau'n sgwennu nes roedd fy mraich yn cyffio'n gorcyn. Pedair oed oedd Robin, y mab hynaf, ar y pryd, ac am hydoedd bu'n cyfeirio at Bob Owen fel y 'dyn fu'n siarad yn parlwr drwy'r dydd.' Mi ddalia' innau mai sylw cynilaf y flwyddyn '58 oedd yr eiddo Bob: 'Fydda i byth yn blino'n siarad, wsti.'

Ar ôl dechrau cofnodi doedd dim i'w wneud ond ceisio dilyn y trywydd i ble bynnag yr âi. I lofft stabal y Wern, i'r 'Merica, i Awstralia, i regi yn y Cyngor Sir, i Swyddfa'r chwarel at Moses Kellow, y rheolwr, i ryw gegin-allan i dryforio ar ôl hen ddogfennau; ar gwtyn motobeic mewn glaw mawr anferth efo Griffith William; gwerthu argraffiad 1752 o *Grey's Elegy* am bymtheg swllt a hwnnw'n mynd am £1,500 yn Sotheby's ym mhen hanner blwyddyn; cael ei fwrw allan o faes 'Steddfod Genedlaethol Pwllheli yn 1925 er ei fod wedi ennill gwobr yno. Bryd hynny John Ellis Williams oedd wedi dweud wrth rhyw glamp o blismon, Sais o ochrau Manceinion: '*See that fellow over there. He's a very bad man. Throw him out immediately*'. Ac roedd hwnnw, y lleban, wedi gafael yng ngwegil Bob a'i fwrw i'r briffordd er fod ganddo ruban enillydd yn llabed ei gôt a thocyn dosbarth cyntaf yn ei law. Do, cafodd y plismon a'i dras ei alw'n bob enw.

Un munud hwyrach y byddwn yn gwrando ar hanes achub cyfrolau o Gronicl yr Oes mewn storm ar y Migneint, a'r munud nesaf o fewn deng munud i farw mewn eira mawr ym Mhentrefoelas. Sut y gwyddai mai deng munud... anghofiais ofyn, mae'n rhaid!

Ymddangosodd y bennod gyntaf yn *Y Cymro* yn Hydref 1958 a pharhaodd y gyfres hyd fis Mehefin y flwyddyn wedyn. Roedd tair pennod arfaethedig i ddechrau, 'gwnewch nhw'n chwech' wedyn ac yn y diwedd aeth y chwech yn ddeunaw pennod ar hugain.

Wn i ddim yn iawn pam nad âi Bob Owen ati i ysgrifennu ei atgofion ei hun. Ac eto, mae gen i amcan go lew. Roedd ganddo, wrth gwrs, fôr o Gymraeg cyhyrog fel llawer o'i genhedlaeth, eithr nid âi i drafferth o gwbl i sicrhau cywirdeb wrth 'sgwennu, chwilota, tyrchu am ffeithiau, dyna'i fyd. Nid oedd gwedd y cyflwyniad ar bapur nac yma nac acw ganddo. Yn wir ysgrifennai yn wasgarog a sobr o ddi-ofal yn aml. Clywais Tegla yn dweud rhyw dro y byddai ef yn caboli popeth a ysgrifennai chwe gwaith cyn ei ollwng o'i law. Go brin y byddai Bob yn ail-ddarllen o gwbl.

Cafodd ei chwipio'n anhrugarog gan R. T. Jenkins am ei ddiffygion iaith yn y traethawd gorchestol ar y testun 'Ymfudiadau o Gymru i'r Unol Daleithiau rhwng 1760 ac 1860' a anfonodd i Brifwyl Llandybïe yn 1944. 'Is-Eryri' oedd ffugenw Bob Owen ond gwyddai R. T. Jenkins yn iawn pwy oedd yr ymgeisydd. Doedd dim ond un yn y ras 'ac yr oedd ei leferydd yn ei gyhuddo ef.'

Wedi canmol cynnwys y traethawd, y diwydrwydd aruthrol a'r craffter chwilgar tu ôl iddo, mae'r beirniad yn dodi'r corn olew o'i law a gafael yn y fflangell ac meddai: 'Nid yw'n unrhyw bleser ddweud pethau heilltion am gyfaill mawr ei barch, a mynych a hael ei gymwynas i mi... ond nid yw darganfod ffeithiau ond hanner y gamp. Y mae'n rhaid eu cyflwyno'n deilwng a'u cyflwyno yn Gymraeg.'

Er gwaethaf y diffygion iaith dyfarnodd y ddau feirniad – David Williams oedd y llall – y wobr yn llawn i Bob Owen a'i longyfarch yn ddidwyll a chalonnog ar lwyddiant ei ddycnwch rhyfeddol a'i fedr fel chwilotwr.

Cytunai Bob mai cowdal o draethawd blêr oedd hwn – ond roedd o'n un mawr! Wyth can tudalen a hwnnw wedi'i deipio'n glos a sgwennu mân wedyn ar ymyl y tudalennau fel y deuai rhagor o ffeithiau i'r fei. Yn ddiweddarach byddai R. T. Jenkins yn pryfocio Bob gan ddweud iddo aros yn rhy hir yn America nes anghofio ei Gymraeg. Y gwir amdani yw yr âi Bob Owen bob cam o Groesor i Gaerdydd, a cherdded petai raid, i chwilio am un ffaith ond ni thrafferthai i droi yn ei gadair i ymgynghori â *Llyfr yr Orgraff* neu eiriadur.

Gan imi sôn am y traethawd mawr, rhaid cofio mai Bob Owen oedd yr awdurdod pennaf ar Gymry America. Roedd pedwar o frodyr ei nain a mab a merch iddi wedi ymfudo yno. Dywedai mai ar arian America y magwyd ef.

Dechreuasai ddarllen am y wlad fawr lle roedd cynifer o'i berthnasai yn byw pan oedd yn ifanc iawn; bu'n gohebu llawer â hwy ar ran ei nain ac aeth ati'n ddyfal i gasglu llyfrau, cylchgronau a phapurau yn ymwneud â gwahanol dalieithiau. Ar un adeg fe gyhoeddid trigain a rhagor o gylchgronàu Cymreig – a Chymraeg gan fwyaf – yn America. Gwerthfawrocach gan Bob Owen na dim arall yn ei lyfrgell oedd y gongl lle cedwid yr adran Gymreig Americanaidd.

Ni bu erioed yn America, ond daethai i adnabod y bobl mor dda nes medru dweud, o'u gweld, o ba dras yr hanent. Ar ei ffordd adref rhyw hwyrnos fe'i cafodd ei hun yng nghanol gwersyll milwyr Americanaidd tua Nanmor. Safai pymtheg ohonynt yn un rhes tu allan i'w pebyll. '*Look here*', meddai wrth y cyntaf, '*you have German blood in you*'. Edrychodd y dyn yn hurt arno. Troes wedyn at yr ail a dywedyd: '*You have Czechoslovakian blood in you*'. Edrychodd hwnnw yn fwy syfrdan fyth. O'r pymtheg yn y rhes llwyddodd, medda' fo, i enwi'n gywir o ba genedl y tarddai tri ar ddeg ohonynt. O'r ddau a fethodd roedd un yn French Canadian wedi croesi efo dyn du!

Ymhen blynyddoedd wedyn roedd yr Athro E. G. Bowen yn teithio ar y trên i lawr yn ne Lloegr gan daro sgwrs ag Americanwr a ddaeth i'r cerbyd. Soniwyd am Gymru, yn naturiol, ac meddai'r gŵr dieithr: '*Once upon a time when I was stationed in North Wales, a little witch came to the camp*'. Fe'i disgrifiodd yn ddigon manwl nes i'r Athro ymateb: '*Oh, I know him well. He's my friend Bob Owen.*'

Ond i fynd yn ôl at y traethawd am funud, wyth gan tudalen, chwi gofiwch, ond yn ychwanegol at hynny yr oedd hefyd 24 o atodiadau, 196 o dudalennau, yn fapiau a siartiau yr oedd ei gyfaill Ifor Owen, wedi eu paratoi dan ei gyfarwyddyd. Ond nid dyna'r cyfan ychwaith. Roedd un atodiad arall yn cynnwys enwau 40,000 o ymfudwyr o Gymru i America rhwng 1760 ac 1860; o ble yr aethant, pa bryd yr aethant ac yn lle yn America y sefydlasant. Ni welodd y beirniaid mo'r rhestr honno. Roedd wedi golygu cymaint o lafur iddo yn ei chywain fel na fentrai ei gollwng o'i law rhag ofn iddi ddigwydd mynd ar goll. Hon, yn wir oedd sylfaen y traethawd.

Mewn blynyddoedd bu'r rhestr yn gaffaeliad mawr iddo pan ddeuai Americanwyr i Groesor i olrhain eu hachau. Roeddwn i yn Ael-y-bryn unwaith pan gyrhaeddodd gwraig o'r enw Mrs King o Galiffornia yno. Hanai ei hynafiaid o Gaerwys a chawsai gyngor gan y Parch. E. Ffestin Williams i fynd i weld Bob Owen. Roeddem ni'n eistedd wrth y bwrdd yn cael te – Mrs King, Mrs Owen, Bob Owen a minnau pan gododd Bob yn sydyn a diflannu i'r parlwr. Ymhen sbel daeth ebychiadau o syndod o'r fan honno cyn iddo ddychwelyd i'r gegin, dechrau dyrnu'r bwrdd o flaen Mrs King a datgan ar dop ei lais: '*Wanwl, one of your ancestors was Siôn Wyn o Wydir, the worst man who ever trod this earth.*' Roedd Mrs King, y greadures, yn gegrwth, wrth gwrs.

Ond cyn imi fynd i sôn am America, dweud

roeddwn i nad oedd gan Bob Owen ddim awydd i 'sgwennu ei hanes, ac oherwydd hynny y bûm yn ymlwybro yn rheolaidd tua Chroesor am hanner blwyddyn i gael rhagor o wair rhaffau. Mwynheais y fraint. Dysgais lawer.

Unwaith, dim ond unwaith, yr aeth hi braidd yn dynn rhyngom wrth y gwaith. Cadwai Bob Owen bob llythyr a dderbyniai. Roedd ganddo fil oddi wrth Doc Tom, yn bigog a dadleugar yn aml. Mynnai Bob y dylid enwi pawb yr oedd ganddo lythyrau oddi wrthynt a daliwn innau y byddai hynny'n ddiflas sobr. Y canlyniad fu cyfaddawdu a chynnwys cyfran ohonynt a ystyriai ef y rhai pwysicaf. Wn i ddim a gefais faddeuant llawn am fy haerllugrwydd mwy nag y cafodd R. T. Jenkins am beidio â chynnwys pob un o'r 150 o erthyglau a baratoisai Bob Owen ar Gymry America i'r *Bywgraffiadur*. I Bob Owen doedd dim synnwyr mewn anwybyddu pobl fel Griffith Griffiths o Lanllyfni a roes barc gwerth can mil o ddoleri yn anrheg i dref Los Angeles, ac Oliver Thomas o Garno a ddyfeisiodd y stemar gyntaf yn hanes y byd. Am wn i na fyddai Bob Owen yn fodlon dadlau fod holl Gymry America yn haeddu lle yn y *Bywgraffiadur*!

Wrth gyd-weithio ag ef bu un neu ddau o bethau o fantais fawr i mi. Un ohonynt oedd yr adwaenwn ef cynt. Oni fuaswn yng Nghroesor lawer gwaith yn chwilio am ryw wybodaeth neu'i gilydd ar gyfer stori

yn y papur? Un tro, daeth fy nghyfaill Dic Goodman ar
y ffôn i ddweud fod rhywun yn dweud fod rhywun arall
yn dweud fod Bob Owen wedi dweud mewn darlith yn
Rhoshirwaun fod Charles de Gaulle yn ysgrifennu
llythyrau Cymraeg. Charles de Gaulle? Arlywydd
Ffrainc? Roeddwn yng Nghroesor cyn i gloch y teliffon
ddiffodd – bron iawn. Ond erbyn deall nid y de Gaulle
hwnnw oedd awdur y llythyrau ond brawd ei dad.
Llydawr ydoedd ac ysgrifennai yr ewythr lythyrau
Cymraeg i Ioan Tegid (1792-1852).

Ond sut meddech chi y bu sôn am Charles de Gaulle
mewn darlith yn Rhoshirwaun ar y testun 'Ffasiynau
Merched yr Oes o'r blaen?' Cawsai Bob ei gyhuddo'n
bur fynych o osod testun a siarad am rywbeth hollol
wahanol. Codai 'sgwarnogod – ac yn y rheini y ceid y
perlau yn aml. Erbyn gweld, fodd bynnag, doedd
crybwyll y llythyrau ddim ymhell oddi ar y testun
oherwydd yr oedd gan fam Ioan Tegid fasnach helaeth
mewn dillad merched yn y Bala yn niwedd y
ddeunawfed ganrif. Ioan Tegid, gyda llaw, yw awdur y
gerdd fach swynol 'I dref y Bala 'raeth y bardd', a bu
hefyd, gyda Charnhuanawc, yn cynorthwyo Lady
Charlotte Guest i gyfieithu'r *Mabinogion* o *Lyfr Coch
Hergest*. Bu'n stori dda i mi.

Ar wahân i adnabod Bob Owen cynt, mantais arall
oedd fy mod yn dod o Fynytho. Roedd Bob yn hoff
iawn o Lŷn. Ond hyd yn oed yn y fan honno, doedd

pobman ddim yn uchel yn y llyfrau. Roedd yno lefydd na chawsech ynddynt wên nac unrhyw anogaeth mewn darlith. Yr unig un a gawsai gymeradwyaeth fyddai'r cadeirydd am ei rodd. Ond nid felly Mynytho. Roedd Uwchmynydd, Rhoshirwaun a Mynytho, o drugaredd, ymysg ei hoff lefydd. Gosodai hwy yn yr un dosbarth â Llangwm, Pentrefoelas a Dinas Mawddwy – a fedrech chi ddim bod yn nes i'r nefoedd na hynny.

Gan fy mod yn frodor o Fynytho bu mantais arall hefyd i mi. Roedd un o'i arwyr mawr yn byw yno, sef Caradog Jones, arloeswr dosbarthiadau Cymdeithas Addysg y Gweithwyr yn Llŷn ac Eifionydd. 'Cymwynaswr mawr, dyngarwr mawr a dewin o drefnydd,' meddai Bob amdano. Y gwir yw mai Caradog Jones a Mrs Mary Silyn Roberts a droes hobi fawr Bob yn gynhaliaeth iddo drwy ei annog i ddarlithio a rhoi cyfleon iddo ar ôl i'r chwarel gau.

Bu'n ddarlithydd poblogaidd iawn, yn rhannol am y byddai'n damio a dweud pethau mawr am ysweiniaid a landlordiaid ymysg eraill. Yn Nhrawsfynydd y bu ei ddosbarth lluosocaf – cant a hanner o aelodau. Ac wedi iddo gael cynulleidfa o'r fath roedd yn ei elfen yn traethu'n ysgubol. Un o'r aelodau yn y Traws oedd Edward Tudor a gerddai filltiroedd dros lwybrau anodd ymhob tywydd, o'i gartref yng Nghefn Clawdd. Dywedodd Bob Owen un noson fod gŵr ieuanc o deulu'r Tudors wedi cipio gwraig rhywun yn yr hen oes a'i dwyn i ryw dŷ yn Llanfachreth, ac ychwanegu: 'Pebai'r gyfraith wedi ei gweinyddu'n deg a'r Tudor hwnnw wedi ei grogi, fuasech chi ddim yma heno Edward Tudor.'

Cawsai stori felly dderbyniad gwresog, wrth gwrs, a chwarae teg iddo fe fwynheai Edward Tudor yr hwyl cystal â neb. Dywedodd Bob hefyd fod pawb yn y dosbarth yn disgyn o ddiawliaid a llofruddion a lladron defaid. Roedd dau hen ewythr iddo ef wedi lladd dyn yn Nolbenmaen, meddai. Roeddynt hefyd yn ewyrthod i Jac Parry o Dremadog a phan glywodd hwnnw beth a ddywedasai Bob dyma ei ymateb: 'Dwed wrth y diawl bach y bydd yna fwy 'na dau lofrudd yn y teulu os na fydd o'n ofalus sut mae'n geirio.'

Soniais eisioes am Bob Owen a'i Wdbeins. Oedd, roedd o'n smociwr mawr, ac yn ei ddydd yn rhegwr mawr. Pan oedd yn aelod o'r Cyngor Sir, âi'n dân eirias rhyngddo weithiau â Syr Evan Jones, Ffestiniog, un o'r *Big Five* fel petai. Pan fyddai mewn tymer ddrwg iawn, rhegai Syr Evan yr aelodau o'u cwr mewn pwyllgorau – ac yntau yn y gadair. Fel un â digon o brofiad ganddo yn y lein honno, âi Bob yn hy arno yntau a'i regi'n ôl weithiau.

'Paid â rhegi Robin,' meddai Syr Evan, rywbryd.

'Mae gen i cystal hawl â chithau i regi, ddyn,' meddai Bob.

'Ond rwyt ti'n flaenor.'

'Ydw, ond roeddwn i'n rhegi cyn bod yn flaenor hefyd,' meddai Bob. Rhoes hynny ben ar y ddadl.

Smociwr mawr, rhegwr mawr a broliwr mawr. Roedd o'n un da mewn rhifyddeg, er enghraifft, ond nid digon yr ansoddair 'da'. Roedd o'n ddiarhebol o dda ac yn well na'r gorau yn Lerpwl, er na wn sut y gallai brofi hynny. Weithiau pan deimlwn fod y canmol yn mynd dros ben llestri, ceisiwn dymheru ychydig ar bethau trwy ddweud mai fo oedd un o'r rhai cyntaf i wneud y peth-a'r-peth, neu'n un o'r rhai mwyaf mewn rhyw faes arall. Wel, dim ffiars o beryg': cynta' un, gora' un, mwya' un.

Weithiau byddai Mrs Owen yn ceisio rhoi brêc arno, yn ceisio ei berswadio i beidio â dweud ambell stori – megis yr un am y forwyn yn y Wern. Tipyn o slwt oedd hi, a ddim yn cael enw da chwaith ar lendid ei buchedd, fel petai. Rhyw noson roedd dyn o'r ardal wedi tynnu llidiart oddi ar ei fachau a dringo i lofft y forwyn wrth fynd adref o'r Ring – o Brondanw Arms. Drannoeth pan aeth gweision y Wern i gael brecwast, cawsant fod y bara yn wlyb socian. Cwynwyd wrth y meistr. Gwnaed ymholiadau a darganfuwyd fod y dyn wrth ymbalfalu yn y tywyllwch wedi troi y pot golch a bod ei gynnwys wedi diferu rhwng 'styllod llawr y llofft i'r car-bara a grogai dan y distiau. Gwaeth na dim roedd y dynion wedi bwyta. Bu yno le, diawl o le, yn naturiol. Doedd Mrs Owen ddim eisiau cynnwys hen stori fel yna. Beth petai rhywun yn perthyn i'r forwyn? 'Duw, Duw,' meddai Bob, 'peth fel'na ydi bywyd. I mewn â hi.'

Pe gofynnid i mi ddewis fy hoff bennod yn yr hanes rwy'n credu mai'r un lle mae Bob Owen yn adrodd am ei berthynas â Charneddog a Catrin fyddai honno – 'yr hen bâr annwyl o'r ddeunawfed ganrif a oedd yn byw yn yr ungeinfed.' Yma y cawn Bob yn ei elfen ymysg ei bobl ei hun. Mae yma rhyw anwyldeb mawr, rhyw edmygu dilys, ffraeo tanbaid, hiraethu, ac amryw byd o straeon bachog a gogleisiol. Ar hyd ei oes bu Carneddog yn darogan ei fod am farw, a doedd hynny ddim yn llawer o syndod yn ôl Bob Owen oherwydd buasai brodyr a chwiorydd iddo farw ym mlodau eu dyddiau. Aeth Carneddog unwaith i Iwerddon i geisio cryfhau, ac ar ei ffordd adref galwodd yn Chwilog i weld Myrddin Fardd. Fe'i trawyd yn wael yno a hwylio i farw, ond ni chafodd ddim cydymdeimlad gan yr hen Fyrddin garw ei dafod. Unig anogaeth Myrddin oedd: 'Paid â marw yn fan'ma i ddrewi.'

Bu ffrae fawr unwaith rhwng Bob Owen a Charneddog pan neidiodd Bob ar ei draed mewn cyngerdd yn Nanmor oherwydd y teimlai i Garneddog ddweud rhywbeth dilornus am Tom Nefyn. Ar ôl mynd adref ysgrifennodd lythyr cignoeth at Carneddog. Adnabu Catrin y llawysgrifen, darllenodd y llythyr a bwriodd ef i'r tân. Ond roedd Bob Owen, yn ffodus erbyn hyn, wedi anfon copïau ohono i ffrindiau yma ac acw. Mae'n llythyr rhyfeddol. Mae E. Namora Williams yn dyfynnu rhan ohono yn ei chyfrol *Carneddog a'i Deulu* ac fe'i ceir yn llawn mewn ysgrif dan y teitl 'Bob Owen y Blagardiwr' gan yr Athro Bleddyn. O. Huws yn *Y Casglwr*, Haf 2002. Cafodd ef afael arno ymhlith papur J. W. Jones (awdur *Y Fainc Sglodion*) yn llyfrgell y Brifysgol ym Mangor. Dyma rai o'r pytiau mwyaf deifiol: 'Catffwl penffol oeddych; penwag, pan feiddiasoch sennu un o broffwydi Duw nos Sadwrn yn Nanmor. Chwi yw y dyn a groeshoeliasai Iesu Grist pe caech gyfle. Y mae eisiau eich rhostio yng nghoelcerth y pwll diwaelod a serio eich tafod yn golsyn â brwmstan uffern. Yr ydych fel dyn o'r co weithiau... Nid cybydd crintachlyd fel chwi yw Twm Nefyn yn myned ag ymenyn i rywle y caiff fwyaf amdano... Dyn sâl ydych i'ch cyfeillion gorau... Dyn diawledig o beryglus ydych... Bradwr o'r iawn ryw... Clown gwylfabsant... Blerwyn digydwybod... Y mae eisiau mynd â chwi i'r Seilam i Ddinbach a chlymu eich tafod â rhefynnau... Bydded i chwi wrido mewn cywilydd hyd ddydd brawd am eich pensyfrdanrwydd a'ch pendifadrwydd anheilwng o Gristion...'

Ar ôl yr helynt bu Bob Owen a Charneddog heb siarad â'i gilydd am flwyddyn gron. Dyna'r flwyddyn hwyaf a mwyaf annifyr yn hanes Bob Owen, medda' fo. Ond pan gymodwyd fe wnaed hynny mewn steil trwy ysgwyd llaw yn gyhoeddus ar ganol y llwyfan mewn cyngerdd arall, ym Meddgelert y tro hwn.

Ond tipyn o sioe oedd hynny, ddyliwn, oherwydd roeddynt wedi dod yn ffrindiau cyn hynny fel y dengys y penillion hyn o waith Carneddog:

Hel hen lyfrau fel rhyw botiwr,
Llond hen sachau, wna'r chwilotwr;
Gwyllt a byrbwyll ydyw Robin,
Ond caredig anghyffredin.

Pan mewn consart mawr yn Nanmor
Methai ddal ei geg heb agor,
Ysgyrnygodd arna'i sydyn
Am grybwylliad ar Dom Nefyn.

Ar ôl inni fyned allan,
Roedd ei wep fel eiddo Satan:
Yn ei ddig yr oedd y cena
Am fy llarpio fel hyena.

Anfon llythyr brwnt wnaeth Robin,
Ond ei losgi a wnaeth Catrin;
Edliw wnai fy holl bechodau
Ond Tom Nefyn waeddodd 'Maddau'.

Ar rhyw ddiwrnod braf ym Medi
Rhedodd Robin i'r Carneddi -
'Gwell yw maddau'r hen Garneddog
Cyn i'r haul fynd dros Foel Hebog.'

Fe wnaed te a thost i Robin,
Ac anghofiwyd am yr heldrin;
Fe gymodwyd fel cyfeillion –
Dyna orchest dau hen Gristion.

Bûm yn byw am fisoedd yn sŵn y straeon. Wedi dechrau dan beth amheuaeth o du Doc Tom, cafodd Bob gerdyn drwy'r post ar ôl y drydedd bennod. Roedd yn bwysig iddo fo, ond yn ganmil pwysicach i mi. Cymeradwyai Doc Tom. Tri gair oedd ar y cerdyn: 'Ewch rhagoch frawd.'

Nid myfi yn sicr yw'r un i ddweud dim am fawredd Bob Owen fel hanesydd a chwilotwr ac achyddwr. Bu rhai amgenach wrthi. Gallaf innau, fodd bynnag, dystio ei fod yn gymeriad lliwgar iawn, yn ganolbwynt pob cynulliad. Os byddai Bob Owen ar lawr uchaf y bws yno y byddai pawb arall hefyd, os oedd digon o le. Roedd o hefyd yn afradus o garedig, yn rhannu'n hael o'i wybodaeth i fyfyrwyr o bell ac agos ac i bawb a ddoi ar ei ofyn.

Er gadael yr ysgol yn dair ar ddeg a hanner oed ac heb gael awr o goleg erioed, fe dyfodd yn brif achyddwr ei genedl ac yn destun chwedl yn ei oes ei hun.

Sgyrsiau Noson Dda

HARRY CATTERICK:
THE UNTOLD STORY OF A
FOOTBALL GREAT

HARRY CATTERICK:
THE UNTOLD
STORY OF A
FOOTBALL GREAT

ROB SAWYER

Published by deCoubertin Books Ltd in 2014.

deCoubertin Books, 145-157 St John Street, London, EC1V 4PY
www.decoubertin.co.uk
First hardback edition.

ISBN 978-1-909245-18-1

A CIP catalogue record for this book is available from the British Library.
Cover design by MilkyOne Creative.

Printed and bound by Svet Print.

In memory of Dad, Billy, Dan and WJ, who showed me the way, and those no longer with us who wore the royal blue shirt with distinction.

A U T H O R ' S   N O T E

For the early years of Harry's story I was fortunate to have access to his unpublished memoirs from 1964 and accompanying notes; any displayed quotes from that source are in italics. For insight into Harry's thoughts after that date I am very grateful for John Roberts' permission to quote from interview tapes John recorded in 1977 in the process of compiling his book *Everton, The Official Centenary History* (Granada Publishing/Mayflower Books, 1978).

CONTENTS

FOREWORD

HARRY CATTERICK was one of the key influences on my career in football. He signed me, nurtured me, gave me my chance in football and always looked after me. I held him in the highest esteem and thought he was a great manager.

The press enjoyed being courted by Bill Shankly, but Harry was an introvert and snubbed them. As a result Don Revie, Bill Shankly, Bill Nicholson and Sir Matt Busby all get mentioned as being the great managers of the era while Harry doesn't. However, he was right up there among them and created three different trophy-winning sides.

Over the years I have been disappointed that he hasn't received the respect and recognition he deserves. I am delighted, therefore, that Rob Sawyer has written a biography which chronicles Harry's life and celebrates his achievements in the game.

Colin Harvey, July 2014

1

INTRODUCTION

GOODISON PARK, 9 March 1985. I was a 14-year-old who sat with my father and sister in the Bullens Road Stand as Everton bundled home a late equaliser to keep the dream of a league and cup treble alive. On the way home, Radio Two announced that Harry Catterick had passed away in the directors' box moments after the final whistle. His untimely passing planted a seed of curiosity in me about Harry, fed by my father's reminiscences and his collection of old match-day programmes. I was keen to learn more about a man labelled an enigma by many observers.

Sadly for Harry, recognition of his achievements in the game has been perfunctory at best. Occasional profiles of the man have painted a picture of a dour authoritarian, grudgingly respected but considered lucky to have inherited Everton's 'Moores' millions' to lavish on the game's top names. Little or no mention is ever made of his playing career, managerial successes in Sheffield or his post-Everton career. In 2013 I placed a post on Toffeeweb enquiring as to Harry's non-executive role at Goodison Park from 1973 to 1975. Things snowballed and within weeks I found myself researching the rich life of a multi-faceted person. To different people he was visionary, introverted, erudite, secretive, demanding, ambitious to the point of ruthlessness, yet sometimes surprisingly kind and thoughtful.

The son of a lower-league footballer and coach, Harry followed his father into the game. After a war-interrupted Everton playing career which failed to attain the heights it might have, Harry embarked on a career in management. For him, football management was a serious business, where only the best was good enough – he served an apprenticeship in the lower divisions before working his way to the pinnacle of the domestic game. Three whirlwind seasons at Sheffield Wednesday, where he came within an ace of winning the league title, paved the way for a return to Goodison Park. Over ten golden years, Everton consistently challenged for top honours, with Harry the equal of Bill Shankly, his more-feted rival from across Stanley Park. While Shankly brilliantly courted the press and the public, Catterick was notoriously protective of his private life and wary of the media, preferring to keep both supporters and players at arm's length. Cultivating an image as 'the thinking man's manager', he was always immaculately dressed – even his training-ground tracksuit appeared to be pressed and crease-free. To his players he was 'Boss' within earshot and 'The Catt' at a safe distance. Both feared and respected, Harry was the, de facto, headmaster at the club dubbed The School of Science.

To the press he was 'Mr Cloak and Dagger', famed for stealthily using John Moores' Littlewoods war chest to secure the services of some of the finest football talent in the land. Less acknowledged was his vision for the club and a youth policy that nurtured young talent and blended it so effectively with established stars. He guided Everton to victory in one of the classic FA Cup finals and crafted two championship-winning teams. Though taciturn in nature, his teams spoke eloquently for him on the pitch – the side that won the 1969/70 title was one of the finest to grace English football and was, tactically, probably 40 years ahead of its time. Sadly, ill-health and some poor judgement brought the glory days to a premature end.

Twenty-five years after his passing in the place he is most closely associated with, Harry received belated recognition with his 2010 induction into the National Football Museum's Hall of Fame – joining other managerial greats of the game. The time is now right to tell Harry's story and re-assess his legacy.

C H A P T E R O N E

BEGINNINGS

THE RIVER MERSEY rises from obscurity in Stockport, to attain fame at its end beside the Three Graces in the great port city of Liverpool. Harry Catterick's life followed a parallel course, his formative years in the industrial town leading, via several meanders, to acclaim and an untimely passing on Merseyside. However, Harry's story began 90 miles from the Mersey in Co. Durham. The only child of Henry Catterick and Lillian Petty entered the world at 26 Union Row in central Darlington on 26 November 1919. Henry was always known as 'Harry' so, to avoid confusion, his son answered to 'Jack' in family circles throughout his life.

In the post-Great War years Darlington's economy was dominated by steel, coal mining and the railways. These were tough times; although his family was never on the breadline Harry would recall seeing free bowls of soup being doled out to the desperate of the town. Perhaps those early experiences of hardship and poverty gave him the resolve and determination to succeed in life and ensure that such a fate would never befall him.

The Cattericks were a typical north-eastern working-class family. Harry's grandfather, another Henry, was a railway plate-layer while Harry's father had been employed at a steelworks before moving to Chilton Colliery. Chilton, a village equidistant from Darlington and Durham, had mushroomed after the first coal mine was sunk in 1873. At its peak approximately 1,500 men and boys were employed, and the colliery produced about 450,000 tons of coal per annum. Part of Harry Senior's maintenance job entailed inspecting the colliery's equipment on Sundays, the miners' day of rest. He was not a man to be scared easily but could never shake off the feeling of dread as he descended into the eerily quiet, all-enveloping darkness of the pit shafts.

Football was an escape from the harsh realities of working life; Harry Senior shared a passion for the game with his younger brother George, who would go on to coach Darlington FC. With support from his employer, he was able to carve out a successful second career as an amateur centre-half with the pit team; indeed, the offer of employment at the pit may have been linked to his footballing prowess. Two years after its formation in 1921 Chilton Colliery Recreational Football Club joined the Durham Palatine League and quickly became a force in amateur football. With Harry Senior as captain, Chilton progressed to the semi-finals of the FA Amateur Cup in 1925, beating Bishop Auckland and then Dulwich Hamlet, in front of 7,000 supporters, before succumbing to Clapton. The following season saw an exciting FA Cup run with victories over league opposition in Carlisle United and Rochdale before elimination at South Shields, then of the Second Division. The club would subsequently gain election to the Northern League at the fifth attempt.

The cup exploits cemented Harry Senior's reputation as a talented centre-half, leading to an invitation by the Football Association to play for a representative XI against Leeds and Durham Universities on 3 March 1926. Despite appalling weather at Darlington's Feethams ground, and a lack of familiarity with his team-mates, newspaper reports praised his defensive dominance in a 5–2 victory over the Varsities.

This appearance, and the high profile of the cup runs, alerted Stockport County's scout in the north-east, prompting the offer of a contract with the Third Division North outfit in the summer of 1926. The lure of professional football was enough for Henry to relocate the family to Pitt Street, in the Edgeley district of the Cheshire town best known as the north's capital of hatmaking. Joining the club as a 'Player-Assistant Trainer', his debut came at Accrington's Peel Park on 11 September, a rousing match in which County came from two goals down to win 4–2. The *Stockport Advertiser* reporter gave guarded praise for the new recruit: 'Catterick, though not over quick in his movements, did quite well in his initial appearance, and there was a constructiveness in his play that stood his side in good stead.' Harry Senior made 14 first-team appearances, briefly playing alongside the future Everton winger Ted Critchley, before being released from his playing duties at the season's end, aged 29. He subsequently secured employment as resident steward at Edgeley Conservative Club on St Matthew's Road, two minutes' walk from Edgeley Park, County's ground; later in life he would run an off-licence on nearby Dale Street. Upon hanging up his boots Harry Senior began a 20-year association with County's backroom staff, starting as reserve team trainer but progressing to the interim manager's position.

Often mistaken for a policeman due to his height and bolt-upright gait, Harry Senior became well known in the town through his twin roles. Family trips on foot became a slow procession as people would hail him in the street and stop for a chat – more often than not about football.

BEGINNINGS

Young Harry was, by his own admission, 'weaned on football'. His first encounters as a spectator would have been the tough, uncompromising world of pit football at Chilton. He learned from his father that there could be no glamour without hard graft; as he basked in the glory of Everton's 1963 League Championship success he would recall the ethos that his father had instilled in him:

> There is no substitute for courage. That is my firm belief, it always has been. It is essential in modern football. Everybody connected with a big soccer club must have it, from the chairman to the lowliest boot boy. Of course you need skill, but no amount of skill can ever compensate for a lack of courage.

Harry remembered being a child of nine or ten in Stockport, sitting in the corner of the dressing room at Edgeley Park, meeting the players and taking in the match-day sights, sounds and smells. As he progressed through St Matthew's School, it was clear that he had inherited his father's footballing genes. He appeared for Brinksway in the Junior Organising Committee League and in 1934, aged 14, he was selected for Stockport Schoolboys who that season won the Cheshire Schools Shield. Interestingly, Harry played at centre-half – his father's position – in the cup campaign. In the final, a 2–1 victory, his deep-lying position did not prevent him from scoring with a long-range shot past the sun-blinded Ellesmere Port goalkeeper. Harry eventually moved to outside-right and then centre-forward as his physique developed to a modest 5ft 9in, weighing just under 12 stone. By his 15th birthday he was representing Brinksway in the Youth Organising Committee League – netting 73 times in one season. Harry would occasionally turn out for Ward Street Old Boys Reserves, a team with links to the Boys' Brigade. The local press reported on one such appearance with the headline 'Catterick's Goal Lust' – he had hit five in a 13–1 thrashing of Marple's Rose Hill 'B'.

Such was his progress that Harry joined Cheadle Heath Nomads. The Nomads were affiliated to Cheadle Heath Sports Club and played in the Lancashire and Cheshire League. Local press reports documented Harry's goalscoring feats, which included frequent braces and hat-tricks against the likes of Old Glossopians.

Harry Senior, although no doubt revelling in his son's sporting development, ensured that Harry Junior had a trade to fall back on. He would tell his son: 'You've got to make as good a life as you can for yourself.' Thus in July 1934 the 14-year-old started a six-year apprenticeship at the Mirrlees Bickerton and Day plant in nearby Hazel Grove; 'Mirrlees' was an engineering firm specialising in the manufacture of diesel engines for marine and industrial use. Harry would earn 11 shillings per week rising (with increments on each birthday) to £1.15s.6d by the time the apprenticeship ended in 1940. Harry is believed to have made a number of appearances for the works football team during his time on the payroll.

By the age of 16, Harry was attracting the attention of local professional football clubs. Stockport County hoped that family links might entice him to sign on at Edgeley Park, but his likeliest destination appeared to be either of the Mancunian football powerhouses, United or City. Louis Rocca, United's scout, was keen to bring Harry to Old Trafford but City stole a march, signing Harry on amateur Manchester League forms. It came as a shock to most observers, therefore, when it was announced on 3 March 1937 that 17-year-old Harry Catterick would be joining the Merseyside giants, Everton Football Club.

CHAPTER TWO

SCHOLAR AT THE SCHOOL OF SCIENCE

THE REASON for Harry signing with a team 40 miles away, when there were suitors on his doorstep, lay in family connections. Charlie Gee was a Stockport-born centre-half who had been coached by Harry Senior as he came up through the County youth ranks in the late 1920s. Such was Gee's impact upon breaking into the first team in 1929 that First Division suitors were immediately making frequent scouting visits to Edgeley Park. When the hard-up Hatters were obliged to cash in during the 1930 close season, Harry Senior encouraged Gee to choose Everton. Within a year Gee was a regular in the Goodison Park outfit's first XI seeking promotion back to the top flight, and a year later he was a full England international. In 1937 the time came for Gee to return the favour to the Cattericks. Aware of young Harry's promise, Gee recommended him to Everton's secretary, Theo Kelly. According to Harry's memoir, Gee 'painted golden pictures of life at Goodison Park' to the Catterick family. The sales pitch was successful and Gee was present as Harry and his parents signed the registration forms, with Kelly, at Edgeley Conservative Club.

Harry had initially joined the Merseysiders as an amateur on Liverpool Combination forms. Thrown into the A team (the club's third team), he scored goals in the County Combination against B.I. Social and South Liverpool Reserves. Impressed, the club moved swiftly to secure his services on a professional basis. Everton offered Harry terms of £3 per week in the season and £2 during the summer break with a signing-on bonus of £5. The board also agreed to grant Cheadle Heath Sports Club £10 in lieu of a transfer fee; a further donation of £25 was made in 1946. The contract was on a part-time basis due to Harry's ongoing five-year engineering apprenticeship with Mirrlees – Harry Senior remained resolute that his son should see through his studies and have a safety net should his football dreams be shattered.

Everton had been dubbed 'The School of Science' after the former Derby County player and journalist Steve Bloomer observed, 'We owe a great deal to Everton. No matter where they play, and no matter whether they are well or badly placed in the table, they always manage to serve football of the highest scientific order. Everton always worship at the shrine of craft and science and never do they forget the standard of play they set out to achieve.' The School of Science tag would sometimes be an albatross around the neck of the club in later, leaner times, but in 1937 they had won four league titles and two FA Cups, and were established as one of England's leading clubs alongside the likes of Arsenal, Aston Villa, Sunderland and Liverpool.

First and foremost in the public's consciousness was record-breaking scorer, and living football legend, William Ralph 'Dixie' Dean. Dean was, by the time of Harry's arrival, in the twilight of his top-flight playing career as injuries, advancing age and disagreements with Everton secretary Theo Kelly took their toll. The goalscoring prodigy Tommy Lawton had been acquired from Burnley in 1936 as heir-apparent to Dixie, while Robert 'Bunny' Bell provided solid competition for the centre-forward position. The squad was also peppered with household names such as Joe Mercer, Cliff Britton, Ted Sagar and Billy Cook.

With such talent in depth it was clear that Harry, still rough around the edges, would continue to learn his trade away from the first team. At A-team level he made an immediate impact, scoring 23 goals in his first full season including two hat-tricks and a five-goal haul against Haydock Athletic. His goalscoring form led to a breakthrough into the reserves – scoring twice on his Central League debut at Manchester United in November 1937. Fittingly, Charlie Gee was also in the team that day and laid on one of the goals. The reserves, who won the Central League that season, contained a mix of promising youngsters and star names such as Albert Geldard, 'Jock' Thomson, Alex Stevenson, Stan Bentham, Jimmy 'Nat' Cunliffe and Torry Gillick. Harry would play a handful of non-competitive games with, and train alongside, Lawton and Dean. This gave him the opportunity to observe and learn from them at close quarters; speaking to the author and journalist John Roberts in 1977 he compared the two forwards:

> I had watched Billy Dean playing in the Lancashire area since
> I was about twelve years of age. There was no doubt in terms
> of heading a ball I have seen no-one like him. He always had
> time. Tom Lawton was a truly great header of the ball but in

that particular skill he did not match up to Billy; with Deany it was only a flick of the head and it was in the back of the net. Tom Lawton was in a tighter era, the game had tightened up defensively so it was more difficult. As an overall player he may have been a bit better but when it came to heading – Deany was the best.

The 1938/39 season saw Everton win their fifth league title, with Lawton's 34 league goals firing the team to glory. A bright future for the Toffees seemed to beckon but, as was the case when the club won the title in 1914/15, war would stymie the momentum and have a catastrophic impact on the careers of many of the footballers.

Pre-season preparations for the following season were overshadowed by the looming conflict in Europe – neighbours Liverpool had joined the Territorial Army en-masse in anticipation of war being declared. Nonetheless the season kicked off at Goodison on 26 August – a 1–1 draw with Brentford. After a mid-week victory over Aston Villa, the following Saturday's match at Ewood Park, in which Lawton scored in a third consecutive fixture, was to be the last Football League match for seven years. By then Nazi Germany had invaded Poland, obliging Prime Minister Neville Chamberlain to declare war on the Axis powers on Sunday 3 September. An emergency meeting of the League Management Committee, chaired by Everton's Will Cuff, led to the indefinite suspension of domestic competitive football.

Looking back with John Roberts, Harry believed the tumultuous world events broke up a team that would have gone on to collect further honours: 'They always played, to my mind, a very good style of football. I think the team that won the 1939 championship would have gone on to win two or three more had it not been for the war. There were so many good players.'

Everton's players were fortunate that, uniquely, their club paid up their contracts – elsewhere contracts were summarily terminated with no payment. Players would be obliged to join the forces or seek alternative employment until such time as peace was restored. Everton's T.G. Jones, doyen of defenders and known as 'The Prince of Centre-Halves', went to work in an aircraft factory while Charlie Gee became a demolition worker with the Air Raid Precautions organisation before training as a schoolteacher.

The clamour for the return of football came from supporters, clubs and businesses. Future Everton chairman E. Holland Hughes, secretary of the Pools Promoters Association, lobbied hard for a resumption of football fixtures – as an interim measure the pools coupons were featuring Irish matches. Soon friendlies and exhibition matches were being arranged in areas deemed to be safe from bombing. One such fixture was a 4–1 Everton victory in a Merseyside derby at Goodison. Fundraising games were arranged, including one in aid of the Red Cross hosted by Everton between a Football League XI and an 'All-British' team. By October the Wartime League had been established consisting of ten regional divisions; Everton were placed in the 'West' section alongside the likes of Stockport County, Liverpool, Manchester United, Manchester City, New Brighton, Tranmere Rovers, Stoke City and Chester. A Football League War Cup was established in lieu of the FA Cup, with regional sections feeding into a national final. A year later the ten leagues were consolidated into two: the Northern Regional League and the Southern Regional League. A 'League West' was added in 1943.

Wartime league football was austere, with neglected stadiums, cabbage-patch pitches and poor attendances as so many young men were working flat-out in factories and pits or serving in the armed forces. That said, the sport played a significant role in boosting morale; in some respects wartime was English football's 'finest hour'. At Everton Theo Kelly, Harry Cooke, Gordon Watson and others played a heroic role in keeping the club functioning – even creating a night-watch rota to ensure that Goodison did not succumb to incendiary bombs. In 1940 Cooke and E. Storey were praised by the Everton board for having dealt with 59 incendiary devices in the environs of Goodison Park; Goodison was damaged by an explosive bomb just once, getting off lightly in comparison to the likes of Old Trafford.

Due to the difficulties of travel and players serving in the forces or other occupations, clubs would struggle to field their regular line-ups. 'Guesting' became commonplace; players billeted in an area would be asked by nearby clubs to make up the numbers. Intended to assist clubs in dire straits, the system would be abused, with clubs bidding for the services of available star names to boost gate receipts. Everton were lucky in that their depth of resources meant they rarely required guests, indeed they provided a rich seam of talent for more needy teams; it was reported that on one Saturday in October 1939 no fewer than 21 Everton players were turning out for teams up and down the country.

The outbreak of war would ultimately prove detrimental to many football careers yet, paradoxically, it offered a short-term boost for Harry. Still based and working in Stockport, he struggled to make it to Goodison Park on a regular basis. Although called up to the RAF, most likely at a nearby location such as RAF Handforth 61 MU stores and maintenance facility, Harry was swiftly demobbed and assigned to a reserved occupation. He would use his recently acquired engineering skills at the Mirrlees plant, where he was by now earning £3.13s.0d per week. A number of Harry's contemporaries, notably Tommy Lawton, recalled criticism for failing to fight on the front line, but Harry never went on record about his experiences. Everton's loss would be Stockport's gain as County enlisted Harry whenever he was unable to travel to Goodison or was deemed surplus to the Toffees' requirements. In fact he would make his Hatters' debut before his Everton bow, facing a Stoke City team including Stanley Matthews on 28 October 1939. Despite falling to a 4–2 defeat at the Victoria Ground, the *Stockport Advertiser* hailed the immediate impression made by the teenager: 'Young Harry Catterick is a decided acquisition and he gave the best centre-forward display I have seen in years.'

As the war progressed the Stockport press hailed the local lad as the best leader of the line since Alf Lythgoe in his pomp, a decade earlier. Despite never playing for them in peacetime football, Stockport County historians credit him with being one of the club's most effective ever forwards. He would go on to live in Stockport for the entirety of his playing career. Being a private man, Harry liked to maintain a division between his work and home life; even in later years as a football manager he kept all his banking in the town as he knew how people could gossip.

As Tommy Lawton was called up as an instructor in the Army PT Corps and billeted to Aldershot, first-team opportunities began to arise for Harry at Everton. In Lawton's absence Harry made his Everton first-team bow in a 2–2 draw with Manchester City on 9 March 1940 before scoring his first goal a week later in a 5–0 rout of Chester FC.

Away from work and sport, Harry married Margery Robinson at Cheadle Parish Church in July 1941. His best man was Grimsby Town's Fred Howe, who had been guesting with Harry for County. Howe was another footballing 'Stopfordian' – a native of Stockport – but in contrast to Harry he had forged his career on the red half of Merseyside. Margery worked at the nearby Cadbury factory but in her leisure time was a keen hockey player with Cheadle Heath; it is reasonable to assume that the couple met through their sporting interests. The newlyweds, after a brief honeymoon in Harrogate, would live on Dale Street in Edgeley; the marriage would last fourteen years and produce two daughters.

Growing up in the late 1940s and early 50s the girls would watch Harry and Margery play tennis at Edgeley's municipal park, close to the family home. Daughter Joyce recalls that for Harry there was always a 'correct' way of doing something – be it holding a racquet, swinging a golf club or rowing a boat – and he ensured that they were taught it. Harry was also a good cricketer and golfer, although Joyce recalls that the latter was not encouraged by football clubs as there was a belief that it 'slowed' players. Although not really interested in the social side of the game,

Harry would get up early and play a few holes at Davenport Golf Club. He would frequently take the girls to school before training and during the close season the girls would be taken out of school early for their summer holidays.

The 1942/43 season kicked off with Harry lining up against Everton in the red of Manchester United, scoring in a 2–2 draw. He had jumped at the opportunity to turn out for United on five occasions, playing alongside future Everton manager Johnny Carey:

> *What an experience, playing alongside magnificent soccer crafts-men: Breedon, Griffiths, Redmond, Bert Whalley, Bill Porter, McKay, Bryant, Johnny Morris, John Carey, Stan Pearson and Jack Rowley. How could anyone fail to learn from these supreme players.*

In July 1943 Harry's father was appointed manager of Stockport County, a position he would hold until the end of the war when Bob Marshall returned from a period in the army and subsequently working in an aircraft factory. Catterick Senior would manage Catterick Junior on 42 occasions. For reasons unclear Harry would also make a solitary goalscoring appearance for Hartlepools United against Sunderland in October 1944.

In the final two seasons of the wartime league Harry was able to become a regular starter again with his parent club – often in place of the unavailable Tommy Lawton. A highlight was a hat-trick in a 7–1 defeat of Blackpool on Boxing Day 1945. The 'make do and mend' approach needed to keep wartime football going was never better illustrated than when Harry's two principal clubs met at Goodison Park in front of 8,699 spectators shortly before Christmas 1944. 'Pilot' (Don Kendall, who would handle some of Everton's press affairs in the 1950s and 60s) of the *Evening Express* bore witness:

> *Stockport County not only arrived late for today's match with Everton at Goodison Park but were three players short. They had to borrow from Everton, Catterick to lead the attack and Bentham to play left back. In addition they enlisted the services of a soldier, Michael Murphy, who had come to watch the game as a spectator. Murphy, who played at outside right, was a South Liverpool reserve player before the war, but this was his first war-time club game. Hill, the County inside right, only came*

out of the mines at 12.30 today having gone on the 4 a.m. shift;
Cleave, a repatriated prisoner-of-war, was at centre half. Had it
not been for the quick thinking and industry of Mr Theo Kelly
we might not have had any match… it was Kelly who got the
necessary registration forms for Murphy to sign and who in the
end dashed to the microphone to announce the team changes. It
was the typical 'Kelly touch'.

An interesting footnote was that a month later Everton travelled to Edgeley Park for a cup fixture, and this time Harry played for Everton, scoring against his father's team. 'Just another of those wartime curiosities,' as Pilot aptly put it.

On 27 January 1945 Harry lined up for County again against The Toffees in a Northern Cup fixture. The game, played in Arctic conditions, was most notable for Tommy Lawton scoring his 400th senior peacetime and wartime goal. Harry would grab Stockport's consolation goals in a 9–2 romp but he'd have another reason to remember the game with less affection than Lawton. In the freezing conditions, with no baths available, a plaster over a cut on his thigh could not be removed and septicaemia set in. His condition was described in the press as 'touch and go' and, in an era just before the widespread availability of penicillin, 'May and Baker' sulfa-pyridine tablets were administered. Harry pulled through and returned to action for County on 17 March, scoring four goals in a hammering of Manchester City. Four days later he was playing for Everton in a Merseyside derby.

C H A P T E R T H R E E

STARTING OVER – THE POST-WAR YEARS

IN MAY 1945, Germany surrendered following the fall of Berlin. However, with Britain still in a parlous state, and hostilities ongoing in the Far East, the wartime league's structure continued for one further season.

In the final season of regional leagues Harry was able to focus on Everton, for whom he hit 26 goals in 28 league and cup appearances, and only turned out twice for County. Sadly he was again hampered by illness and injury: having recovered from a bout of flu he succumbed, again, to blood poisoning – this time in his arm. On this occasion the bout was less serious and he managed to play through the pain, as Pilot described when reporting for the *Evening Express* on a victory over Newcastle:

> *Everton had an unknown hero in their latest championship quest victory... This was Harry Catterick, their 25-year-old centre-forward and one of the inside trio whose value in the market is more than £25,000. Only a player with as big a heart as Catterick would have played at all. Six days before Harry contracted blood-poisoning in an arm and was under continuous treatment. Despite this handicap, however, Catterick insisted on playing, but only after trainer Mr Harry Cooke had made special business to protect the arm. Mr Cooke did a grand job and I am certain that not one of the 54,700 spectators knew that Catterick was operating under such a handicap. Certainly the centre-forward went into every tackle with all his balance unaffected – proved by the magnificent manner in which he took*

his goal late on – a splendid drive right along the ground.

A week later he sustained another injury in a match against Sheffield Wednesday and Pilot, once more, praised his fortitude:

> *Only 'guts' enabled him to carry on at outside right in the second*
> *half. Catterick's poisoned arm was still troubling him and the*
> *kick under the knee was so severe that he could not walk after*
> *getting out of the bath and had to be driven to the station in a*
> *director's car. Harry was walking with a stick when Secretary-*
> *Manager Mr. Kelly went to see him yesterday. I say, after deep*
> *consideration, that had Catterick been at centre-forward all*
> *through Everton would have won well.*

Competitive domestic football finally returned on 5 January 1946 with the resumption of the FA Cup. After seven years in the wartime school of hard knocks, Harry was determined to make up for lost time and seize the opportunity to be the club's peacetime centre-forward. However, the lack of top-class action and coaching in the preceding years had undoubtedly stunted his development, added to which his appalling luck with injuries meant he would not fulfil the potential that had been evident when he joined Everton in 1937.

Though no world-beater, Harry was a competent top-flight player who was unlucky to be judged in the context of his illustrious Everton forebears rather than on his own merits. The journalist Len Capeling recalls interviewing Tommy Lawton and suggesting that Harry was a limited player: 'I had this in my head that he was not a very good player just like Alex Ferguson and some other top managers. I was fortunate enough to meet Tommy towards the end of his life, living in Nottingham, and I ventured this opinion of Catterick. Tommy had the opposite opinion, he thought Catterick was not a bad player and was not thought of as a good centre-forward as he had come after two greats. He felt that he'd had a bad press and was a decent centre-forward.'

As a teenager, Everton supporter Ray Terry watched a lot of Everton's wartime fixtures in which Harry led the attack, or played in a wider role if Lawton was in the side: 'My recollections of Harry as a player are that he was fast, fearless, never shirked a tackle and had good ball control but limited heading ability. I suppose he suffered somewhat from being a contemporary of Tommy Lawton, who was a big man and a very accomplished footballer.'

The shock departure of Tommy Lawton to Chelsea, due to marital problems, was Harry's gain as secretary-manager Theo Kelly handed him a long-awaited competitive debut in a two-legged tie against Preston North End (this season was the only time in the FA Cup's history that two-legged ties have been used). At right-half on the opposing side was a player named in the *Evening Express* as 'Willie Shankly'; the man subsequently better known as 'Bill' had only been demobbed the previous day. Harry did not disappoint, channelling six years of frustration to notch a debut goal in a man-of-the-match performance. He was on hand to fire into the roof of the net when Preston's goalkeeper, Fairbrother, failed to collect a Wally Boyes cross. Pilot was effusive in his praise for Harry in the *Evening Express*:

HEROIC CATTERICK
Pilot's Log

Of all the Everton players who trudged through the sticky Deepdale mud I thought Harry Catterick stood out on his own. Yes, and the fact that Harry failed three times in the last four minutes with only Fairbrother to beat did not cause me to change my opinion that in Catterick, Everton have a great leader in his ability and enthusiasm.

Do you know why Catterick missed those openings which would have given Everton a nice lead? Well, Fairbrother's cunning in narrowing the shooting space, and more important, the fact that for 85 minutes Catterick had been subjected to the toughest buffeting I have seen for a long time. Harry was bumped by everything and everybody, but he still battled on to the last gasp of his endurance. And it shows the wonderful spirit of Catterick when I tell you that as soon as he got into the dressing-room after the game Harry said, 'Sorry, boys, that I missed those chances.' No excuses, no alibis, just a genuine expression of regret. Yet Catterick, as he was assured quickly by his colleagues, need have no cause for regret. He did all that was humanly possible and to my mind, he was something of the hero of the game.

Of course, they were all heroes to a degree for it needed doggedness to stick to a hectic pace on that morass.

Everton's Cup campaign came to an abrupt halt in the second leg four days later. With the match tied at 2–2 on aggregate after 90 minutes, Preston consigned the Blues to a 3–4 aggregate defeat in extra time. Perhaps inevitably, Bill Shankly scored the deciding goal from the penalty spot.

The spring of 1946 brought wartime league football to an end. In all Harry had made 71 Everton league and cup appearances in wartime football, scoring 55 goals. For Stockport County his 98 goals in 122 appearances included eight hat-tricks and a four-goal salvo against Manchester City.

The Football League programme finally resumed in August 1946 but the reigning champions were shadows of their illustrious 1939 vintage. Pre-war stars such as T.G. Jones and Joe Mercer were falling foul of Theo Kelly while others were nearing the end of their careers. The 1940s and 50s would see Everton recruit a sizeable Irish contingent – pioneered by the arrival of Peter Farrell and Tommy Eglington from Shamrock Rovers to form a left-sided partnership. Bandy-legged Londoner Wally 'Nobby' Fielding was signed after being spotted while on army service in Italy. The season retained the fixture list of the aborted 1939/40 campaign and so kicked off with a home fixture against Brentford. As he lined up with his team-mates on the Goodison pitch that afternoon, Harry had honour of being the first Everton player to wear the famous royal blue number nine shirt in an official league fixture (numbered shirts were first introduced for the 1939/40 season that was voided after the first three games).

After a disappointing 0–2 opening-day reverse, and two further goalless appearances, Harry broke his elbow at Ewood Park. Determined to retain his standing as the first-choice number nine, he rushed back with undue haste, fracturing the arm again shortly before Christmas. The ill-timed injury forced the Everton board to seek reinforcements. Having had Liverpool steal a march on them in acquiring Newcastle's Albert Stubbins, Theo Kelly drafted in Ephraim 'Jock' Dodds from Blackpool. Harry, fit again by mid-February, was unable to reclaim his first-term berth for the remainder of a bitterly disappointing season on both personal and club levels. Everton finished the season in tenth place; salt was rubbed in the wound when their neighbours across Stanley Park, inspired by Stubbins, Billy Liddell and Jack Balmer, claimed the first post-war league title.

It would be mid-September 1947 before Harry was recalled to the first team – it was reported in the Merseyside press that he 'revitalised the attack' and he scored his first league goal in his second outing of the season at Stamford Bridge. Sadly, further goals failed to flow, moving Pilot to comment: 'Everton's deputy centre-forward Catterick tries hard – almost too hard – and is still a little luckless. As big-hearted as they come, Catterick fights every inch and my only criticism of him was a tendency to overdo trapping instead of more use of the first-time pass.'

In March 1948 Harry requested a transfer having been overlooked, despite an injury to Dodds, for a first-team match against Arsenal. Stockport County made a bid to bring him to his home-town club but were unable meet Everton's asking price. An approach from Nottingham Forest seemed more promising but did not come to fruition, as the *Liverpool Echo*'s 'Ranger' explained:

> *Manager Billy Walker of Nottingham Forest watched him play against Burnley Reserves. Satisfied with what he saw Mr Walker contacted Everton and agreed on the fee – which was exceptionally reasonable. Catterick declined to sign for Forest as it required him to live in Nottingham. He would have been obliged to find a home, and possibly a job. But as all his friends and relatives are in Stockport, where he also had a good job, and is on regular top money with Everton, he felt he had nothing to gain in the Midlands.*

Pilot also reported Stoke City to be in the running for Harry's signature but the forward claimed to have declined in view of the fact that he was 'in the running for the post of Youth Organiser in Stockport' – presumably a reference to the Youth Organising Committee, which ran a local football league.

In October 1948 Cliff Britton became Everton's full-time manager with secretary-manager Theo Kelly reverting to a purely administrative role. Britton, after a distinguished playing career at wing-half for Everton and England, had made a promising start to his managerial career at Burnley. Once ensconced at Goodison he restored Harry, his former Everton reserve and wartime team-mate, to the number nine shirt. Britton's strict disciplinarian approach, and preference for leaving the coaching staff to take training sessions, is likely to have been an influence on Harry as his thoughts turned to a post-playing career. After a promising return to first-team action, yielding winning goals against Huddersfield and Aston Villa, Harry's injury curse struck again when he pulled a muscle in the annual match against the Army in Aldershot.

Harry soon overcame this latest setback but, against Wolves on 4 December, worse was to follow. 'Pilot' was reporting at Molineux:

> *Catterick chased a ball to the line and after hooking it behind*

crashed into the concrete surround and lay flat... Both trainers dashed across and then a stretcher was called; fortunately no stretcher was needed. Trainer Harry Cooke removed Catterick's left boot and the player walked behind the goal where he insisted on having his boot put on again. This was done and Catterick then left the field. Catterick must be one of football's unluckiest players, for this was his first game following injury. Catterick came back in the 70th minute, going to outside right with Corr in the centre.

It would not be until the 1949/50 campaign that Harry was able to re-establish himself as first-choice number nine, his 25 appearances producing 12 goals. The 1950 close season was enlivened by 'Radar', in the *Evening Express*, revealing that Harry's former rival for the number nine shirt, Jock Dodds, was acting as an agent for the Millonarios club of Bogota. A number of cash-rich Colombian teams, with no affiliation to FIFA, had been actively recruiting English players; the offer of riches was tempting for players stuck on the English maximum wage of £12 per week. Perhaps the most notable exile was Neil Franklin of Stoke City and England, who spurned the chance to appear in the 1950 World Cup in Brazil, accepting instead an offer to play for Independiente Santa Fe. Independiente also secured the services of Charlie Mitten, who had left Manchester United during a South American Tour. The 'Bogota Bandit', as Mitten was dubbed, returned to England within a year only to be met with a fine and six-month ban by the FA.

With former Evertonian Billy Higgins having signed for Millonarios, Dodds turned his attention to Harry and centre-half Jack Humphreys. Although Humphreys gave the offer short shrift, Harry was tempted by the alleged £4,000 signing-on fee and £100 monthly salary, as he told the *Express*: 'If nothing materialises I shall re-sign for Everton, it will have to be a good offer to induce me to leave a club of Everton's standing. They have shown me every consideration and although I am in football for my livelihood, I want to show the same consideration to them.' After re-flection, influenced by family commitments, an imminent second benefit payment from Everton and potential FA sanctions, Harry elected to remain at Goodison.

The 1950/51 season, though disastrous for Everton, saw Harry enjoy a period of good form which reached its zenith in October with a hat-trick in a 5–1 away victory at Craven Cottage. Ironically Cliff Britton was not there to witness it as he was scouting another striker at White Hart Lane – Burnley's Harry Potts. In Britton's absence the *Daily Post* hailed Harry's performance: 'Catterick's change of fortune came deservedly. His three goals were all excellently taken. He will derive much confidence as will the side as a whole from succeeding so outstandingly.'

Symptomatic of Harry's woeful luck, injury struck again two days later in the annual match against the Army, with Harry up against 'Gentleman' John Charles. Leslie Edwards in the Liverpool *Daily Post* reported:

> *Harry Catterick, the Everton centre forward, who jumped into form with three goals at Fulham on Saturday, pulled a thigh muscle playing against the Army at Aldershot yesterday and is likely to be out of the game for three weeks at least. Catterick was two yards ahead of the Army centre half, Charles, when the damage was done. Charles, who is the biggest and probably the best to arrive in football since 'Dixie' Dean, saw Catterick go down. He banged the ball straight to touch and bent down to attend to the Everton player.*

Harry would play only four more top-flight matches for Everton and looked on helplessly as the team spiralled towards the relegation zone. Despite appearing to be safe from relegation at the start of March, the team could muster only three goals in the final 11 matches of the season. A disastrous sequence of seven defeats, three draws and only one win culminated in a 0–6 humiliation at Sheffield Wednesday on the final day of the season. While newly promoted Tottenham Hotspur romped to the title with a revolutionary intricate passing game, Everton were relegated on goal difference and would not return to the top flight for three seasons.

CHAPTER FOUR
PLAYER-MANAGER

IN THE SUMMER of 1951, as Everton started life in the unfamiliar surroundings of the Second Division, Harry was, as he reflected in 1977 to John Roberts, 'over the hill'. Advancing years and frequent injuries had diminished his effectiveness and he was all too aware that his Goodison career was nearing its end. With commendable foresight he had already been looking to the future, as he recounted in his unpublished memoirs in 1964:

> *One naturally has always to look ahead… no matter what your walk of life. I was thrilled with life at Goodison and with football generally, so it was an early decision that, given the chance, I would remain in the game after my playing days. It was an early decision and I never changed it. Theo Kelly was of great assistance. He revealed to me how the soccer machine 'ticked over', the little (but so important) points of administration and all the angles. I became convinced that an administrative role was my destiny.*

Kelly was a divisive figure at Everton – his flair for administration and dedication to the club during the lean war years were counter-balanced by a prickly personality that led to fall-outs with most of the club's star players of the 1930s and 1940s. Harry, however, held him in high esteem, as he told John Roberts: 'Theo was a great PR role man, the best I have ever known. He could open doors that were closed anywhere. He had a wonderful personality required for the role and was a great organiser as a secretary. Any of the shortcomings he had were compensated by his ability to open doors.'

Harry's praise for Kelly's public relations skills was at odds with the prevailing view of the club secretary. Although a talented administrator, well connected in football circles, Kelly was regarded as having poor interpersonal skills by many of Harry's contemporaries. Harry went on to reveal to Roberts how other players sought his counsel:

> As a player, in my later years at Everton, most of the players would come to me and ask questions about contracts and what one could do or couldn't do – which wasn't a lot as the dice were loaded in favour of the clubs. They would always seek my advice – why I don't know. I was the guy in the corner that took things seriously and they'd come and ask me about terms – whether they should accept or not. I wasn't the union man but they thought I'd come out with a little bit of common sense.

After a playing career that had failed to reach expectations, Harry would be relentless in his pursuit of a second career in the sport – as a manager. To this end, in 1951 he attended a course to receive an FA coaching certificate. Twenty years later Harry recounted to Geoffrey Mather of the Daily Express how, as he prepared for management, he attended debates and discussion groups: 'So many managers are unable to express themselves...and the very place it matters is not the pitch, it is the boardroom. If one can't put one's ideas over in the boardroom, effort during the week, on or off the pitch, falls by the wayside.' Despite thoughts of moving on, Harry started the 1951/52 season as Everton's first-choice number nine. This was to prove only a stay of execution and he was dropped after a barren run of four games. In the next match the centre-forward's shirt was worn by debutant Dave Hickson – the start of an illustrious career for a man destined to become known as the Cannonball Kid. As one Everton playing career blossomed another withered – Harry had played his final match in royal blue, his peacetime league career bookended by defeats to Brentford.

Within days Harry's name was on a list circulated by Everton listing players for whom the club were 'open to offers'. Blackburn Rovers expressed an interest in Harry but no firm offer was tabled. By November, Harry was in Goodison limbo, festering in the reserves, and becoming increasingly frustrated by the club's stance on his request for a free transfer. On 17 November the board had deemed it not 'timely' to grant a free transfer. Four days later Harry broke his silence in a telephone conversation with 'Radar', the Liverpool Echo correspondent, who reported that Harry, 'a grand club man', had 'never given the club a moment's trouble all these fourteen years'. Radar reminded his readers that Harry had been loyal when approached by Millonarios: 'Unlike some of those who did a midnight flit, he took the straight course and advised the club, and finally turned the offer down… Catterick felt that after his long service he could not let Everton down. He was thanked by the then chairman for his straight-forwardness, and honesty.' Radar concluded by arguing that the board should repay this integrity by dropping the asking fee for him to move to another club: 'The idleness is doing him no good in playing and certainly not helping him to get away. I don't know the exact fee they are asking for him. But if it is such that the player's chances of getting away are then perhaps prejudiced then perhaps the board will consider the position.'

Within days of Radar's article going to print, Stan Cope, chairman of Third Division North Crewe Alexandra, enquired of his Everton counterpart as to Harry's availability. A transfer fee of £2,000 was agreed. The *Crewe Chronicle* had been speculating for weeks about the identity of the new manager before revealing in early December that Harry was the 'bright, young managerial talent' the board had identified. The news of Crewe's interest reached Harry in Stockport:

> *I was playing a round of golf with my old friend [the Stockport County and later Scotland manager] Andy Beattie when a messenger came up breathlessly saying, 'There's a telephone call for you.' The call? 'Was I interested in taking up the player-manager position at Crewe Alexandra?' My immediate reaction was 'This is it, take it!'*

Everton's board minutes gave a more sober version of events. Harry watched Crewe lose at Rochdale on 30 November and then entered into two hours of negotiations which broke down. Despite agreeing a salary of £14 per week, plus bonuses, the Railwaymen would not accede to Harry's other stipulations, which Crewe secretary Tom Bailey described as demands for 'lavish terms'.

A few days later Everton's board minutes recorded that Harry 'did not appear keen to go to Crewe but agreed to reconsider'. Following further negotiations at Goodison, a three-year deal was agreed. Harry bade farewell to his footballing home of the past 14 years and became Crewe's player-manager on Thursday 13 December. His peacetime Everton career had seen him play 71 times, notching a respectable if unspectacular 24 goals. The *Crewe Chronicle* welcomed the new manager: 'Harry Catterick, who was signed as player-manager on Thursday, has soon got down to business. He is a qualified coach on the FA coaching scheme and is on the panel of players who have been coaching at Cheshire schools.'

Two days after being appointed as player-manager Harry debuted for Crewe at centre-forward. Fittingly the away fixture was at Darlington, his birthplace. Being based in a railway town, Crewe travelled to away matches by train. Harry's recollections of his managerial debut centred not on the 1–0 victory but the shock discovery, upon pulling into Darlington station, that Crewe's scout in the north-east was female. He later remarked, 'No doubt my astonishment was evident; the two directors with me looked sheepishly at me and remarked that it might be a little unusual but that she was a good scout. I found the lady very knowledgeable on soccer and a great friend of the directors.'

The ever-supportive *Crewe Chronicle* celebrated the new appointment and debut victory. Harry also used the newspaper article to outline his blueprint for the Railwaymen: 'My main concern is to improve the standard of play... and my chief medium will be coaching. Playing myself does give me the opportunity of seeing the younger players, but I am going to get them together for as much coaching as my other work will allow.'

After the grandeur of Goodison, the reality of life as a player-manager in the lower leagues soon hit home:

> *The discrepancy between a club of Crewe's standing and Everton*
> *was enormous but nevertheless I learnt a lot. My first duty was*
> *to look at the team – not easy as I was in it! I soon realised that*
> *playing and managing was not possible. Like oil and water the*
> *two do not mix if consistent success is your objective. At Crewe*
> *I found a limited playing staff, inadequate facilities and every-*
> *thing on a small scale – like living on a shoestring.*

The Crewe board, Harry remarked, was made up of an ever-changing 'mixture of farmers, local shopkeepers and businessman. It seemed that at every board meeting I was introduced to someone new... another of those people who supply the cash and enthusiasm to keep such clubs in existence.'

In September 1966 Harry collaborated with journalist Mike Langley on a series of articles for publication in the *People* where he gave another insight into the approach of the board: 'A lot of the Crewe directors were farmers and countrymen; every time I discussed signing a new player two questions were invariably asked: "How big is he? What's his weight?" I often wondered if there was anything significant in the close proximity to the cattle market!'

The *Chronicle*'s sports editor was, as ever, gushing in his praise for the early impact made by Harry: 'It is no exaggeration to say that Catterick's leadership has inspired the team... it is just the tonic they have needed.' Harry was more circum-spect: 'We are not a great team but I am very well pleased with the grand spirit in the side.'

Harry would go on to make 17 appearances that season, scoring eight goals including a hat-trick in ten minutes in front of 2,800 spectators against Halifax. The team would finish the 1951/52 16th.

Despite the paucity of funds at Gresty Road, Harry was fortunate to inherit two gems in the left-sided partnership of local lads Johnny King and Frank Blun-stone. As part of Harry's transfer to Crewe, Everton were given first refusal on Blun-stone and an assurance that should he be transferred to another club Crewe would pay Everton £1,000. Blunstone, while still a teenager, made a lasting impression on Harry:

> *I was impressed by one amateur in particular. Frank Blunstone developed into one of the best outside-lefts in Britain. He was a man who dedicated himself to the game... so enthusiastic was he that I often had to curtail his training and practice. Voluntary training is one of the secrets of success; Blunstone was determined to reach the top and did with Chelsea.*

Frank Blunstone recalls: 'Harry signed me as a pro, as you couldn't sign until you were seventeen. We had another good young player in Johnny King, who was two years older than me and later went to Stoke and Cardiff. We were both inside-lefts so Harry switched me to outside-left and I never looked back as a number eleven. Harry once had us both in one afternoon as we were both very left-sided players and he wanted us to work on kicking with our weaker right side. So he had us chipping balls to each other with our right feet but Kingy and I kept missing it, so he said: "For Christ's sake, go back to your old ways!"'

Blunstone appeared alongside Harry on ten occasions and remembered his manager as 'not very big but a bustling, hard-working centre-forward; his control was quite good but you don't take much notice when you are sixteen!' Blunstone recalled that Harry, despite being a youthful managerial novice, was determined to stamp his authority, a facet he would take to his subsequent clubs. 'He was quite a disciplinarian; we did have some experienced players so he was quite strict and keen on the coaching side. He was very friendly with Eddie Lyons, who played at left-back. Harry brought him to the Alex from Millwall and then he took him to Rochdale with him. They were good friends and the families used to go on holiday together.'

When Blunstone's transfer to Chelsea came about in February 1953 it suited all parties concerned, as the winger recalled: 'Stoke came in and offered £15,000 for Kingy and myself but I turned it down – despite only being seventeen! Not long afterwards Harry called me in and told me that Chelsea had come in with an offer of £8,000 and said that the club were keen to take the money. He was very good about it and suggested that we went down there, as Chelsea were a top club. So we went on the train with the club secretary just for a look round and to see what the situation was – but I was so impressed I signed there and then.'

At Chelsea Blunstone would make over 300 appearances, taste League Championship success in 1955 and earn five England caps. Everton had not taken up their option of signing Blunstone on the basis of a negative director's scouting report. After the sale of Blunstone, cash-strapped Crewe asked Everton to reconsider the £1,000 payment clause triggered by the transfer; eventually a compromise payment of £500 was agreed upon. Harry, foreseeing the Blunstone transfer, had already brought in Eric Betts from Rochdale for a four-figure fee. The season, despite the loss of their star player, had been one of consolidation with a creditable tenth place finish. The consistently obsequious *Crewe Chronicle* was fulsome in its praise:

> *Crewe Alexandra's continued success has created a feeling of optimism within the club... and among the supporters. Much of this is due to the extensive coaching and prepared plan of campaign initiated by Harry Catterick, who is grateful to the players for their enthusiastic response. Basford for instance has changed his style completely.*

Harry restricted himself to just eight appearances in the forward line in the 1952/53 season, his second in charge, due to injury and the good form of centre-forward Jack Basford. Harry told the *Chronicle*: 'I have never known such a grand team spirit. One question is repeatedly asked: What is going to happen when I am fit – as I hope to be in the next six or seven days? Well if the team is playing well I will be content to continue with coaching and organising.' Harry would indeed focus on coaching, alongside trainer Archie Capper, making his farewell appearance as a professional against Grimsby Town at Blundell Park in the penultimate fixture of the season.

Harry became frustrated by the demands of being a player, and also with boardroom politics and the limited potential at Crewe. Gates were averaging only 5,800 despite the club having their best post-war season. He would bemoan this fact through the pages of the *Chronicle*; complaining to the press was a method he would use at all the clubs he managed.

In March 1953 Harry made it onto a four-man short-list, from over 60 applicants, to succeed the late Angus Seed at Barnsley. Not only did this post offer second-tier football but also, as Harry admitted to local journalists, a salary far in excess of what Crewe could offer. The post was eventually awarded to Barnsley player Tim Ward but it was abundantly clear that the ambitious young Crewe manager, determined to make up for the disappointments of his playing career, would be leaving Gresty Road at the earliest opportunity.

CHAPTER FIVE
ROCHDALE

IN THE SUMMER of 1953, shortly after the Queen's Coronation, Harry was successful in his application to succeed Jack Warner as manager at Rochdale FC. Crewe chairman Frank Cottrell released a joint statement with Harry confirming that they were 'parting on the best of terms' with Harry's contract being terminated by mutual consent with 18 months left to run. He left Crewe in better shape than when he had joined them, and the club posted a profit of £654 in his second season there.

The *Rochdale Observer* reported: 'He will have charge of team selection at Spotland and will be manager in the full sense of the term'. In retrospect 'Dale' seemed a strange choice for career progression; the club had just finished 22nd in Division Three North, only narrowly avoiding having to apply for re-election. The club also had a constant battle to galvanise interest in a town whose loyalties were split between football and rugby league. However, the role of manager without playing commitments was attractive to Harry, who was ready to hang up his boots after 16 years as a professional. In 1966 he explained to the *People* newspaper the physical impact life as a footballer had had on him: 'I've broken both arms and my nose. I carry the playing-day scar of eighteen stitches on my head and, occasionally, there's a twinge from a smashed-up ankle.' Other factors in accepting the post were a pay rise and the promise of an atmosphere created by the board that was considerably less claustrophobic than the one at Gresty Road. He intimated as much to the *Rochdale Observer* upon his appointment:

> One of the factors that swayed me to come to Rochdale was the
> progressive outlook of the board of directors whose views on policy
> were similar to my own. Much can be done by coaching and
> I shall be out there with the players all the time I can, giving
> personal supervision to coaching and training. First of all it is
> imperative that we cultivate local talent in a club in Rochdale's

position; I shall arrange as many trials as possible.

He was not exactly over-burdened with players. As pre-season training got under way there were only five professionals on the books, two of whom were tarrying about re-signing. With some hurried wheeler-dealing in the free-transfer market, 'trying to build bricks with straw', a small squad was assembled just in time for the season's opener against Carlisle at Brunton Park. Harry recalled to the *People*: 'I hadn't enough players even to stage a practice match.' There was no fairy-tale opening though as the Cumbrians notched seven goals without reply. As a dejected Harry trudged off the pitch at full-time, Carlisle's manager tapped him on the shoulder and offered words of consolation and encouragement: 'Don't let this worry you, son. We all have to start somewhere and you will get things going – keep at it.' Harry would frequently need to draw comfort from those words of wisdom as the team lost 6–0 to Hartlepools and Port Vale in the early-season fixtures and 'amassed' a meagre five points from the opening 12 fixtures of the season.

The Fred Radcliffe-led Rochdale board demonstrated, according to Harry, 'unswerving support and enthusiasm'.

> *Fred was an ideal chairman who let the manager manage – was discreetly out of the way if you didn't want him but on hand if needed. We had played at Bradford Park Avenue and lost to a dubious last-minute penalty. The team had played their hearts out for the bonus and away point. Mr Ratcliffe came into the changing room after the game and said, 'Harry, the ref cost the lads. I can't do anything about the point but I can give you this and tell you to treat the boys to a drink and a meal during the week.' I looked down and saw a bundle of notes – some £20 – the gesture was typical of the man and his love of soccer.*

It was no mean feat to, in Harry's words, 'buckle-to' and climb up to 19th place by the season's end. The battle was helped by the £2,000 acquisition of the veteran, former England, striker Jack Haines from Bradford Park Avenue. Haines would go on to make 60 league appearances for the club and was an astute acquisition, despite his advanced years.

The club's finances, despite the best efforts of Ratcliffe, remained in a dire state throughout Harry's five-year stay at Spotland. After a string of low attendances the bank manager decided 'enough was enough' and refused to increase the club's overdraft, which had reached its limit. An emergency board meeting was called without resolving the pressing issue of how to pay the players' wages, as normal, at midday on Friday. Harry was left to handle the situation:

> *By 11:30 the Club Secretary was still without the money and training had finished. The Secretary had hopes of someone providing a cheque but said it could take an hour and then he had to reach the bank and subsequently make-up the wage packets. Meanwhile the players were bathed, dressed, and waiting for the wages and an afternoon off training... I called the trainer and told him I wanted the players in the dressing room for a tactical talk about Saturday's fixture – it was the only way I could find to take up time. The players were livid but at last, at 2pm, I was called to the phone – the Secretary had achieved the improbable and secured the wages. Under their breath the players called me the biggest '#*X!' for keeping them so long but never knew how close they came to being without wages.*

On another occasion the electricity was cut off after a bill had remained unpaid. Harry recounted the tale to the *People* in 1966:

> *The trainer came in complaining: 'I've got two of the lads under heat treatment but the radiant lamp's broken down.' 'That's funny,' I said, 'my office light has just gone off too.' Then the groundsman burst in: 'Hey, Boss, the electricity men have just cut us off, we've not paid the bill.' No manager dare let his players know when a club is that hard up so I sent the trainer back to the treatment room saying, 'Just tell those two that a main fuse has blown and we can't repair it right away, then get them out of the ground – fast.*

On a more positive electrical subject, there was a considerable innovation at Spotland in 1954 with the introduction of floodlighting for a series of exhibition matches – several years ahead of the likes of Everton and Liverpool. As he had done at Crewe, Harry took to the press to bemoan a low turnout, labelling the 7,000-odd through the turnstiles for the St Mirren encounter as: 'The lowest so far for the opening of any floodlight installation in the country.'

With income suffering from the low attendances, the club's parlous financial situation forced Harry to pass on opportunities to sign future internationals Ray Charnley and Harry Gregg, despite respective asking prices of only £1,000 and £1,500.

The 1954/55 season saw progress and, despite the occasional heavy loss, Rochdale finished a creditable 12th; they also enjoyed a cup run which was halted by Charlton in a 3–1 defeat in front of a Spotland crowd of over 16,000. The following season saw the previous league placing repeated, but Harry was looking to improve the squad and made a bold, but doomed, moved for FA Cup final and England legend Stan Mortensen of Blackpool. Instead Dale secured the services of Andy McLaren, a former Scotland international striker.

A more significant signing was behind the scenes as Harry brought in promising coach Joe Fagan. Fagan, a Liverpudlian, had made his name as a defender at Manchester City before moving into non-league coaching at Nelson. Harry, aware of Fagan's potential, brought him in to replace Joe Duff, the club's trainer/coach driver, who had been injured in a road accident. One of Harry's greatest gifts was recruiting talented backroom staff to support him; Fagan was an inspired selection. Despite having a coaching team of only himself, Fagan and Arthur Griffiths, Harry was able to start his gradual transition from being a tracksuited coach to a suit-and-tie manager.

In Joe Fagan's biography, written by his son Andrew and Mark Platt, the former Rochdale player Brian Green recalled how Harry delegated the training pitch work: 'Harry would leave the training to Joe. "Work them hard," he would tell him. But Joe was great and training was always fun.'

Harry was now living in Heywood with Nancy, whom he had married in London in 1955, once his divorce from Margery was finalised. Harry's daughter Joyce recalls, 'We saw my dad every Sunday at eleven in the morning and we'd usually go to my grandparents for Sunday dinner and then go out for the afternoon. Of course the conversation between my dad and my granddad was always about football.' Despite his often austere public persona Harry was far from being a strict father. Joyce says, 'He'd take us along to Crewe and Spotland saying, "Do you want to go to the ground today, kids?" He'd have us tagging along with the groundsman doing stuff.'

The 1956/57 season, in which Harry was reunited with former Everton teammates Jackie Grant, Eddie Wainwright, Gwyn Lewis and 36-year-old veteran Cyril Lello, saw another mid-table finish. By now the coaching triumvirate was starting to make headway and the team hit its stride in the 1957/58 season. This would prove timely as league re-structuring was on the horizon with a four-tier national format being created. The top-half clubs in the Third Division North and South would constitute the Third Division in 1958/59, with the rump forming the Fourth Division.

The chase for Third Division football and improved form on the pitch led to a welcome surge in attendances, with 18,000 witnessing a Lancashire derby against Bury. The team's form faded in the later stages of the season, due in part to Fagan's departure for Liverpool FC, the start of a 27-year association with the Anfield club. Harry had, perhaps unwittingly, set the wheels in motion by praising his coach to Liverpool's directors while attending a match at Anfield. The ringing endorsement, and Fagan's subsequent appointment, would come back to haunt Everton in the years ahead.

After a late-season wobble, with a ten-match winless streak, Rochdale finished the season in tenth position, just doing enough to secure a spot in the new Third Division for the start of the 1958/59 season. However, by then Harry had swapped mill-town Lancashire for a South Yorkshire city. Reflecting on his early years in management in 1964 he stated:

> *Crewe and Rochdale taught me the hardships of football life, I knew how the poor of soccer lived and began wondering 'Has my "apprenticeship" ended?' I decided 'Yes'.*

Looking back with John Roberts on his time at Spotland, Harry reflected: 'I had five happy years there – really managing where you really had to scrape around.'

CHAPTER SIX
THE YO-YO CLUB

SHEFFIELD – the Steel City – is a football hotbed split, like Liverpool, between two tribes. It can lay claim to the 'world's oldest Association Football team' in Sheffield FC, but by the mid-20th century Sheffield United and Sheffield Wednesday were the dominant forces. The post-war Wednesday was the archetypal 'sleeping giant'. The League Champions of 1930 and FA Cup winners in 1935 had oscillated, with depressing regularity, between the first and second tier of the league, resulting in the mocking sobriquet of 'The Yo-Yo Club'. Although Wednesday had generally overshadowed United, whose last silverware had been an FA Cup triumph in 1925, both teams found themselves floundering in Division Two as the 1960s approached.

In a throwback to the Theo Kelly era at Everton a decade earlier, Eric Taylor had been combining the roles of Wednesday's club secretary and team manager. A calamitous 1957/58 season saw the Owls relegated back to the Second Division in last place with only 31 points.

An atmosphere of supporter and shareholder unrest was reaching a crescendo as the Hillsborough hierarchy desperately sought to make changes that would appease the critics and right the listing club. Taylor was moved to the new position of general manager, ironically a promotion in some respects, as the club started its search for a team manager to focus on coaching the first team and scouting.

The preferred choice of the board had been Tottenham Hotspur's first-team coach Bill Nicholson. Nicholson was approached in Sweden by Eric Taylor with the job offer while on England coaching duty at the 1958 World Cup. The former Tottenham player told Taylor that he was happy at White Hart Lane and was subsequently rewarded with the Tottenham managerial position just weeks later. Press speculation linked a myriad of potential candidates for the vacancy, from Raich Carter to Ron Greenwood. Tim Ward, who had pipped Harry to the Barnsley job in 1953, was strongly tipped. It was a shock to most observers when the board announced the appointment of Harry at a stormy AGM on 14 August 1958. Harry, whose managerial experience had been limited to struggling minnows on the other side of the Pennines, was not the big-hitter that the supporters had been hoping for; however, he had impressed the board with his ambition and strong personality, as vice-chairman F. Gardiner recalled to the *Sheffield Star* newspaper in 1977: 'We interviewed a number of people who had experience with the top clubs but felt that perhaps they were on their way down. Catterick impressed us with his positive approach and forceful personality. We had a few problems then and felt that Catterick might be the man to sort them out.'

Harry recounted to the *Sheffield Star* how the Owls appointment came about: 'I had a tip to apply, subsequently getting on the short-list. By some coincidence, on arrival for the interview, I saw Tim Ward who was being interviewed for the same position. Tim and I were rivals for the Barnsley job. This time I was fortunate enough to beat him.'

The announcement of Harry's appointment had been delayed for a week as the Rochdale chairman and two other board members were on holiday in Italy. It took a series of frantic phone calls to officially secure his release – although he had to work his notice to the end of August. Harry left Spotland on good terms and the *Rochdale Observer* was swift to praise his five-year contribution: 'His policy has never been to sell players unless he wished to do so to better the team generally. He has given more youngsters their Football League baptism than any other manager the club has ever had – practically half of the current professional side has been signed from junior football.'

These words would prove prescient for the remainder of Harry's managerial career. He would never shirk from moving on a player he did not rate or thought was 'going stale' – regardless of that player's status with the supporters or board members. Nor was he averse to giving young players their head – a policy that would come to glorious fruition 11 years later.

There is little doubt that he had some influence on Hillsborough affairs before his official start date of 1 September 1958. When interviewed by the *Sheffield Star* upon his selection being made public, he made his priority clear: 'Get Wednesday back into the First Division, that is their proper place... there's nothing more I love than a fight.' Also interviewed was Nancy, who gave an insight into Harry's personality: 'Whether Rochdale win, lose or draw Harry never shows his feelings. It is the same about this new move but I feel deep down that he is very pleased.'

In his first meeting with the Wednesday chairman, Dr Andrew Stephen, Harry recalled receiving 'assurances that I would have his maximum support from the board; but there was a warning that finances were limited and that support was poor because of relegation'. In fact the new management structure ensured that Taylor would retain great sway in the Hillsborough corridors of power, having the 'ear' of the board – something akin to a modern-day 'sporting director'. Having two strong characters, each with his own ideas on how to take the club forward, was a recipe for friction which precipitated the departure of Harry two and a half years later.

Dr Stephen laid down Harry's duties, which centred on the team: training, preparations, team selections, scouting and transfer transactions – the latter only with the approval of the board, a caveat that would have ramifications. Nominally Taylor focused on the administration of the club and the development of the Hillsborough stadium; in fact there were numerous grey areas and turf wars:

> *Eric is probably the finest club secretary in the game, for whose administration I have the greatest admiration. He was a long-serving employee of the club who had never kicked a ball professionally. Despite bringing the club down he had been promoted to general manager and appeared to rule the club and dictated much of the board policy.*

Waiting to welcome Harry on arrival in Sheffield was his former Everton team-mate Joe Mercer who was, at the time, managing at Bramall Lane. Their paths would only cross briefly, however, as Mercer was Villa Park-bound by the turn of the year. A decade later at Manchester City, Joe, in tandem with Malcolm Allison, would provide intense competition for Harry in the higher echelons of the First Division.

Harry's first 'signing', as the first team's trainer-coach, was Tommy Eggleston. A fellow north-easterner, from Consett, 'Eggo' had played for Derby County, Leicester and Watford but, like Harry, had seen his career disrupted by the Second World War and injuries. Having made a name for himself as the trainer at Brentford, and gained qualifications in chiropody, he was invited to join Harry in plotting the Hillsborough renaissance. In over a decade of working with Harry he would become one of the few people to gain the trust of the notoriously private and wary manager. As Harry continued on his path (started at Rochdale) towards becoming an office-based manager, Eggleston would be his eyes and ears on the training ground. Don Megson, who became a full-time professional within days of Harry joining Wednesday, recalls, 'Harry went "arm-in-arm" in partnership with Tommy. They were as thick as thieves.'

Inside-forward Billy Griffin backs up Megson's view: 'Tommy Eggleston was as hard as nails and a great number two to Harry, they had a great rapport. One morning I came down to the ground and Tommy wasn't happy with what I was wearing. I thought it was alright but maybe it was a bit casual – it was shirt and tie, blazer and slacks at Hillsborough in those days He just pointed to me and said, "Hey, back home and get changed please." And you used to have to get your hair cut. Sometimes I let it grow that little bit longer, I'd walk in and he'd say, "There's a hair appointment for you on Middlewood Road".'

With Harry still in the wings Wednesday started the 1958/59 season in impressive fashion and quickly became the bookies' favourites for promotion straight back to the First Division. Harry was fortunate to inherit a squad ripe with potential. His task was to nurture it and ensure that it blossomed. Despite the latent talent, he was struck by the de-motivated state of his new charges when he met them on 1 September:

> *The air of doom and despondency amazed me; never in my seventeen years in soccer had I met such a dejected, dispirited set of players. My first task was to lift the spirit of the side which I knew had the skill, but to me lacked the essential courage and will to apply it. I think it arose from playing a too-rigid system.*

In the preceding seasons Wednesday's supporters had queried tactics that betrayed Eric Taylor's absence of playing experience. Nearly 50 years before the advent of Prozone, a former RAF officer had analysed all the matches played by Wednesday. The resultant charts were subsequently studied and tactics made to suit. Harry recalled the basic points hammered home to players:

> • *The more often the ball was in the opponents' half, and penalty area in particular, the more often Wednesday were likely to score.*
> • *Players in defence must not hold the ball but get it first-time into the opponents' half or, better still, penalty area.*
> • *No passes between defenders in their half of the field.*
> • *Players were confronted with their respective charts some two to three days after the fixture.*
> • *Forwards were instructed to shoot at goal whenever possible and to get X number of shots per match or they would be dropped.*

He then elaborated on the effects these instructions had on the players:

> *My first coaching sessions amazed me. Talented forwards needed*
> *to receive passes from defenders but they refused to give them*
> *the ball and booted it far in the air into the opponents' half.*
> *Norman Curtis, the tough, gruff defender, shouted to Alan*
> *Finney: 'Bugger off up the field. If I give thee t'ball, and not get*
> *me quota, I'll be out of team.' I found out that forwards were*
> *shooting from prodigious distances instead of passing or centring.*
> *I was informed that every forward must get x number of shots in*
> *a match or be in danger of losing his place.*

This account was corroborated by centre-half Peter Swan in the *Sheffield Star* in 1977: 'I was not allowed to pass the ball more than ten yards. It was big boot, long ball stuff because the plan was to get the ball into the opposition's penalty area as quickly, and as often, as possible.' Derek Wilkinson had similar experiences: 'We were told that everyone in the forward line had got to get at least three shots in – so Albert Quixall said, "I'm going to shoot from the half-way line and get my quota in."'

Harry continued:

> *Dr Stephen asked me if I would care to use the charts and services*
> *of the gentleman concerned. I declined and expressed my belief in*
> *a more skilful approach to the game. Since the Chairman and*
> *Mr Taylor were disciples of the method, I am sure that from there*
> *on I was unwelcome at the club. I had to face the fact that play-*
> *ers went onto the field with preconceived ideas of the dreaded, in*
> *my eyes, charts. I wanted confidence to hold the ball and play the*
> *game with more skill. The best way was to implement practice*
> *matches as often as possible.*

Harry then made the surprising discovery that a club of Wednesday's standing had no training ground:

> *Eric Taylor had very strict rules that no-one should train on*
> *his, beloved, Hillsborough pitch so the arrangements were as*
> *follows: the local greyhound stadium had a good playing area*

inside the dog track which was ideal for training purposes. The players changed at Hillsborough and proceeded to the greyhound stadium three-quarters of a mile away. Imagine my amazement, having organised a vital training session, to be told that training would not be possible because the greyhounds were having time trials! That morning training was restricted to a run around the local park.

He was furious that a club boasting a fine stadium had, in his opinion, neglected the facilities for coaching and training, but got no support from his employers, as his memoirs record: 'I stormed back to Hillsborough and confronted Eric Taylor. Eric's cool, calm exterior was certainly ruffled but his only comment was, "That's your problem".'

Harry's frosty relationship with Taylor cooled further one snowy morning:

The gym was barely big enough to train half a dozen players and we felt the only alternative would be to organise a single-file circuit within the main stand. The session had been underway some twenty minutes when I received a typewritten note delivered by a member of staff. This note, signed by Eric Taylor, informed me that training had to stop immediately as it would damage the stand and create dust. Needless to say I ignored the request, feeling that the welfare and fitness of the players mattered most. Eric reported the incident to the chairman and the outcome was that Eric no longer spoke to me but sent typewritten messages across a twelve-foot corridor from his office to mine. I would sometimes receive as many as seven or eight notes, headed as 'Internal Communications', each day. I found the situation ludicrous.

Billy Griffin was only 17 when Harry arrived at Hillsborough. The new manager made an instant impact on the teenager: 'Harry was a tremendous person, he treated everybody the same. He was fantastic to me, every day I went to the ground and put a big shift in – I had endless pace and stamina and Harry loved that. But if you tried to pull one on him he'd have you, make no mistake about it. If he saw you in training and you tried to short-change him, well, "look out". He'd show you up in front of the other players, which nobody liked as it gave them a warning that they had to be careful.'

In a practice game just days into his Hillsborough tenure, Harry was already running the rule over the younger players in the squad. Billy Griffin recalls: 'Tommy took the training but Harry was sat in the stand – so you had to play like it was a first-team game. I was running the line with the flag but after about forty minutes Tommy came up and said, "Harry wants you to get Albert Quixall's shirt." I thought it was a joke as I was only running the line. But Albert came off, I put the shirt on and scored two past Springett – that really perked me up. Harry was just testing me, to see where I was with my game.'

As well as demonstrating Harry's interest in nurturing young talent, the practice match incident served as an omen of events about to unfold with Albert Quixall. At 25 years old, the flaxen-haired England international was the darling of the terraces. He had a scoring record of 63 goals in 241 league appearances since his debut in 1951; despite having sought a move in the past he held the captaincy. In a reflection of himself as a player, Harry always favoured strikers who would 'pull their weight', both at home and away, and would happily give and take the hard knocks. He considered Quixall to be a flair player whose performances away from home failed to mirror his impact at Hillsborough. Matt Busby's Manchester United were seeking to rebuild after the Munich tragedy and made enquiries about the inside-forward. Harry made his first major decision only 18 days into the job.

Knowing that United were desperate to recruit Quixall, Harry, with John Fantham waiting to be promoted from the reserves, sought to maximise the transfer fee, as he told the *Sheffield Star* in 1977: 'Albert over-elaborated at times and did not fit into my pattern of play. I let Matt know that he was available. I turned down the first offer of £35,000, having consulted the board. I remember hearing Matt whistle when I told him that Quixall would only move for £45,000. Matt came back to me on the phone and said he would agree to it.'

Don Megson, still a Central League player at the time, recalls: 'When Harry first arrived at Hillsborough he got rid of the "blue-eyed boy" straight away as he would not fit into his "get stuck in" team – he was too flowery for Harry's taste.'

On 18 September, Busby, accompanied by United's chairman Louis Edwards, drove to Hillsborough to complete the deal. In a photo opportunity that would seem an anachronism now, the United delegation were joined by Harry and Eric Taylor as the striker put pen to paper. Upon Quixall's departure the wonderfully named inside-forward Redfern Froggatt assumed the club captaincy. Looking back with John Roberts Harry cited Froggatt, a former England international who was 34 when Harry arrived at Hillsborough, as a key influence on the side's resurgence: 'He had skill, finishing ability, and he was a hell of a good skipper. I would put him high on my list of all-time players.' The influence and support of both Froggatt and fellow veteran Norman Curtis proved invaluable to Harry in his first months. He was happy to acknowledge their contribution when penning his memoir: 'I must pay unstinting tribute to two players in particular – never shall I forget Norman and "Red".'

Having hit the ground running in the Second Division – beaten only once in the first 13 outings – Harry started to mould a settled line-up. On 22 November in a fixture at Cardiff, a Sheffield-born, fiery redhead by the name of Anthony Herbert 'Tony' Kay dislodged Don Gibson from the left half-back position and made the number six shirt his own. This 2–0 win saw the establishment of the half-back line of Kay, Tommy McAnearney and Peter Swan that would be the team's bedrock over the following four seasons.

Looking back in 1977 with Tony Pritchett of the *Sheffield Star*, Catterick's admiration for Kay shone through:

> *Tony Kay had everything. If we get away from the problems he ultimately had and just think of the football then he was a great player. He was arrogant, hard, a good tackler and he could make others around him play. He had a lot of qualities which, in later days, Bremner showed at Leeds. Kay had twice as much as Bremner – for me he was the ultimate in midfielders and I never handled anyone better in this position.*

Acknowledging Kay's impetuous streak to Pritchett, Harry regretted not managing him in his formative years: 'Kay had a bit of a reputation as a tearaway but I had no problems with him. Remember he was young, had a little bit of success and it would go to his head a little, but I could always handle him. My regrets are that I hadn't handled him right through; I'm quite sure I would have resolved a lot of the problems which subsequently came about for him.'

According to team-mate Keith Ellis, McAnearney, the Dundonian right-half, was 'a skilled, perceptive, passer over long and short distances'. Harry told the *Sheffield Star* in 1977: 'McAnearney was never very popular with the crowd but he made a great contribution to the team's success.' McAnearney concurred: 'Catterick put me in the team when the crowd – and some sports writers – were against me. I was grateful for this but nevertheless we argued all the time. When I think about it now I realise how tough Harry was… Harry once physically threatened one of our players… and a great player at that. But such was his personality and such was our respect for him that he could get away with it.'

Harry would be accused over his management career, with some foundation, of lacking empathy and motivational skills with his players, yet McAnearney recounted to the Star how Harry gave him confidence to overcome negative reactions from supporters and the media: 'Catterick used to tell me not to worry about the crowd or the press. He used to say, "I pick the team here," and said that I made mistakes because I had twice as much of the ball as anyone else.'

While Kay delivered bite and verve on the left and McAnearney the skill, stability and passing range on the right, the centre-half position was dominated by the statuesque Swan. Aged 21 when Harry arrived at Hillsborough, he would go on to make 19 appearances for England between 1960 and 1962, travelling with the squad to the 1962 World Cup finals in Chile. Peerless in the air and comfortable with the ball on the ground, Swan is rated as perhaps Wednesday's finest ever centre-half.

The rest of the team became fairly settled with Ron Springett in goal, Curtis at left-back and Peter Johnson eventually seeing off the challenge of Ron Staniforth and Jack Martin for the right-back position. The inside-forwards, Froggatt and Fantham, would support Roy Shiner, the traditional centre-forward who Harry admired for his 'huge heart'. Fantham would become Wednesday's leading marksman during 'The Catterick Years', notching 48 goals over three seasons. Fellow forward Billy Griffin recalls: 'John Fantham was a top man. Strong as a bull, with legs like tree trunks – but with pace. I've never seen a large lad get off the mark as quickly as he did.' Operating wide on the flanks were Derek Wilkinson and Alan Finney, who Harry described to the *Sheffield Star* as 'superb'.

Griffin recalls: 'The defence picked itself with Springett, Johnson, Megson, McAnearney, Swan and Kay, but the forward line could be anything with myself, John Quinn, Alan Finney, Derek Wilkinson, John Fantham, little Bobby Craig and Keith Ellis – there were about fourteen players for five slots. Harry was clever – he knew the team to pick and if you were left out and it disappointed you it was tough – but you got used to it. He gave everybody a chance, there were no favourites. Harry was always looking and played you on merit.

The only signing made during the season was Roy McLaren as goalkeeping cover for Springett. Even this modest acquisition raised eyebrows in the boardroom, as Harry recalled to the *People* in 1966:

> The deal was only £4,000 for Roy McLaren of Bury to come as
> an understudy. The directors, although they allowed me to spend

the money, were muttering, 'When we've got Springett, £4,000 for another keeper is sheer extravagance.' Now I've always believed that any club without adequate goalkeeping cover is courting disaster, it's a specialist position. I was proved right that Easter when Springett injured his hand and McLaren came in to play splendidly for the final eight matches. You need foresight, and luck, in football.

When Harry arrived at Hillsborough he was disturbed by the fact that Springett lived and trained in London, only coming to Sheffield for home matches. This was an agreement reached when Eric Taylor had signed the goalkeeper in the spring of 1958 from Queens Park Rangers. Springett, who achieved full England honours in 1962, recalled to the *Sheffield Star* in 1977 that Harry used the press to try and force him to relocate:

I got to the station (in London) one day to be met by reporters and cameramen. They had got hold of a story that Harry had issued an ultimatum: I was to move to Sheffield or be transferred. When I got to Sheffield I was driven to the ground. I arrived to see the chairman and some members of the board waiting for me and I assumed the worst. But Dr Stephen told me that there had been no ultimatum and as long as I kept my part of the bargain and trained properly there was no question of the club going back on its promise. Mr Catterick was asked to apologise for all the publicity and he did. After that it was never mentioned and Harry and I got on well together.

This would be one of the very few times that a player won a battle against Harry during his 25 years in management.

In late January 1959, with Wednesday comfortably on course for promotion, but out of the FA Cup after being defeated by First Division West Bromwich Albion, Harry gave a statement to *South Yorkshire News Service* press agency. In it he reaffirmed his belief in bringing through young talent but also sent a clear message to the board that the purse strings would need to be loosened in the summer:

People are now asking if Wednesday are really equipped for the top grade and are wondering if they are again for the 'yo-yo' role. It is true that we are riding high in the Second Division table but believe that we have a tough fight ahead before we gain First Division status. I say, quite frankly, that we could not survive in the First Division with our present style of play. If we win promotion we shall need replacements – I am prepared to state that we need four new first class players. Each player I want would cost from £15,000 upwards. That is, of course, nothing more than a pipe-dream as far as my cheque book for new players is concerned. When I took over the team manager-ship at Hillsborough, shortly after this season began, the club had a £40,000 overdraft. Because I had complete faith in young Johnny Fantham filling the inside-forward gap, I negotiated the transfer of Albert Quixall to Manchester United for a record £45,000 fee. I have no misgivings about that, it was good busi-ness because I knew Fantham would not fail me – I regard him as my key forward. But forget once and for all that I can go into the transfer market with a £45,000 cheque as a result of the Quixall deal. Times have changed and that is the problem. If I had had time to build up my reserve strength it would have been easier. I must, however, make it clear that whatever I do spend on new players for ensuring a long stay in the First Division there will always be a chance for the youngster who makes his way successfully through my reserve side.

Despite the tensions off the pitch, the Owls were virtually unstoppable in the league, hitting seven past Lincoln, five past Rotherham United and four past Derby County, Stoke City, Huddersfield Town and Scunthorpe United. The season's tally of 106 goals was shared out across the team, with each of the five regular members of the forward line getting into double figures. Promotion, and the Second Division title, was secured with a 5–0 hammering of Barnsley in the penultimate fixture of the season – Harry secured a £500 bonus in the process.

Wednesday finished the season on 62 points – two clear of Fulham, who had inflicted a 6–2 defeat on the Owls in February. Cross-city rivals Sheffield United – where Joe Mercer was succeeded by Archie Clarke and, later, John Harris – fin-ished in third place, narrowly missing promotion. Journalist James Lawton recalls that Harris, a gentlemanly manager who later became a lay-preacher, had come up against Harry when playing in defence for Chelsea against Everton. Matters came to a head as their rain-sodden shirts began to sag: 'Harris was once so inflamed by the roughhouse tactics of his Everton opponent he delivered the most ruthless of retribution. In one penalty-area scuffle he noticed that just below the neckline of Catterick's shirt was an extremely large and angry boil. Soon after he took the chance to ram down his elbow on the vulnerable spot, sniffing: "Take that, you blighter."'

Sadly, there is no record of Harry's reaction!

CHAPTER   SEVEN

BACK IN
THE BIG TIME

DESPITE AN encouraging start to Harry's debut managerial season in the First Division – Fantham scoring the game's only goal at Highbury – he cut a frustrated figure. After the previous season's pronouncement that the addition of four top-class players would be required to prevent Wednesday becoming opposition cannon-fodder, the 11 players fielded were unchanged from the promotion campaign.

Harry had intimated to the *South Yorkshire News Service* that, should Wednesday start the next season in the top flight, some of the attacking élan would have to be sacrificed in favour of defensive solidity:

> *We are playing the free scoring type of football which I'm sure*
> *pleases supporters and it is the type of football which is admirably*
> *serving our immediate purpose of promotion. I know however*
> *that it will not be sufficient for a long reign in the First Division.*
> *Our first job will be to tighten up defence, whether or not we get*
> *new men, there will have to be a considerable adjustment but*
> *all our efforts are directed to a long stay in the premier division.*

In fact the team only won one of the first six fixtures, losing three; this poor run seemed to end when Blackpool were hit for five without reply, but the somewhat topsy-turvy form continued until November 1959 with the arrival of Bobby Craig from Third Lanark. Craig would be the only significant outfield transfer in Catterick's three years in Yorkshire. The Scot's arrival, for £6,500, signalled the fast-approaching end for Froggatt's first-team career, which stretched back to the Second World War. It was an inspired acquisition; Craig would score on his debut, a 7–0 pummelling of West Ham United. Harry praised Craig to the *Sheffield Star*: 'A small clever ball player; a fiery little chap but he had great creative quality.' The description suggests that Craig was a template for the midfield players he would mould together a decade later.

With the financial restrictions in place, Harry relied on the deep pool of talent in the reserves. One such example was Keith Ellis, who replaced veteran centre-forward Roy Shiner. Brilliant in the air, if slightly less adept on the ground, he would become the attacking fulcrum in Harry's team. Ellis had made his debut as a part-timer in 1955 under Eric Taylor and, in a parallel with Harry, he had followed his father's wishes by combining mechanical engineering studies with being a part-time football professional. Ellis recalls: 'We had a very good young side at the time, we were all in and out of National Service. I didn't do my National Service, in the RAF, until I was twenty-two, and when I came out Harry was the manager. My first impression was that he was immaculately dressed. I never saw him as a tracksuit boss – don't think I ever saw him in a tracksuit – but he certainly changed the mind-set. Harry and Tommy were hand in glove – it was Tommy who did all the hard work in the rain! The inside-forwards were generally small and agile and they would feed off me quite often. Harry didn't come and ask, 'Now then, Keith, how are you doing," he wasn't a players' man – he was more a directors' man. Harry was on a different wavelength from the players – he used to class footballers as the "rough" while he was the "smooth".'

Winger Derek Wilkinson has a contrasting view of Harry: 'Harry Catterick was the best manager I played under, he had control over everybody and they respected him. Harry was a hard man, a bit ruthless, but you had to respect him because if you didn't you were out! He was very fair with me and I liked him – if he dropped you he'd have you in to explain. He made a lot of changes – you need to get all the players playing for you and he did.'

Harry had made enquiries with Huddersfield Town's manager, Bill Shankly, about signing their left-back Ray Wilson in part-exchange for Don Megson. Shankly was tempted, having seen Megson play for Wednesday's reserves. Megson's subsequent ascent to the first team saw the deal stall, but Harry would covet the cultured Wilson for the next five years.

Speaking to the *Sheffield Star* in 1977, Don Megson, who quickly cemented his place in the first team, summed up the impact Harry had on Hillsborough:

> *Harry Catterick was a man completely without frills and this was the character of our football of the time. We were skilful, hard and forceful and we soon found that he had the personality to command discipline. You were under no illusions as to what he wanted from you, as far as we were concerned we had a job to*

do on Saturday and nothing else mattered. Under Eric Taylor we
had the tag 'The Yo-Yo team' and Harry's mind-set was, 'That
isn't going to happen to me.'

Speaking in 2014 Megson adds: 'Like Harry as a player, I took a long, long time to break through to the first team. To give credit to Eric Taylor, he kept me on for all those years without getting a shot. I had been in the army and part-time – National Service was reckoned to be the ruination of many a professional. When I came out in 1959 I had no idea that football might give me a full-time career. I just knew from the full-time pros that Harry was a hard taskmaster and didn't suffer fools very much. When Harry first saw me I was virtually a centre-half. In my first week back at the club he brought me into the office and told me he wanted me to play at left-back as he had four good players at centre-half whilst the left back, Norman Curtis, was the oldest in the squad at thirty-four. It is possible that Harry was watching me in the Wednesday reserves when he was manager of Rochdale – I doubt that he made a snap decision to put me at left-back. After about fifteen games in the reserves at left-back I got my chance in the first team.'

Having broken into the team in November 1959 Megson had it drilled home what was expected of him: 'Behind the stand was a little grass base where we warmed up on Friday mornings before the game. Harry had told me that I was playing and then we went over to train. Tommy Eggleston came up to me and said, "Don't change anything about your game. If it's in a different-coloured shirt, and anything above two foot from the ground, tackle it as hard as you can." Harry did not like fairy stuff, I think he had been a bit of a batterer as a player – he liked a bit of that personality in his team.

'He had me on the left whilst on the other flank he had Peter Johnson, who was very quick but didn't tackle to destroy – he tackled to nick it, but we played well together. We had basically the same team as under Eric Taylor, the only player that he actually bought in was Bobby Craig from Third Lanark a week after he brought me into the team. We went nineteen games without defeat and I got established. I think Tony Kay was his favourite: quick, strong, hard as nails and determined – his ideal player.'

Megson also picked up on Harry's body language, which indicated that this naturally quiet, even shy, man was not comfortable addressing audiences: 'Harry had a mannerism; he was not all that comfortable at team talks; he would stand in front of you and wring his hands.'

Although results in the First Division were mixed at times, the team lost only four games from January until the season's end to finish in a very creditable fifth place. Harry had completed the second phase of his plan – he had not only got Wednesday promoted but then kept them in the First Division – the 'Yo-Yo' tag could be discarded.

More thrilling, but ultimately disappointing, that season was an FA Cup run that saw the Owls defeat Middlesbrough, Peterborough and Manchester United – courtesy of a Tommy McAnearney penalty at Old Trafford – on the way to a quarter-final tie at Bramall Lane against their city rivals. A Derek Wilkinson brace set up a semi-final tie against Blackburn Rovers at Maine Road in front of 74,000. Despite being favourites the team would succumb 2–1 to the Lancastrians. The players would recall that, on this occasion, Harry's plan of playing long balls to Keith Ellis backfired, with the centre-forward being muzzled by the Blackburn rearguard. Looking back, Peter Swan told the *Sheffield Star* in 1977: 'I think we'd have won the game if we'd played the ball on the ground more. Instead we had to keep sending it over the top to Keith and it just didn't work out.'

In the late 1950s Wolverhampton Wanderers had whetted the appetite for floodlit challenge matches against foreign opposition. Sheffield Wednesday were one of the clubs to follow suit, playing several matches against Eastern bloc teams. Having hosted Torpedo Moscow in November 1959 the team packed their bags at the season's end and traversed the Iron Curtain for a tour, taking in fixtures against CSKA Moscow and Lokomotiv Moscow – punctuated by a trip to play Dynamo Tbilisi in Georgia. The tour came at a time of heightened tensions in the Cold War – just 23 days before the first fixture an American spy plane, piloted by Gary Powers, had been downed over Soviet territory. Despite the tensions, Keith Ellis retains fond memories of the tour: 'It was marvellous, it was just after the Russians shot down the U-2 spy plane. We were the first Western team to visit after the crisis and it was a very official sort of tour. We went to meet the ambassador etcetera.'

After the CSKA fixture the team boarded a flight for the three-hour trip to the Georgian capital, which contrasted starkly with Moscow. On arrival at the airport they were festooned with floral bouquets before making their way to a hotel. Keith Ellis noted the political contrast with Moscow: 'Tbilisi was Stalin's place and they idolised him there, everything was Stalin with statues, whereas in Moscow it was all Lenin.'

Tony Kay would recall that the cable-car trip up Mount Mtatsminda was the only time the party were offered fruit during the entire trip.

Away from the pressures of home turf Harry allowed himself some fun, as Don Megson recalls: 'Harry could be very stern but he could have a laugh with us.

A few beers were knocking around and Harry was happy to join in. One evening some of us went out in Tbilisi. Peter Johnson had brought a balalaika or something similar, Harry had had a few drinks and made a beeline for the instrument and poured a beer in the hole... he had this big grin on his face and gave a big chuckle! Peter was well peed off. That evening this drunk fellow was following us all over the place and Harry was peed off with him. There was a roadworks hole in the road and Harry beckoned the man to come over and look down this hole – Harry had lifted his foot to push him in then we grabbed hold of him. We didn't see it very often but he had that wild side in his nature.'

Back in Moscow Harry was nonplussed at the quality of hotel accommodation on offer, especially as the directors were given the best rooms, leaving the dregs for the squad and coaching team. The next day the directors were taken off for a tour of the local distilleries – returning well-lubricated at 5pm, whereupon they retired to their bedrooms. Harry then received a curious request:

> I received a message to go to one of the director's rooms. I knocked
> rather loudly on the door and it was duly opened. I was surprised
> to be greeted by a toothless and pale-looking Mr Gunstone who
> had apparently been violently sick and lost his dentures down the
> toilet. Why he should consider I could do anything I do not know
> but obviously he did not fancy travelling around Russia toothless.
> After much explanation via an interpreter, a plumber appeared,
> the dentures were recovered and Dick Gunstone breathed a hefty
> sigh of relief.

Derek Wilkinson recalls the mischievous side of Harry being revealed on the roof garden of what was then the world's tallest hotel: 'We were on the roof of the Ukraina, our hotel in Moscow – it was very high as there were about forty storeys. We looked down and Harry Catterick said, "Who the bloody hell is that down there? It's Billy Griffin!" Billy was sunbathing on a lower roof balcony in just a pair of shorts with no shirt on – he was only eight stone – from above he looked like a bone. Harry started throwing pebbles from a plant pot down at him – luckily his aim was that bad that he got nowhere near him!'

Griffin recalls: 'I was near the top of the hotel sunbathing. They went up top and started throwing bit and bobs down and they were landing on me. They were a wonderful bunch of players!'

Reflecting on the tour, Griffin adds: 'It was a magnificent trip. There was me, a teenager, staying in the Hotel Ukraina. It was massive, I have never seen a building like it in my lifetime. I played in the Central Lenin Stadium, there were 80,000 in – it was unreal. We all had bunches of flowers and threw them to the crowd before kick-off.'

CHAPTER EIGHT
MR SUCCESS

AFTER THE RELATIVE success of the previous season, the 1960/61 campaign saw Harry, and Wednesday, aim for the very top. Such was his impact at Wednesday that the *Daily Herald*, with a nod to the popular Frank Sinatra song of the time, dubbed the manager 'Mr Success'.

Certainly Harry was a man who knew his own worth and saw an opportunity to improve his lot. As the 1959/60 season was drawing to a close, aware of interest from another (nameless) First Division club, he requested a salary increase from the board. The directors offered a £1,000 bonus for the progress achieved in the season but no salary increase was tabled. Harry was not impressed, as he informed the *Sheffield Star* in 1977: 'I felt that since I was doing the dual role of team manager and chief scout, and having brought success, I was worthy of a higher reward than I was getting. My salary was probably the lowest in the First Division; I went for an increase and was disappointed with the offer.'

In mid-April Harry requested to be released from his contract and went public with the dispute. In 1977 the *Star* reproduced Harry's press statement from the time:

> *Two months ago I was approached by a Football League club of considerable repute, offered the position of manager with full control of playing matters, a five-year contract and an increase in my present salary of some 40 per cent. While I would much prefer to remain at Sheffield Wednesday I felt I must give the matter some consideration and give Wednesday the opportunity of matching the offer... I was informed that they were not prepared to match the offer made to me... I felt that this left me no alternative but to be released from my present contract which has sixteen months to run.*

After a further three hours in the boardroom, Dr Andrew Stephen announced that Wednesday would not accede to Harry's request for release.

Away from intrigue in the corridors of power, the settled team did not have any significant additions. Ellis was now established in the number nine shirt as Shiner had moved on to Hull City, while age and Fantham's excellent form had seen Froggatt eased out of the first team. Wednesday embarked upon a 12-game unbeaten run until mid-October, when Wolves inflicted a 4–1 defeat at Molineux. It became clear that Wolves, along with Tottenham Hotspur and Wednesday, would be challenging for the title.

In September 1960 – in the midst of the unbeaten run – another off-pitch distraction sprang up. First Division Nottingham Forest made a move to secure Harry's services. Harry recalled to the *Sheffield Star*: 'A number of clubs were interested in me and Forest had expressed a wish for me to take over. An old friend and very able manager, Billy Walker, was retiring and he had personally recommended me to the Forest people.' Twelve years earlier Walker had attempted, unsuccessfully, to lure Harry as a player from Everton to the City Ground. The battle of wills as to whether Harry stayed in Sheffield or headed to the Midlands was played out in the press and it appears that Forest's interest was used by Harry as leverage in another attempt to increase both his power and financial reward at Wednesday. He continued: 'I had an interview with them and they made me an offer in excess of the salary I was receiving at Sheffield Wednesday. I went back to my club and told them of the offer and that I was greatly tempted to take it. Nottingham Forest did not hire and fire managers willy-nilly and it would have given me a fair amount of security.'

With the board due to discuss the situation on 19 September, Harry did a volte-face and elected to stay at Hillsborough; he would tell the *Sheffield Star*: 'I stayed because of my love for the team... and the public were behind me. I hoped that in future the board would make an offer of a more substantial salary.'

With peace apparently restored, the team could continue with their challenge for the league title. On 2 November, on the back of 15 wins and one draw, Spurs came to Hillsborough for a match billed as an indicator of the destination of the league crown. In a physical match, watched by 56,363, Fantham and Griffin's goals ensured a 2–1 victory. Harry told the *Sheffield Star* in 1977: 'My boys, at that time, would have taken anyone on. They were a great bunch of players... the success at the time was built around a wonderful team and dressing room spirit. In all modesty I must say there was also a great relationship between myself and the players.' The euphoria of victory was quickly dampened by three consecutive defeats, including one at Goodison Park, which would prove critical at the climax of the season.

Despite getting things back on track with a 5–4 victory over Blackburn Rovers, Don Megson received a Catterick-style wake-up call: 'I must have got a little bit complacent. We went to West Bromwich Albion and I went into the dressing room to look for my number three shirt and get the coat on the peg. Harry came up to me and said, deadpan, "You're not playing today" – no reasons for it and that was that – virtually, "Get out of the dressing room". The next game was against Arsenal and they didn't do too bad after he'd also dropped me for that one. The older pros encouraged me to go and ask him what it was all about. So I knocked on his door and went in the office. He was writing and didn't even look up but said, "You are the best left-back in this club, now get out and prove it." Then he put me back in the team and I was never out after that. Maybe he'd thought I was getting too cocky and wanted to bring the wind out of my sails.'

When selected for the first team Billy Griffin revelled in a floating attacking role which bore similarities to Jimmy Husband's at Everton in the late 1960s: 'I went where I wanted. I used to fly across to the right, fly back across to the left and go down the middle so no one could pick me up. Everywhere I went I made an extra man. That was the game that Harry wanted me to play because I had the stamina. He used to say, "Bill, I don't want to see you back there, I want to see you up there."'

A tragic incident occurred on Boxing Day 1960 as the team headed back from a creditable 1–1 draw at Highbury. Normally the team travelled to away fixtures by rail but the restricted services over the festive season had obliged the party to travel by coach. Harry had called up a young prospect called Dougie McMillan to the squad, primarily as it stopped him being alone in digs over Christmas. After a meal and drink the coach headed home for Sheffield, conscious that temperatures were dropping. Harry recorded:

> *A voice called to Dougie to change the radio station, he duly dashed to the front of the coach. At that moment the bus appeared to develop a skid; the next moment we had run off the road and hit a concrete gate-post. The bus was tilted at 45 degrees, with the near-side wheels in a sort of ditch and windows were smashed. Peter Swan had been thrown some five rows forward and was damaged about the shoulder. The engine was still running – the driver was knocked out – and I could hear the cries of injured players. Tommy Eggleston and I opened the emergency door at the rear, this was a feat because of the angle of the bus, broken glass and total darkness. After ten minutes all*

A press photo of Harry as a teenager. (Catterick family)

Harry Catterick Senior captained Chilton Colliery's football team to FA Cup giant-killing acts before joining Stockport County in 1926. (Catterick family)

Chilton Colliery football team 1924/25 season– Harry Catterick Senior is seated third from right. (Chilton Library)

Harry's Catterick's home from the age of six – Edgeley Conservative Club in Stockport. (Author's photo)

Harry with the Everton "A" team shortly after joining the club in April 1937. (James Corbett)

Harry on the 1937/38 Everton squad photo - middle row – 5ᵗʰ from left. (George Orr)

Team sheet for Harry's Everton reserve team debut against Manchester United – 13 November 1937. Harry, playing alongside family friend Charlie Gee, scored twice. (Catterick family)

Harry guesting for Stockport County on 21 September 1940. (Marcus Heap)

A 1945 Caricature of Harry - probably in Stockport County playing strip. (Catterick family)

Harry in wartime football action for Stockport County against Chester – Harry is second from left. (Marcus Heap)

Everton's team photographed at Villa Park on 2 September 1946 before the second match of competitive post-war league fixtures. Harry is seated third from right. Theo Kelly, wearing the hat, was credited by Harry with teaching him about football administration. Harry broke his arms five days later at Ewood Park. (Catterick family)

Everton players (Harry third from left in a light suit) inspect the pitch at Roker Park in November 1945. (Getty Images)

Portrait photo of Harry in Everton colours – probably taken during the early post-war years.

Opposite page: Harry training will the ball in the mid to late 1940s.

Harry attempts to charge down a clearance by Wolves' Bert Williams at Goodison Park on 4 October 1947. (Catterick family)

Everton line up at Goodison Park 30 October 1948. Newly appointed manager Cliff Britton is on the left of the photo. Centre-forward Albert Juliussen, seated third from right, was a record signing but played only ten matches for Everton. (Catterick family)

Harry in ball-striking pose at Villa Park on 20 November 1948. Harry scored the only goal of the match, Cliff Britton's sixth at the Everton helm. (Catterick family)

After some haggling over terms, Harry accepted the player-manager post at Crewe Alexandra in December 1951. He is photographed here upon his appointment. With a non-existent transfer budget, his primary work was to improve players on the training pitch. (Catterick family)

A business-like Crewe player-manager trots out onto the pitch. (Catterick family)

In the early 1950s, Harry presents trophies to teenage Brownley Green FC players in the Wythenshawe area of Manchester. (Catterick family)

Sherlock Catterick putting his players under close scrutiny.

On 12 April 1952, the Crewe Chronicle's cartoonist suggested that Harry was keeping a close eye on his first team squad. (Catterick family)

Harry and Tommy Eggleston taking training on the muddy Hillsborough pitch – presumably whilst was General Manager Eric Taylor was not looking. (Catterick family)

Harry at the manager's desk at Rochdale in the mid-1950s. (Catterick family)

The Sheffield Wednesday squad, photographed at Hillsborough circa 1959. (Catterick family)

Harry and Sheffield United's manager, John Harris, walk towards the tunnel in inclement weather – probably before a FA Cup tie in March 1960. (Catterick family)

Harry with the Sheffield Wednesday team early in the 1959/60 season. Back row L-R: Tommy Eggleston, Tom McAnearney, Peter Swan, Ron Springett, Tony Kay, Peter Johnson, Harry Catterick. Front row L-R: Derek Wilkinson, Roy Shiner, Redfern Froggatt, Alan Finney, John Fantham, Norman Curtis. (Catterick family)

Harry poses for a joke with (L-R): Tom McAnearney, Alan Finney, Ron Springett, Tommy Eggleston, Don Megson. (Catterick family)

A bequiffed John Quinn receives one-to-one advice from Harry. (Catterick family)

Some of the Sheffield Wednesday travelling party outside Moscow's Hotel Ukraina in May 1960 (Back row L-R: Peter Johnson, Eric Taylor, Tommy Eggleston, Harry Catterick, Peter Swan, Jack Martin. Middle Row L-R: Tony Kay, Ron Springett, Gerry Young, Don Megson, Billy Griffin, Alan Finney, Derek Wilkinson, Bobby Craig. Front row: John Quinn, Roy McLaren). (Catterick family)

Bouquets of flowers to hold in Tbilisi, as the teams stand for the pre-match anthems. (Catterick family)

The Owls are greeted with flowers shortly after touching down in Georgia prior to their match against Dynamo Tbilisi in May 1960. (Catterick family)

the players were out except the little Scot stuck at the front with his leg trapped – his only remark was 'My leg is stuck Boss'. Tom and I did all we could to free him but to no avail. A passing motorist sent for an emergency accident unit from Huntingdon Hospital. Tom, although badly cut himself, saw everyone into hotel or hospital beds.

Meanwhile I was standing outside the damaged coach with the doctor and accident unit who had tried every device to free up young Dougie – he was losing blood. The surgeon present told me that he had little option but to amputate the leg below the knee to free Dougie and save his life. My feelings, standing whilst the operation was being carried out, left a permanent scar on my managerial experiences. To think he was only with us to provide him with a treat at the festive season. Dougie would have been a fine player and his stamina and courage was never more evident than in that coach.

After the accident 19-year-old McMillan travelled with the squad to away games for a while, as he later recalled: 'It was good that they kept me as part of the squad. I worked in the office at Hillsborough for about six months with Eric England and Ted Gibson but I knew I was going to have to leave.' His Hillsborough testimonial, attended by 26,000, saw a combined Wednesday–United team face a Select XI including England internationals Billy Wright, Bobby Charlton and George Cohen. Dougie went on to run a post office and even played in goal in a five-a-side league wearing a prosthetic lower limb.

Nothing was totally straightforward with Harry; the stern exterior seen by players occasionally slipped to reveal a surprisingly compassionate side. On 1 February 1961 Wednesday travelled to Old Trafford for an FA Cup fourth round replay and hammered a Manchester United side including Owls' alumnus Albert Quixall in their line-up. Young Northern Irish goalkeeper Ronnie Briggs had been drafted in due to injuries and was on the receiving end of a seven-goal Sheffield salvo, with Ellis notching a hat-trick. The shell-shocked Briggs was surprised to receive a letter two days later with a Sheffield postmark. In his autobiography, when comparing the various managerial styles he had encountered, the former England goalkeeper Gordon Banks recalled the contents of the letter:

Dear Ronnie,

I felt that I must write to you to let you know how highly some of our players, and Ron Springett in particular, rate you as a goalkeeper of the future. I should not like to feel that the fact that we beat you 7–2 was in any way going to shake your confidence. All the great goalkeepers have had days where they are beaten several times and of course, being a goalkeeper, when they pass you they are in the back of the net.

You showed sufficient ability at Hillsborough in the first cup tie to convince me, and many good judges of the game, that you have a bright future. The game is full of ups and downs and I feel it is part of the fascination to players, managers and spectators, but I am equally sure, Ronnie, that you are going to have far more ups than downs. In addition to which you are probably with one of the finest clubs in the British Isles and in the very capable hands of Mr Busby and Jimmy Murphy.

Yours sincerely,

Harry Catterick

Despite Harry's words of encouragement it is arguable that the 18-year-old never recovered from the mauling that day. He left Manchester United in 1964 after making 11 appearances and continued his career at Swansea and Bristol Rovers before slipping into non-league football.

Wednesday would be knocked out in the sixth round by Burnley but in the league they continued to press Tottenham for the title. On some occasions they were irresistible – hitting Fulham, Preston and Manchester United for five. Despite the dazzling displays, Harry was unimpressed with the gates at Hillsborough. True to form, he declared his opinions to the press, claiming that the attendances were 'poor reward' for the football on offer.

On 8 April the championship challenge, which had stuttered with two consecutive draws, effectively ended with a 2-2 stalemate against Leicester City.

Unbeknown to the Wednesday faithful, Harry would never take charge of the team again as, within 48 hours, matters came to a head. The strained relationship with the board over wages and resentment about the failure to sanction the signing of Hibernian striker Joe Baker – who Harry believed might have made the difference in the title race – were instrumental. Harry told the *Sheffield Star*: 'I felt that a signing of some importance, say a centre forward, was a big need. I looked around and felt that Joe Baker was the man I wanted. One Sunday night in the winter I drove to Scotland with Mr Bob Peasegood, one of my directors. We made an offer of £50,000 which was turned down. I personally would have gone to £60,000 or £70,000 because I felt the team justified it and we were doing reasonably well in the First Division. I felt that had Baker come to us in mid-season he would have made the difference. However, I didn't get him and it was a matter I deeply regretted. I felt the board could have been more helpful in this than they were.'

Billy Griffin recalls: 'There was some magnificent football and it was all moulded by Catterick. The one piece that was missing in the jigsaw was Joe Baker, and Harry tried his hardest to sign him but they would not release the money. Keith Ellis was very good in the air but not so good on the floor, But Baker, who I played against when he was at Arsenal, had the lot.'

Don Megson adds: 'It really upset Harry that he could not have Joe Baker; he wanted him badly and resented that he couldn't get him as he felt with him we'd have got the title. Harry's objection was that the board would not give him money to buy him.

The spin from Harry was that the board preferred to ring-fence the cash for building a new stand at Hillsborough, but Megson disputes this: 'It's not true – the money for the North Stand cantilever was given to the club purely for the stand and not player acquisitions.' Nonetheless, the episode strengthened Harry's view that his voice was being drowned out and he tipped off journalists about his discontent. On 4 April the national press had carried a story suggesting that the Wednesday board had reneged on a promise made to Harry during contract renegotiations at the time of the Forest approach. The chairman 'refuted categorically' any truth in the story – however, Harry, in what was becoming almost open warfare, retorted to the *Sheffield Star*: 'I am equally convinced that the directors have failed to fulfil promises.'

Harry would observe in 1964:

> *The ambitions of Mr Taylor and I just did not mix. Mr Taylor's number one aim was the improvement of Hillsborough as a soccer stadium. My number one aim was the improvement of the team. It was as simple as that. When an unstoppable force meets the immovable object something has to give. My departure followed a very stormy scene with Eric Taylor and Dr Stephen. I*

had been promised an increase in salary and improved contract but this failed to materialise.

On 10 April 1961 came the bombshell that Harry had resigned from his post:

To me the atmosphere was fast becoming untenable. There were a lot of special meetings and a lot of plain speaking. Matters had gone beyond human endurance, it was that unhappy that I decided to leave the club, motivated by my own principles.

Harry appeared on the steps of Hillsborough to make a statement to the assembled press: 'I expect to be leaving as soon as possible, I have one or two things to clear up as I have been combining the role of chief scout with team manager. I have no job to go to immediately and, for a time, I shall be out of work. I am sorry to have to leave such a fine bunch of players, I am quite sure that this team will go on to have further success.' Then, with the passing Dougie McMillan looking on, Harry turned round and headed back up the steps to enter the stadium foyer only, in a moment of bathos, to find himself locked out.

Although aware of tensions between Harry and the board, the sudden departure came as a shock to the players, including Keith Ellis: 'There were paper rumours flying around but it was quite a shock really that he left.' Derek Wilkinson was disappointed by the news: 'The players didn't want him to go. He was a really good manager and I liked him, he was really up front with you. Once I went in to see him and I said, "I think you should drop me as I'm not playing that well," and he said, "Well, you just anticipated that – an hour later you'd have been in here anyway!"

Billy Griffin recalls being devastated by the departure of the manager who had developed him: 'If Harry had stayed I can honestly say he would have kept Wednesday up there for as long as they wanted to be – and they'd have won in Europe as well. He was the best manager in England for me at the time and the finest manager I ever played under. I believe that I would have played for England if he had stopped on at Hillsborough.'

Reflecting, Don Megson laments Harry's premature departure and a lost opportunity: 'Harry Catterick is still held in high esteem for what he did here – a lot of people were really sorry to see him go. We thought he had nous and the drive; you could see that if he'd had carte-blanche to bring in players that he wanted Wednesday could have become quite a power. Some years later I asked him why he left as it was going so well and Harry said: "Eric had built a brick wall around himself – I tried to knock it down and I didn't succeed in moving one brick.'"

Even today many of the older generation of Owls supporters look back wistfully at the events of April 1961 and think 'what if?'

Harry would return to Hillsborough just ten days later – however by then he would be with the visiting team – Everton Football Club.

CHAPTER NINE
EVERTON RETURN

BY 1960 Everton had been transformed from the relegation fodder of the early 1950s to an ambitious First Division club, hungry for success and with the financial means to achieve it. The catalyst for change had been the strengthening of ties between the club and John Moores.

The Eccles émigré had settled in Liverpool in the mid-1920s and, with Colin Askham, pioneered Littlewoods Football Pools. In the decades that followed, the pools grew alongside a mail order business and a department store arm, which operated over 50 branches. By the late 1950s Littlewoods was a behemoth – the largest private company in the UK, with thousands employed on Merseyside alone. Despite its size, Littlewoods continued to be dominated by the Moores family. Due to John's football involvement, his brother Cecil took on the pools business to avoid a conflict of interests, leaving John to focus on the mail order business and department stores.

Moores was a brilliant businessman with a keen eye for money-making opportunities – he was ruthless yet loyal to those he trusted. Graham Wilson, who would become his link-man to day-to-day affairs at Goodison and Anfield recalls: 'John Moores was a genius, there are no two ways about it. He was incredibly bright. If you convinced him of something he would drive a tank through a wall to get to it.' His diminutive stature did not detract from an aura that instilled fear at all levels of the business. Being told that 'Mr John' was displeased was enough make the toughest employee break out in a cold sweat.

In 1977 Moores related to John Roberts his earliest memories of watching football at Manchester's Bank Street Stadium, early in the century: 'I used to watch Manchester United when I was a little boy, I must have been seven or eight. They played in Clayton. My father bought a season ticket and he lifted me over the barrier and let me sit on the grass. These men looked enormous to me, thudding around when I was so near to them.' Once settled on Merseyside he had watched Everton and Liverpool but the Blues had the greater pull: 'When I came to Liverpool I began to watch Everton and you get the flavour for one side and stupidly you keep going for that side. I'm one of the stupid buggers who is a football fan, I like watching football.'

Business and footballing interests would eventually lead him to the Goodison Park boardroom: 'Littlewoods had a supplier called Dick Searle. He had got nearly a majority of Everton shares but during the war he was in a little bit of trouble financially so he offered to sell me half his shares on the understanding I'd always vote with him. So I took half his shares and he gave me an option to buy the others if he died; I suggested they put Holland Hughes on the board.'

In fact the Littlewoods influence on Everton matters predated Moores', as his former business partner and friend, Colin Askham, had been a shareholder since the 1930s and was elected to the board in 1955. In the late 1950s Moores was persuaded to have a hands-on influence at the struggling club. He told John Roberts:

> Everton were overdrawn by £30,000–£40,000 and there was a credit squeeze on. The bank wouldn't give them anything and they wanted to put floodlights in – they wanted money for players too. So finally Mr Hughes said, 'The only way you will do any good, Mr Moores, is to come on the board.' I wanted to give them money, we had bingo running at the stadium, which I controlled, and I let them take all the money they made from this. I lent them money interest free. We tried to make them produce it for themselves. You have to have directors who can find some way of producing money.

Reflecting on this symbiotic relationship with the journalist and broadcaster Charles Lambert in 1976, Moores felt it was a win-win situation: 'The Littlewoods connection is good for Everton and good for the Liverpool public. It benefits the company from publicity and it gives the club the benefit of a wide range of professional advice and expertise, which is readily available to it.'

Less publicised was that Moores also held a significant shareholding in Liverpool FC. He would exert arm's-length control on Anfield affairs, most notably through the appointment of Littlewoods' finance director, Eric Sawyer, to the board. Sawyer would work closely with Bill Shankly and Peter Robinson to revitalise the club, finding the funds to lure Ian St John and Ron Yeats south of the border.

In 1960, the new chairman Moores set about transforming Everton into title contenders. He had inherited as manager Johnny Carey, the former Ireland international and Manchester United captain, who had played briefly alongside Harry in wartime football. Since arriving from Blackburn Rovers to replace Ian Buchan in 1958 Carey had steadied the ship, but once Moores opened the cheque book he was able to assemble a stellar squad boasting some of the finest players of any Everton era. The expensively assembled roll call included captain, and heartbeat of the side, Bobby Collins, the rapier-like striker Roy Vernon, left-wing maestro Tommy Ring, the muscular Jimmy Gabriel and the graceful Alex Young.

Moores would be a regular visitor to the Bellefield training ground, famously once giving a bemused Derek Temple a lesson in how to cross the ball. Though respecting Johnny Carey as a 'good practitioner', Moores had reservations about the Irishman's ability to deliver silverware. The chairman knew what he required, as he recounted to John Roberts in 1977: 'Everton expects success, we have a very good crowd and they are very loyal. But, of course, they pay their money and they expect to see us do well. If we don't do well then something should be done about it – and something will be done about it.'

He continues:

> The important thing is to get a good manager who can enthuse his team. Carey was a good, honourable man and a good tactician but he was not completely involved. He wasn't a tracksuit manager, he thought he could give his instructions to (Gordon) Watson and didn't need to go and watch his men train. Before I went on the Board they had passed a resolution, asking Johnny to give more time to the team. There wasn't too much discipline amongst the players in training.

Team captain Bobby Collins, in his biography *The Wee Barra* (also titled *Scotland's Mighty Atom* in some editions), echoed some of Moores' concerns: 'Johnny insisted that we enjoyed our football. The only flaw was that he was not hard enough with the players and some did take liberties. Discipline was not tight enough and this stopped him from becoming a great manager. Top managers need a ruthless streak, as players do, if they want to make it at the highest level.'

Centre-forward Frank Wignall, who played under Carey at Everton and Nottingham Forest, concurs: 'He was a gentleman; he didn't like upsetting people. I don't think he had the right character to be a manager if things started to slide.'

Matters came to a head in the most unlikely of settings, just six days after a 4–0 demolition of Newcastle United. On 14 April 1961, with Everton sitting in fifth position, John Moores broke the devastating news to the incumbent of the manager's chair, as he told John Roberts:

> *Somehow or other the word had got round that we were very*
> *dissatisfied with Johnny. There had been a League Management*
> *Committee meeting in London and afterwards Johnny wanted*
> *to speak to me but the journalists were all about with their*
> *ears cocked. So I said to Johnny, 'Well come along with me to*
> *the Grosvenor House Hotel.' He wasn't fired in the taxi but he*
> *wouldn't be quiet and wanted to know what I wanted to see*
> *him about. So I said, 'Well I want to see you about that, Johnny,*
> *because I want to see if we can make an agreement and give you*
> *a golden handshake and see if you can leave us.' Then we stopped*
> *for an hour and a half in the hotel until we finally decided that*
> *it was best for him to go.*

Shortly after the parting became public Moores sought to reassure the *Liverpool Echo* that the decision to dispense with Carey's services had not been a knee-jerk one: 'The question of a managerial change had been discussed by the directors for some time and it was agreed unanimously at our last meeting that Mr Carey would be given the opportunity to resign.' The outcome was harsh on Carey who, many believed, had put together one of the most entertaining sides ever seen at Goodison Park and deserved to be given more time to bed in his stars properly. Carey, gentleman that he was, agreed to oversee the team's fixture at Goodison Park the following day, with Cardiff City the visitors. After being given a vote of thanks by Bobby Collins in the dressing room before kick-off he saw his charges hammer the Bluebirds 5–1; the irrepressible Bobby Collins claimed a hat-trick and Alex Young added two more. One further injustice for Carey is that his dismissal coined the refrain 'Taxi!' which, to this day, is shouted at under-pressure managers.

At a board meeting held at Goodison Park the following Monday, Moores introduced the manager-elect: Harry Catterick. His appointment was rubber-stamped there and then. In fact, Moores had been casting envious glances across the Pennines for some time; perhaps Everton were the unnamed club that had made overtures to Harry back in the spring of 1960. In his unpublished memoirs Harry related the fact that Goodison emissaries had ventured to Sheffield on more than one occasion:

> *For some months Everton had put out feelers for a successor*

> *to John Carey and various unknown characters, one a lawyer,*
> *called at my home to ask if I would be interested in the Everton*
> *job. I was very happy at Wednesday at the time and spurned any*
> *other offers of employment. But of course after parting with Shef-*
> *field I eagerly accepted the terms offered by the Everton board.*

This style of indirect approach was the Moores way. Twenty years later Howard Kendall, then Blackburn Rovers' player-manager, received similar home visits enquiring if he would be interested in succeeding Gordon Lee at Everton.

Having walked away from Hillsborough, Harry would claim that he was 'on the breadline for the first time since leaving school'. Les Gore, the Leyton Orient manager, invited Harry down to the England–Scotland match on 15 April to discuss the possibility of teaming up at Brisbane Road. Harry accepted the Wembley hospitality but declined the employment offer. Reading between the lines, Harry had been expecting a call to return 'home' to Goodison Park. Whether his resignation kick-started the removal of Carey, or whether Harry had been 'tipped the wink' by Everton that the job was waiting for him if he resigned at Hillsborough, is open to question. The answer was taken to the grave by both Harry and John Moores.

Harry's recollection in his planned memoir, perhaps mindful of his potential audience, was thus:

> *I heard that a vacancy had arisen at my old club Everton, the*
> *club always dearest to my heart. Maybe I indulged in a pipe-*
> *dream or two. Those dreams became a reality when Everton*
> *approached me to take over. Just imagine my feelings, being*
> *invited to manage the club I loved – a chance to go back to*
> *Goodison Park, towards which my mind had been drifting for*
> *years. Once an Evertonian, always an Evertonian! I was there*
> *on the dot, 17 April 1961, for an interview with the Chairman,*
> *Mr John Moores – who I have to rate as 'the greatest thing' that*
> *ever happened to soccer in this century. A forthright interview*
> *with this firm, but extremely kindly, business genius and Mr*
> *Moores was satisfied that I could bring more glory to the greatest*
> *club on earth.*

Some years later Moores told journalist Ian Hargraves about the interview: 'When Harry joined us I asked him if he could try and recreate the type of team that made

Goodison known as the School of Science. He replied: "If I build a team that plays brilliant football, but goes down to the Third Division, will you still keep me as manager?" I'm afraid the answer was "no".'

In 1977 Moores explained to John Roberts the decision to approach Harry: 'Harry was a good manager – he was a tracksuited manager, he enthused the players and got with them and knew their problems. Bill Shankly was another perfect example. Harry was totally committed and he was a big step forward for us.'

Moores' statement would have raised a wry smile from Harry's contemporaries at Goodison. He, like Everton, had changed dramatically over the preceding decade.

Although not a complete stranger to the training ground, he increasingly delegated coaching duties to his staff. To keep up appearances, however, the tracksuit would always be on stand-by – cleaned and ironed – ready to be pressed into service. It became a standing joke among the players that when Harry trotted onto the training pitches in his blue tracksuit, John Moores or cameramen would not be far behind. One wonders if Moores ever did rumble the ruse.

By now the physical centre-forward had morphed into a self-styled 'thinking man's manager' who conducted his business in fine, tailored, suits. Like his father, Harry had never possessed a particularly strong northern accent but had, by now, developed a broadcasting voice, with clipped tones, to be used for public consumption – the harsher northern inflections would be saved for dressing-down players. Keen to improve himself socially, he took dancing lessons and developed a taste for quality cigars and fine red wine – always in moderation. He had successfully transformed himself from blue-collar to white-collar, as comfortable in the boardroom, managing the expectations of directors, as in the dressing room.

This transformation bears parallels with managerial contemporary Alf Ramsey, who was reputed to have hidden his East End roots by taking elocution lessons – although Catterick never seemed embarrassed by his roots in the way that Ramsey seems to have been.

Len Capeling, formerly of the *Liverpool Daily Post*, recalls: 'He got on very well with the right people within the hierarchy; that was where he was happiest. Had he stayed in engineering he'd have become a top man; he'd have always moved with a certain class of people – you could not imagine him turning up at a Christmas party to play as Santa Claus or glad-handing the players. He didn't need that because, then, you were the boss and they were the workers. To me Catterick was like an Agatha Christie character – a cipher – there was nothing there. With Shankly you can place him with the things he did, but Harry was like a cardboard cut-out that moved around to certain points.'

Moores' favourite mantra was, 'Anyone who lives on high hills should expect high winds'; in other words, with high rank comes high expectations. Harry knew that by becoming, in all but name, the head of the football division of Littlewoods he had a serious and demanding job with great responsibility on his shoulders. His attributes made him ideal for a role where keeping Moores, and his Littlewoods acolytes, onside was as important as managing the playing and coaching staff. He told John Roberts why he believed John Carey had been removed from post and outlined how he avoided the same fate:

> *If John Carey had a weakness, and we all have, he would let things develop rather than hurry them along. When you have a driving personality like John Moores and a laconic type like Carey they won't necessarily get on together. If John said he'd do it tomorrow John Moores would want it done yesterday. Possibly there was a conflict. You not only had to be busy – you had to be seen to be busy.*
>
> *John Moores' main contribution has been an astute business acumen which I was fortunate to be able to study. He loved the club which he gave so much of his heart, and financial backing, to – but one still had to run a business and money was available when I needed it but a lot of it was also returned as and when we made it. He liked it that I had an eye to the business end of it, I was not a glorified coach who did not want to know about the financial side – a manager needs that. It is important that you do get involved in the finance to a point, you can't ignore it.*

Graham Wilson, of Littlewoods, recalls: 'Harry, like everyone, was scared of Moores. Whereas Bill Shankly moved his office from next to the Anfield boardroom to next to the players, Harry was a directors' manager.' It is certain that Harry was always wary of Moores, but he was able to develop a solid working relationship with the club's main shareholder over his 12 years at the helm. He would become accustomed to being summoned to Moores' home in Freshfield, Formby, on Sunday mornings to conduct a postmortem of the previous day's match. However, when speaking to John Roberts, Harry sought to downplay the shadow of Moores:

> *I felt I did have a good relationship with Moores. He likes a*

fellow that can discipline himself and can work hard at the job. In those two factors we had a lot of common ground but he didn't like a 'yes' man deep down; he wanted men who would ask questions. He would ask me questions as to how situations were in football but never presumed to be able to tell me about how to do my business. He'd merely make an observation – if you could give a logical answer to a reasonable question that was fine. I found him very approachable, I talked to him on the most personal matters in his office or home. We had common ground on how the game should be played.

Upon walking through the doors of Goodison Park, Harry knew that a ruthless streak would be required to change the mindset at the club.

There was an air of complacency about the place, everyone seemed too easy-going. Some of the staff seemed afraid to make even minor decisions affecting training and coaching. I had to make changes and I didn't like what I had to do because I had known some of them as players.

Despite any feelings of discomfort expressed, no sentimentality was shown to people Harry had known for over 20 years: 'The major complaints brought to my notice were that no qualified physiotherapist was available, that the training system was not up-to-date and not in keeping with such a great club. Matters were quickly sorted out. We had to retire Harry Cooke, for instance, he was nearly seventy years old then and I had been a boy under him.' Cooke, a Goodison institution, was in fact 82 at the time of Harry's arrival. In his 58-year association with Everton he had been a player, trainer and physio. Harry himself, as a player, had been on the receiving end of Cooke's ministrations in the 1940s but his techniques, once cutting edge, had become decidedly 'old school'. Brian Labone said that Cooke reputedly still rubbed down players with a rag that had seen service in Dixie Dean's time. Harry promptly advised Cooke that he would be retiring that summer. In his place came Norman Borrowdale, a qualified physiotherapist who had already done some ad-hoc work at Goodison while employed by St Helens Rugby League Club.

Cooke's grandson, also known as Harry, had joined the club in 1939 as a player and was appointed head scout in 1958. He would forge a strong partnership with Catterick over the coming 12 years as they scoured Britain for the best talent.

Cooke junior, who would himself serve Everton for 51 years, became one of the few to truly gain the ear of Harry. They would often head off on scouting trips, with their golf clubs in the boot, to assess the rich pickings in Scotland. Catterick and Cooke were not just interested in the natural talent of players they scouted but also their character. Gordon Lee worked with Cooke at Everton from 1977 and recalls: 'Harry Cooke always had this saying – "Has he got the desire?" As well as ability, he always paid a lot of attention to the player's attitude and as to whether he wanted to do well as a football player.'

Gordon Watson, a former playing colleague of Harry's, was unceremoniously removed from his position as first-team trainer and obliged to accept a demotion to become reserve team coach. In Watson's place Tommy Eggleston followed 'The Boss' across the Pennines in the close season. Discreet enquiries were made to Joe Fagan about a switch across Stanley Park, but these were politely rebuffed; Fagan was now well established in the Anfield boot room set-up. Fagan's wife said in his biography: 'He was more than happy at Anfield. He had made good friends there and the club was progressing as he would have hoped. He felt part of something and saw no reason to go elsewhere.'

On the playing staff only Tommy (T.E.) Jones remained from the first-team squad of Harry's playing days. Jones would suffer a shattered knee-cap shortly after Harry's arrival, effectively ending his playing career, but would coach the 'A' team in later years. In *Three Sides of the Mersey*, he recounted to the authors how striking the change was in Harry from player to manager: '"The Catt", as they called him, was the iron man. He was certainly a man-manager but you never knew where you stood with Harry Catterick. He was the type of person who could talk to you as if the best of friends and the next day he'd walk past you as if you didn't exist.'

Upon starting work Harry showed an iron fist to certain players when he found that not everything was as it should be. He recounted to John Roberts:

> *I've always set very simple principles about people who earn wages that they should work hard to get them. I had a very strict upbringing – not only in football but in life – possibly that was an extension of that. I think he (Carey) was a bit easy on discipline and one or two players, who were outstanding in terms of ability, had run a little wild. It was one of my jobs to straighten them up, which didn't make me very popular. Any player playing badly but working hard was never in trouble with me. The player I didn't like was the fellow who wanted to play about at*

night and still wasn't doing his stuff on Saturdays. That fellow
I wouldn't tolerate and he would catch it from me. My problem
was with fellows who had been at other clubs and brought one
or two habits which I wouldn't tolerate. Eventually we ironed
them out and eventually many players have said I was right; I
could have been a bit too harsh with one or two but I don't think
it did them any harm really. But I had many players under me
that I never had to speak to – particularly the group that came
up under my theories like Husband, Hurst, Harvey, Wright and
West. I never had trouble with them off the field.

Taking up the same theme with Mike Langley in 1966 he opined: 'There's a general tendency among British players to live it up off the field. So few of them can foresee the day when the glory's over at 32. In my opinion a footballer should dedicate himself to ten years of self-discipline – no alcohol, no parties, but plenty of steady saving. I've given this advice to every man I've ever signed but sometimes it's like talking to a wall.'

The playing staff would soon learn the value placed on punctuality and discipline in the Catterick regime:

Players appeared to be reporting for training at times which
suited them and not the club. Players under me can expect strict
discipline, but they know they will always get fair treatment for
a fair day's work.

Stories became legion of 'The Bollocking Room' located in the Goodison Road stand where Harry would tear a strip off players who, he felt, were not giving their all or meeting the high standards demanded of them. To up the ante it was customary for Harry to keep the players waiting an hour before entering the room – just to let them stew.

Harry Bennett, who joined the club as an apprentice in 1964, recalls the contrast between Harry and his predecessor: 'Harry just had the persona about him that he was the commanding general and we were the troops. What he said was the word of God and there was no argument about that. I think one or two of the people left over from the Johnny Carey regime thought that they could be on the same footing with Catterick as they were with Carey – quite informal, I believe. But that was not the case. For him you were there to do a job of work in the way and the manner he said. If you were not prepared to do that you kissed the place goodbye.'

One employee anticipating Harry's arrival with a sense of foreboding was Alex Young. The Scottish forward, signed from Hearts in 1960, had had little opportunity to establish himself at Everton before the managerial coup. A modest, softly spoken man, Young was not your typical centre-forward as he lacked bulk and brawn but more than made up for it with intelligence, sublime skill, body-swerve and an uncanny heading ability for one lacking great height. Young heard through *Liverpool Echo* journalists that Harry was 'gunning for' him even before he sat in the manager's chair.

The situation shared some parallels with the Quixall conundrum Harry had faced upon his arrival at Hillsborough. Both Young and Quixall were fans' favourites: though devastating on their day they had a reputation for being less effective away from home. But having dispensed with Quixall, Harry persevered with Young and the Scot would repay this in spades. He was near ever-present in their first two seasons together. Young would remain at the club for a further seven years of supporter adulation – yet he felt, with some justification, that Harry was always on the lookout for a more muscular replacement. Colin Harvey agrees with this view: 'Alex was a lovely touch player but Harry wanted a little bit more – touch, hard work and someone who would tackle.'

Ironically, Harry's first game at the helm took him back to South Yorkshire for a duel against his former employers. His appearance in the stand prompted boos from sections of the Hillsborough terraces but it was Harry who was smiling at the end as two goals from centre-forward Frank Wignall secured a 2–1 victory. The season ended with a 4–1 triumph over Arsenal in Harry's first match in charge at Goodison Park.

Upon Harry's appointment Everton were already committed, much to his chagrin, to a summer tournament in North America – he wanted to spend the close season making changes to the set-up. Everton's participation in the International Soccer League had been in doubt until the eleventh hour, as FIFA was reluctant to sanction the tournament. On the pitch, in New York and Montreal, the Blues won their eight-team mini-league, containing the likes of Besiktas, Kilmarnock and Bangu of Brazil, to claim a £10,000 prize. After travelling home to England the team were then obliged to return to New York for the final against Dukla Prague, the winners of the other group. John Moores travelled with the squad to New York but witnessed a humiliating 9–2 defeat over the two-legged final at the famous Polo Grounds baseball stadium. Personal photos taken by Harry during the tour show a surprisingly relaxed squad. While in New York players took in shows, horse racing at Belmont Park in New Jersey and there was a visit to the United Nations building. However, there were also numerous issues with the organisation of the tournament and the standard of hotel accommodation, which Harry reported to the board on his return to England.

For Frank Wignall the tournament sowed the seeds of his Everton exit. The six-foot Lancastrian, who broke his toe on the tour, crossed swords with Harry in unusual circumstances: 'Harry was a bully but he wasn't the only manager like that at the time. He used to put the fear of God into the players, you couldn't have a joke with him. We didn't have a reserve goalkeeper on the tour so Harry said: "Have any of you flaming lot ever kept goal?" I'd always been an emergency goalkeeper so I said, "Yes, I'll do it for you, boss." So he said, "All right then, come on and let's fire a few shots at you." After ten or fifteen minutes firing shots at me he said, "That's all right." As it happened I had to go in goal during a match and he started criticising me for one or two incidents in the game – "You should have done that and should have done this." I said, "Hang on a minute. I think you're a bit out of order. I haven't played in goal for two years!"'

An incident at the team hotel pool perhaps helped seal Wignall's fate. 'Harry didn't like the water. He was in the pool, standing, I dived in and grabbed hold of his legs and pulled him under – I think that was it for me! When we got back to England he took me out of the first-team squad for training – I had a few words with him then!'

Another player who fell foul of Harry was Roy Vernon, who crossed the disciplinary line by breaching a curfew. The manager took the harsh – but perhaps necessary – step of sending Vernon home in disgrace, putting down a 'don't mess with me' marker to the rest of the squad. Vernon was quietly made available for transfer but remained at the club for a further four years. Harry, hoping that giving Vernon more responsibility would control his temper and excesses, actually made him captain for the 1962/63 season, recalling in his memoir: 'Roy Vernon was a bit of a problem but a very fine player – I made him skipper and we got a better response from him.'

The Vernon incident underlined to Harry's new charges that discipline and punctuality were paramount; non-adherence would not be tolerated. After the more laconic approach of Carey it came as a shock to some. Derek Temple remembers: 'Harry quickly let them know who was boss – he got the opportunity to prove himself very quickly. If you were doing your job he was OK with you, he never actually complimented you – you had a job to do and you were getting paid for that. He would almost come across as critical of players but he would delegate that. If we played away and we lost we knew what would happen, then Tommy would get up and walk along the bus and say, "You, you and you!" and he'd have us in on the Sunday just lapping around.'

Flint-born Vernon was renowned for his propensity to smoke almost any time and anywhere. In 1966 Harry told Mike Langley of the issues he had experienced in dealing with headstrong young players, perhaps referring to the Welshman:

> *A player, although youngish, started puffing and blowing like a veteran towards the end of every match. I called him into the office; he arrived with a cigarette in his hand while I was on the phone. Before I'd put the phone down he'd stubbed that cigarette and lit another. I said: 'How many of those are you going through a day?'*
>
> *'About five.'*
>
> *'Well you've smoked two while I've been watching.'*
>
> *'No, I mean packets, not fags.'*
>
> *'Five packets of tens?'*
>
> *'No, twenties.'*
>
> *I was horrified – 'That's a hundred a day.'*
>
> *'Yes,' he just grinned, 'it ain't half expensive.'*
>
> *'Well save yourself some money by putting that one out for a start and don't light up in here unless I give you permission.'*
>
> *Then I gave him the lecture about how he was wasting his talent and taking several years off his career. It made no difference for I heard the scratch of the match almost as he closed the door.*
>
> *I decided this player needed a scare. He was told to report for a medical examination. The doctor checked him over, looked suitably concerned as he sounded the player's chest and said: 'There might be trouble here. I think you ought to have an x-ray.'*
>
> *That would have been enough to frighten any other footballer off cigarettes for life but not this fellow. He lit up even before putting his shirt on again.*

Back in England, the Cattericks – Harry, Nancy and his third daughter Diane – swapped Beauchief in Sheffield for Knowle Avenue in Ainsdale; a safe yet commutable distance from Liverpool surrounded by some of the finest golf courses in the country. The very word Ainsdale still sends shivers down the spines of ex-players, as it was the scene of brutal pre-season training runs along the beach and sand dunes. Harry would turn up in his Rover 110 (registration: '1 EFC') to see them off and then leave the slog in the capable hands of Eggleston or, in later years, Wilf Dixon.

Frank D'Arcy, an Everton squad player throughout the 1960s, recalls: 'In pre-season we'd jump on the bus at Goodison and it would take us to Southport; Harry would jump in the car. They used to drop us off and we'd do a five- to eight-mile trot. We'd get to Ainsdale and they'd have us up and down those sand hills – they killed you. They wanted you one hundred per cent fit. Norman Borrowdale, the physio, used to come with us and you used to think that your heart would give way – that's how hard it was. Norman would come along and say, "Take deep breaths – take it easy".'

Howard Kendall concurred with D'Arcy in his autobiography: 'He [Catterick] would be there for pre-season training on the sand-dunes at Ainsdale. Maybe it was the sadist in him as, to a man, we all detested it. It was carnage. Harry would sit in his Rover at the bottom, looking up at us, just to keep a check on it. Of course, like fools, we tried to go faster when he was there!'

C H A P T E R T E N
TOWARDS THE TITLE

AS THE 1961/62 season kicked off with a win over Aston Villa there were few changes to the squad. Harry believed that discipline combined with his fitness and coaching regime would make a material difference to results on the pitch.

After years of campaigning by the Professional Footballers' Association, one significant change that year had been the abolition of the wage cap for footballers. Tommy Trinder, Fulham's chairman, offered captain Johnny Haynes £100 per week but Harry and the Everton hierarchy were in no mood to be so generous, as Frank Wignall discovered: 'In my own mind I thought: "Johnny Haynes is getting £100, I should get £40 at least." Harry came down to the dressing room and said: "Right, four at a time come to my office and we'll get you signed on for next year." Bobby Collins went in the office for five minutes and came out rubbing his hands saying, "That's me sorted for the next two years." I was in next. As I was sitting down he slipped a contract across the big desk and said, "Get that signed." It was for £25 a week. I said, "Boss, I was expecting a bit more than that, Johnny Haynes is on £100 a week." He picked another contract up and slid it across to me saying, "Have a look at that. That is Bobby Collins, your club captain, the Scottish captain, the best player in our club. He has just signed for £35 a week and you're trying to tell me you are in line with him – get it signed or get out!" So I signed.'

Harry would rue the disruption to his pre-season plans caused by the two trips across the Atlantic, blaming it for a poor start to the season; an invitation to a further tournament in North America for the following close season was firmly declined. Injuries sustained in the opening-day victory over Aston Villa contributed to a run of five defeats in the next six matches, including a 4–0 home mauling by Sheffield Wednesday. The poor run of form persuaded Harry to make a rare written foray into the club programme. The article underlined the contrast with his predecessor's ethos 'to give Everton entertaining and, if possible, winning football':

The great feeling of optimism has been dampened by the un-
happy start which we have made. Nevertheless there is every
reason to believe that the results will come, particularly when we
are free of the injury bug which has struck at such a vital time.
My main concern is for the team to play not only attractively
but effectively. Indications are that teams will be playing harder
than ever before, and if we are to enjoy a high position, then
determination as well as ability must be displayed in every game.

In a nutshell, Harry's recipe for success was to win home matches and avoid defeat at away grounds – 'Two points at home and one away is championship form'.

Bobby Collins was one of the most formidable and gifted players ever to don the royal blue shirt of Everton. His arrival from Celtic in 1958, just before Johnny Carey's appointment as Everton manager, had transformed a team that had struggled under Ian Buchan. His displays at inside-forward mixed skill, passing ability, goalscoring prowess and a vital nasty streak. He was also opinionated and strong-willed off the pitch – a natural leader whose diminutive 5ft 4in stature earned him the nickname 'Pocket Napoleon'. Almost single-handedly, through his ability and sheer force of will, he ensured that relegation worries were banished at the turn of the decade and became a vital cog in the squad that Carey was assembling at considerable cost. Frank Wignall is effusive about his former team-mate: 'As a player he had everything, absolutely everything. He was a tough little bloke and he used to get stuck in. He played twice above his weight. He helped me quite a number of times and I heard him helping other kids there. Every Tuesday morning there used to be a match between the first team and reserve team. I used to play as hard as I could to get a bit of recognition. Before the game Bobby said, "You've got to be a bit harder when you try to win the ball." During this match the ball came loose between me and Bobby and I just went full at him. I caught him and he went down on the floor, snarling away, and I said to him, "Bobby, I'm just doing what you told me to do." And he just said, "Give us a lift up." And that was it forgotten.'

Harry saw the incumbent captain finish the 1960/61 season with 18 goals to his name – second only to Vernon. He retained the captaincy at the start of the next campaign but succumbed to two injuries that saw him miss 11 games by the end of November. The absences caused Harry to reflect on whether the 29-year-old's powers were on the wane. Perhaps with this in mind, Harry reported at the first board meeting after Christmas that squad reinforcements were required, and
the minutes recorded: 'Mr Catterick reported that having seen two games on heavy

grounds he did not think our present league position would be maintained with the present playing staff.'

Despite returning to the team in good form over the festive season, Collins would claim, in his 2004 biography, to have been upbraided by Harry despite scoring twice against Fulham: 'Catterick told me I was not the player I used to be. I was not happy and told him so. I'd been the best Everton player that day and I'd got a rollicking. I knew that my days were numbered.' His pride was further piqued when John Moores sided with his manager: 'As Captain I was first to receive his opinions and was unhappy when Mr Moores inferred I wasn't giving my all. Nobody criticises my work-rate, winning is all to me.' The livid Scot briefed a journalist on the meeting with Moores and the story made the sports headlines. Despite a subsequent conciliatory meeting with the chairman, Collins' card had been marked.

Harry, at odds with Collins' version of events, cited injury and loss of form as key factors:

> Bobby, after injuring a knee, came back in indifferent form and got the bird from the fans who idolised him. He was shocked. In any other area it might have been possible to 'hide' Bobby for a month whilst he regained his touch but not on Merseyside where fans don't wait for the tide to turn.

Collins would disagree with Harry's assessment: 'Harry Catterick was the only one giving me the bird.'

Whatever the truth, the path was being paved for a controversial exit, as Harry recalled:

> During one of our many chats Bobby said that he was of the opinion that certain players were not playing with him as they should. I kept a close watch and failed to see the point that Bobby made. I felt that in the interest of Collins he should have a spell in the second team, yet an adequate replacement was not available so negotiations were started for Dennis Stevens of Bolton Wanderers. Whilst we were in the midst of these negotiations Bobby pointed out that he was quite happy at Everton but asked, as manager, would I mind telling him if another club became interested? I agreed and that promise was kept when Mr Harry Reynolds, Chairman of Leeds United, and manager Don Revie

came through.

Years later, in 1978, Harry would reveal to Charles Lambert a twist in the tail to the Collins transfer:

> *Billy Bremner had played a handful of games for Leeds but had*
> *by no means established himself. I was interested in Bremner*
> *but Don Revie was very browned-off with him. The lad had*
> *been homesick and going home to Scotland at weekends and not*
> *coming back until several days later. Don spoke to me about*
> *Collins and we agreed a fee of around £20,000. At the same*
> *time I asked about Bremner and it was agreed that I could have*
> *him for the same amount. But Leeds had a series of matches*
> *coming up and they wanted to keep Bremner for a couple of*
> *weeks longer. I agreed, the lad played for them, did exceptionally*
> *well and the deal was off. The whole destiny of Leeds probably*
> *hung on that and you can imagine how I felt when I saw how*
> *Bremner developed.*

Speaking to Mike Langley of the People in 1966, Harry admitted publicly to a rare lapse of judgement in selling Collins: 'Of all the sales I've made the sale of Bobby Collins to Leeds was the only one which would have been better delayed.' Perhaps more than losing Collins a year too early, Harry regretted inadvertently helping to kick-start the Leeds United revolution under Revie with Collins as his general on the pitch and Bremner his apprentice.

Mick Meagan, who played alongside Collins for three years, links the transfer of the Scot to the development of Leeds into the tough yet talented team that would challenge Everton for supremacy in the late 1960s. 'Bobby was a great player, one of my favourites, and it was a surprise when he left. Maybe Harry thought he was just hitting the veteran stage. He was a brilliant footballer but by God he was a tough little customer. At Everton he used to come up to me and say, "You bloody Irish, you had it too good over there; you should have been born in Glasgow during the war – you'd have had to fight for your crust of bread!" But Bobby was a brilliant signing by Revie – he gave Leeds an awful lot of backbone. I remember playing against Leeds' second team when Bremner, Hunter, Madeley and Reaney were all brilliant players but lovely lads – a pleasure to play against. A few years later we played them with Bobby in the FA Cup and they had changed completely – the lovely lads had become Rottweilers and I'm convinced Bobby Collins had a great influence on that. That's why Revie signed Bobby – to give those lads a little bit of what was missing. He did wonderfully well for Johnny Giles who was a brilliant player but too nice – Bobby gave him his needle.'

Collins would spend five happy years at Elland Road. His Leeds team-mate Johnny Giles emphasised to Collins' biographer David Saffer the Scot's contribution to the Revie revolution: 'Bobby's impact on Leeds United was immeasurable. He was older than the rest of the players and set the standards of how a top professional should look after himself. Bobby thought he could and should win every match he played in. Long after Bobby had left, his influence stayed with the players.'

Despite the adverse reaction and secret regrets brought on by the sale of Collins, Harry remained on course to blend a team that could go all the way in the league the following season. Whatever the merits of the deal, the Collins episode demonstrated his guts in trusting his instinct and not pandering to what others wanted. It was also the catalyst for a round of transfer activity at Everton.

Dennis Stevens was an industrious 28-year-old inside-forward but no Bobby Collins – a player almost on a par with Young in the affections of the Gwladys Street End. The change in personnel went down like a lead balloon with the incredulous Everton supporters. Poor Stevens, a cousin of the late Duncan Edwards, felt the wrath of the Goodison crowd and would take some time to work himself into its affections. However, his energetic displays saw him become a vital, if unsung, cog in a wonderful footballing machine. After making his debut he became an ever-present for two seasons and pitched in with his quota of goals. Looking back 15 years later Harry would say to Mike Langley: 'Stevens was not a popular signing. He didn't have the thrills of the others but his work-rate, determination and sheer guts away from home added steel to the artistry of Alex Young and Roy Vernon. Stevens protected Young a lot physically, he would take on people on who were trying to bounce Alex, and add a bit of toughness.' He added: 'They said he was too old and didn't like his style but Stevens was a manager's player, not a spectator's player. He put hard work and effort into the forward line.'

Derek Temple concurs that Harry valued Stevens' contribution in his four seasons at Everton: 'He rated Dennis Stevens very highly: he was his type of player – a great little worker and a good footballer. He'd get the tackles in and give somebody else the ball. There were no lost causes. He had the misfortune to follow Bobby Collins, there was a gulf in class but Dennis was a good player to have on your side.'

Arriving just days before Stevens was Harry's first transfer and a real statement of intent – a record fee for a goalkeeper was agreed with Blackpool for their young custodian, Gordon West. Harry had decided that Albert Dunlop, who had been in the junior ranks when Harry was playing for Everton, was lacking in height and would not form part of the spine of the side. Barnsley-born West had been a late-comer to goalkeeping but was quickly challenging Tony Waiters for Blackpool's number one jersey. An eye-watering £27,500 for the 18-year-old was required to draw the Blackpool board to the negotiating table.

Although Everton would finish the 1961/62 season in a respectable fourth place, the building bricks had been laid for a sustained assault on the title the following season:

> Eventually I believed we had a team which could win the championship. We had acquired experienced reserve strength and had players with the skill necessary to fall into the pattern of play I had designed... a pattern I believed was correct for our type of player.

Perhaps in a tacit acknowledgement of the situation with Alex Young he added:

> Quite often managers become too stereotyped as too defensive or too offensive. He must adjust his tactics and style of play to his playing resources. This over-riding principle can very often mean the omission of a highly-skilled player in the interest of the club as a whole. Much the same can be said of a player whose main attributes are courage and tenacity. The interests of the club always come first – it's far more important than the players.

Even before it kicked off, the 1962/63 season promised added spice as it saw the return of neighbours Liverpool FC to the First Division. It also reunited Harry and Bill Shankly after their earlier rivalry in Yorkshire. The two managers were yin and yang. Taciturn Harry would find himself overshadowed by the publicity-consciousness and loquacious Scot, not that this perturbed him unduly. They were never close – Shankly would sarcastically dub the Everton Manager 'Happy Harry', while Harry would retort by mockingly call the Scot 'Rob Roy'. That said, suggestions of a deep antipathy have been overplayed – they were two fiercely competitive managers hell-bent on securing supremacy on Merseyside and nationally.

Harry Bennett, who progressed to the fringes of the Everton first team in the late 1960s, recalls the similarities between the rivals. 'They were both serious, hard taskmasters. I knew from chatting with Liverpool's Roy Evans and Ian Ross, who was a good friend of mine, that with Bill Shankly, you did what you were told – just like us with Harry Catterick. All Shankly and Catterick were interested in was what you could do for their football club. If you were an asset to them and did as you were told then you were fine but if you were injured, you ceased to exist. At the end of the day they took the can for anything that happened so they were quite right.'

Harry told Mike Langley in 1966 of the pressures that they both faced once reunited on Merseyside: 'No two managers in the country are under greater pressure than Bill Shankly and myself. Our fans believe success is their right and they'll give us the hammer if they don't get it. Everton and Liverpool – there's no rivalry like it in Britain apart from Rangers and Celtic. We could finish as low as sixth and still keep our fans happy provided the other club finished lower. The same goes for Liverpool.'

Harry would seek to set the record straight about the relationship with Shankly to John Roberts in 1977, several years after he and Shankly had stepped down from their respective positions:

> *My relationship with Bill Shankly has always been misrepresented. There was this terrific rivalry; he has had a go at me in the media, in the way he jokes, and I have had a go at him. There was no animosity. I was at Sheffield Wednesday when Bill was at Huddersfield so we saw a lot of one another. When I moved back to Merseyside, after he'd gone to Anfield, was yet another situation. If his brother was in the opposition he'd kick him as much as anyone – that was professionalism and that's alright. I wasn't as good a friend of his as I had been when I came here; we could never be pals as we were on opposite sides but there was never any animosity as such. It would have been wrong if we had been pals, on Merseyside you can't be.*

Shankly, also in conversation with John Roberts, summed things up with his usual humour: 'We respected each other and we'd be happy to be first and second in the league – the other fellow second, of course... But deep down we were very friendly – we spoke to each other once a year!'

In the context of this rivalry, Harry showed real chutzpah to raid across Stanley Park in August 1962 and secure the signing of left-sided forward Johnny Morrissey for £15,000. Morrissey had been a bit-part player at Anfield so the approach to take him to Goodison, made once a bid for Chelsea's Peter Brabrook had fallen-through, came as a surprise to many – none more so than Bill Shankly. The Liverpool manager was apoplectic when he discovered that Harry, in trademark fashion, had bypassed the manager and persuaded the Liverpool board to sanction the transfer. Shankly would never let the Liverpool directors go above his head again. Almost inevitably, his goalscoring Everton debut would come in a Merseyside derby match.

Morrissey lacked the high profile of later singings such as Pickering, Ball and Kendall but would prove, over 344 appearances in a decade of service, to be one of Harry's most astute acquisitions. An unorthodox winger, with a build more akin to a rugby league player, he offered a potent blend of skill and steel. He would become an invaluable member of the team challenging for honours as the 1960s drew to a close. Jack Charlton of Leeds identified him as one of the toughest opponents he had faced, familiar, when required, with the dark arts. Mick Buckley recalled, in *Gwladys Street's Holy Trinity*, the physical aspect to the winger's game when he made his debut alongside him in 1972: "My lasting memory was of the respect everyone on the pitch, including the officials, gave to Johnny Morrissey. It wasn't until half-time that I noticed Bernard Shaw, the England Under- 23 defender, hobbling towards the tunnel. His legs were black and blue. His gold socks were in tatters and covered red with his own blood.…The unfortunate right-back would have to endure another 45 minutes against the Goodison hard case."

The Morrissey swoop illustrated vividly why Harry would gain a reputation for being the master of the 'cloak and dagger' transfer, a tactic he tried to explain:

> *It isn't politic to let fans know about your transfer intentions; that is only inviting competition. We would like to take fans into our confidence every time but it cannot be done; better a blanket of silence and a star captured than publicity and a star signed by somebody else!*

As with all Catterick teams, success started at the back, with Gordon West now established as the first-choice goalkeeper and two out of Alex Parker, Mick Meagan and George Thomson selected at full-back. The maturing Labone was the centre-half 'pivot', flanked by Jimmy Gabriel and Brian Harris. Gabriel was, in his own description, the team's 'policeman', while the versatile Harris was the team joker off the pitch. At various stages of the 1962/63 season Bingham, Temple, Ray Veall and Morrissey would raid down the wings. Dennis Stevens consistently put in shifts as a hard-working inside-forward who freed up Vernon to concentrate on what he did best – scoring goals. With Young at centre-forward, spectators witnessed perhaps the finest striking partnership ever to grace Goodison. Young's stylishness, creativity and surprising aerial ability blended superbly with the waspish Vernon's darting runs and unerring finishing.

John Moores set the bar high in the programme notes for the first home game of the season, with Manchester United the visitors: 'This season, we hope to go further up the League, nothing below top place will satisfy.' There was no ambiguity in the message to Harry, evoking the club motto: 'Nothing but the best is good enough'. Fortunately for all concerned, the season started strongly with four consecutive wins.

Everton approached Christmas 1962 having lost only three league games, one of them to Leyton Orient managed by Johnny Carey – victory must have tasted sweet for the Irishman. The team hovered between the top two positions in the table, with Spurs and Burnley offering the stiffest competition. A humbling by Dunfermline in the Inter-Cities Fairs Cup was a rare blip – the fact that the great Jock Stein was their opponents' manager, four seasons before his glory with Glasgow Celtic in Lisbon, was only partial mitigation. Alex Young has admitted that the team had displayed uncharacteristic complacency: 'Our approach had been unprofessional and we paid the price for our arrogance. Harry Catterick went ballistic and ordered us to go straight into training when we returned to Bellefield.'

In December, with Everton heading the league table, the season ground to a halt as an arctic winter descended on the UK. In an age where undersoil heating was virtually unheard of, football was put on hold for nearly two months. Foreseeing the fixture backlog once the season resumed, Harry moved, with trademark stealth, to make two key signings in an effort to push his title challenge over the line. He returned to Hillsborough to tie up a £60,000 deal for Tony Kay, the cocksure yet brilliant left-half whom Harry had developed into the Owls' team captain. In fact it was a surprise to most observers that Kay, a left wing-half, had not been recruited earlier. Despite subsequent events, Harry would always credit Kay as being his greatest signing. The transfer took some negotiating as the player was settled in Sheffield. On Christmas Eve Harry drove into Hillsborough's car park to begin negotiations in his former office. Kay recalls: 'The manager, Vic Buckingham, said, "I'd like to see you in the office, your pal has come to see you." I said, "Who's that?" and he replied "Harry Catterick". He assumed that Harry had been in touch with me but he hadn't. So Harry talked to me but I told him that I didn't want to go. Then a week or so later Vic said, "Your pal wants to see you again," and Harry made me an offer I couldn't refuse.'

In an era of 'under the counter' bonuses, few managers were complete strangers to brown envelopes. Kay would claim to the Sunday Mirror in 1997 that he was finally persuaded to swap Sheffield for Merseyside by an 'unofficial' £2,000 signing-on fee plus a promise that he would become the leader of the team. He recalls: 'Harry said he wanted me to win the title for him. He came back a bit later and told me Roy Vernon would be captain for the toss-up, but I'd be the real boss of the team. Brian Harris was playing really well that season so Harry was such a brave man to replace Brian and bring me in. I thought, "Wow, he must have a lot of confidence in me." He was proved right. I was a good player to have on your side – you don't make an enemy of Tony Kay. You know the expression "kick his own granny"… there were no 50/50 balls, it was always mine.'

Brian Harris had performed consistently well under Harry and was unfortunate to lose his place to Kay. Harry explained why he added Kay to Gabriel and Harris in the half-back ranks:

> There must be strong cover for every position. That was just not there. The importance of 'cover' reminds me of the criticism which greeted the Everton signing of Tony Kay at a time when Jimmy Gabriel and Brian Harris were playing so well. The general verdict from the terraces was 'unnecessary'. I am one that believes emphatically that to be an outstanding First Division club you MUST have three star wing half-backs. It is impossible to carry on week after week with only two.

The recruitment of Kay, recounted by Harris in his biography, emphasised how guarded Harry was with transfer dealings:

> The day Tony Kay arrived was a very strange day for me. There were rumours going around that Tony Kay was about to sign so I'd gone in to see Catterick that very morning to find out what was going on. After all, my position was in jeopardy and I wanted to know where I stood. Harry told me that he had no intention of signing a wing-half and totally denied that Everton were even talking to Tony. He convinced me that the whole story was media rubbish. I was out in Liverpool that very afternoon when the Echo announced that Everton had actually just signed Tony Kay; I was stunned and upset to say the least! I know he had a reputation for being secretive about incoming transfers…

*but felt that he could have given me a hint. I felt that I'd been
bull-shitted by my own manager and I was not very pleased to
put it mildly.*

Despite initially seeking a transfer, nothing materialised and Harris went on to play
a key role in the following three seasons.

At £40,000 the second major incoming transfer of the severe winter was just
as audacious. Alex 'Chico' Scott was a fast, direct and stocky winger with Glasgow
Rangers who had seen his first-team place come under threat from Willie Hender-
son. There was no shortage of suitors for the Scottish international and it appeared
that Tottenham were in pole position to clinch his services.

Nicholson, the Scarborough-born Spurs manager, was held in high esteem by
Harry, both for his honesty and principles on how the sport should be played. Harry
recounted to Mike Langley how he took a call from Nicholson when it was clear that
Rangers would listen to offers for their winger:

'Are you interested?' he [Nicholson] asked.

> *'Yes,' I said.*

> *'Well so am I,' said Bill, 'and we don't want to make this
an auction, so if you tell me your maximum figure I'll tell you
ours.'*

> *We exchanged prices and they were the same.*

> *'Right,' I said, 'it's up to the player.'*

> *But Nicholson beat me comfortably into Glasgow. I
drove up and got caught in a snowstorm. I got stuck in a drift,
tried to dig my car out and finally abandoned it near the border
and took a train from Carlisle. I'd hardly checked into the St
Enoch's hotel when my phone rang. A reporter was on the line.*

> *'You've lost Scott,' he said. 'He's going to Spurs.'*

> *I phoned Scot Symon, the manager of Rangers. 'What's
going on?' I asked.*

> *'Well,' said Scot, Bill Nicholson's negotiations are well
advanced but I'll keep our part of the bargain. I won't let the boy
sign before you speak to him.'*

> *I jumped into a taxi and went to Ibrox.*

> *I talked to Scott and his wife for an hour…and the rest
you know. He came to Everton.*

Bill Nicholson, although leaving Scotland under the impression that Scott would sign for him, and obviously disappointed when he didn't, has never complained to me about that Everton swoop.

Scott told Jon Berman and Malcolm Dome in 1997: 'It came down to a straight choice between the two clubs, and it looked for a while as if I would end up at White Hart Lane. I met up with both clubs on the same day and had to make a decision. After meeting Bill I had all but made up my mind that Spurs were the team for me. But then Everton made me a very lucrative offer that I would have been mad to turn down. So I reversed my original choice and opted for Everton.' Scott's wife, Annette, had a slightly different take on the reasons for selecting Everton, as she told Becky Tallentire in *Real Footballers' Wives*: 'Spurs had been after him too, but the deciding factors were that his brother Robert lived in Bury and, of course, it was far easier to get to Scotland from the north of England so we could go home for the weekend.'

Scott replaced Billy Bingham at outside-right, heralding the demise of the Irishman's playing career at Goodison – however, he would return a decade later in another capacity. The new additions made their debut in Everton's first league match since 22 December – a 1–3 defeat at Filbert Street on 12 February. There would be two further away defeats that season but Goodison would prove to be a fortress in the final push towards the title. Vernon and Young had, by now, blossomed into one of the game's most effective strike duos. Scoring 49 goals between them, they missed only one competitive game all season. No goal was more important than Young's salmon-like leap to convert Vernon's cross and secure a narrow, but fully deserved, victory over title rivals Tottenham Hotspur in April. The header, captured for posterity on grainy Pathé footage, has gained legendary status and it is claimed that the roar which greeted it could be heard in Bootle. Aside from – in the words of David France – the 'Golden Goal', the match saw the imperious Gabriel and Kay deliver perhaps their finest performances in royal blue as they rampaged over their Spurs adversaries.

The title was now Everton's to lose and, with Harry and Tommy Eggleston's hands firmly at the tiller, there would be no more slip-ups as four consecutive victories rounded off the season. Having demolished West Bromwich Albion 4–0 at the Hawthorns in midweek, the coveted crown was finally secured on a memorable Saturday in front of the 60,000-strong Goodison gallery. Fittingly Roy Vernon, Everton's captain, scored a hat-trick, including a trademark penalty, to seal a 4–1 victory over Fulham. In the absence of a trophy presentation the players joined the board members, and the immaculately attired Harry, on the balcony of the Main Stand for a champagne toast above the delirious throng. 'I have never seen anything like it,' Catterick told John Roberts. 'You should have seen the ground that day; it was packed to capacity, seething. You could almost get out and touch the atmosphere. It was terrific and very moving as I had come in for a fair amount of criticism after Bobby Collins' departure. Here it had all gone and this was the thing they had waited for since 1939 – a hell of a long time for a top-class club. It was most moving at the time.'

For the manager it was a justification of some unpopular decisions – the sale of Collins and the purchase of Stevens chief among them. Within two years of his return 'home' he had turned Everton into winners in a style befitting of the School of Science tag and sated, albeit temporarily, John Moores' thirst for silverware. In a piece in the *Liverpool Echo* Harry celebrated the season which, true to his mantra, had seen Everton unbeaten at home in the league: 'We won the title as I wanted to win it, with brilliant teamwork, sound methodical football and brimming confidence.'

CHAPTER ELEVEN
PRESSING MATTERS

IN THE SUMMER of 1963 there was scant opportunity for Harry to rest on his laurels with the defence of the title and an assault on the European Cup only a few months away.

Several players had left over the summer, including Billy Bingham to Port Vale, while George Thomson headed for the bright lights of London with Brentford. Frank Wignall, after falling out with Harry, had become a peripheral figure, appearing only once in the 1962/63 campaign. Despite an impressive 22 goals in 38 Everton appearances he moved to Nottingham Forest where he rebuilt his career and won two England caps.

Shortly after the start of the 1963/64 season, as the club enjoyed its championship celebration dinner, Harry moved stealthily to recruit a utility player who would provide loyal service for eight years. In 1966 Harry recalled the episode to Mike Langley:

> It was midnight in our championship dinner. The players were celebrating and the cabaret was onstage but neither I nor the Everton directors were watching it. No, we were huddled in a corner holding an emergency board meeting.
>
> 'We need cover at full-back,' I said, 'and I've just heard where I can get someone.'
>
> 'Carry on, Harry,' said the directors.
>
> I left the hotel immediately, still in my dinner suit, and drove alone to Scotland. At breakfast time I was changing clothes at a small hotel in the Lowlands. At nine I was parked outside Partick's main entrance. At ten I'd signed Brown and was driving home again.

He added to Charles Lambert in 1978: 'When the manager Willie Thornton arrived he wondered what the hell it was about. I said, "I want to sign Brown." A £38,000 fee was swiftly agreed for the player Harry described as 'a good servant and a great character in the dressing room'.

A collective groan could be heard in Liverpool 4 when the draw for the first round of the 1963/64 European Cup was announced. Harry's memoirs recorded: 'We weren't a lucky club in Europe and, in the preliminary round, were drawn against Inter Milan, the best team in Europe.' The Italian champions were managed by the legendary Argentinean Helenio Herrera, who had won La Liga titles twice each with Barcelona and Atlético Madrid. Like Harry, Herrera enforced a strict disciplinary code – forbidding players to drink or smoke and controlling their diet.

Wearing their away colours of white, Everton threw everything at Inter in the first leg at Goodison but the Italians, who used the 'catenaccio' system with a sweeper, stood firm and also threatened West's goal on a number of occasions. Having a 0–0 score to take back to the San Siro, Herrera predicted an easy victory in the second leg.

Ahead of the return leg in Milan, Harry picked up some pointers for future European adventures, as he recalled in the *People* in 1966: 'I'll be ready with all the lessons I've already learned from Europe. For instance, never let continental opponents arrange your travelling and hotels. Perhaps it was just a remarkable co-incidence but when I went to Milan all the hotels we were shown overlooked tram routes, railway lines or scooter-infested streets. "My players," I said diplomatically, "would prefer to stay in your beautiful Italian countryside." So we moved miles out of Milan and booked into a hotel in Monza.'

Arriving in Italy ahead of the fixture, Jimmy Gabriel was carrying an injury sustained in the previous weekend's win over Sheffield Wednesday. The upshot was the launch of the first-team career, at 18 years of age, of one of the club's finest players and servants: Colin Harvey.

Harry waxed lyrical about Harvey to John Roberts:

> We took Colin Harvey from school and he always looked a player
> of immense potential with lots of skills. Colin was always quiet
> and shy in my presence, the most he ever said was 'Good morning'
> and 'Hello Boss'. He was no trouble. I don't think anyone could
> have had a better professional to handle, and he was absolutely
> superb as a player. Colin had to come into the side, we only went

*down 1–0 but he had a superb game in the San Siro. My God,
he did show a lot of character and ability. From thereon in he
never looked back.*

Colin Harvey recalls: 'I played in the reserves on the Saturday at Sheffield. On the way back we stopped for a meal and Gordon Watson, who was in charge of the reserves, got a message that three of us were to travel with the team to Italy. I just thought I was going to carry the skips. On the Wednesday afternoon, we'd had lunch and were just about to go for a lie-down. Then Harry announced, "Jimmy Gabriel is injured, Dennis, you drop back to number four, Colin you'll wear number eight." He had given me no prior indication so I went to bed and I didn't have any nerves – I did not have time to get worried about it. I didn't play brilliantly well but did OK considering we were playing the team that would eventually win it. It was just his way of taking pressure off me.'

Harry withdrew Harvey from the first-team picture almost as soon as he'd entered it, either to keep his feet firmly on the ground or to shield him from the limelight. This action would be repeated with many other young debutants under Harry. 'I'd played in a couple of reserve games afterwards,' Harvey recalls. 'In one we got beaten away at Derby and I got the call to his office and I thought "Here we go". But when I got there Harry said, "We had this given to us by Inter Milan – do you want it?" It was a state of the art record player so I walked out with it under my arm!'

Harvey's rapid progress was vindication of an incoming transfer made the previous summer that, on the face of it, had been a relative failure. Jimmy Hill, the Northern Irish international inside-forward, had been signed from Norwich for £20,000 but only played seven first-team matches for Everton. Unbeknown to the supporters, Hill had been brought in largely to have a nurturing influence on younger players in the Central League squad. Harry recounted the background of the acquisition to Mike Langley in 1966: 'As the forms were on the desk I said to Hill: "Now you'll only get the occasional league game. I'm really buying you to bring on some youngsters in the reserves." It paid off, and Hill's influence and guidance went a long way towards producing two of Everton's best ever home-grown players, Colin Harvey and Tommy Wright.'

The fixtures against Inter gave Harry an insight into a different way of playing football, albeit not one he felt inclined to emulate. He recalled to the *People*: 'This is the era of team play, of players who sacrifice their own individuality for the sake of the other ten. This discipline struck me forcibly in those matches against Inter. I had expected a packed defence but not so many players who could dedicate themselves to a dull role without the slightest deviation. I thought that British clubs would find it difficult to persuade players to restrict themselves to a negative job but now everyone's doing it.'

A vignette noted in the Everton board's minute book from October 1963 highlights Harry's adherence to the Everton motto Nil Satis Nisi Optimum: 'Mr Catterick reported that the motor coach put at our disposal and the service were not up to standard. It was agreed to write to them advising them that we would change if there was no improvement.'

In early March 1964, with Everton lying fourth in the league and still in the title race, Harry once more delved into the kitty. He had been strongly linked with Sheffield Wednesday's David 'Bronco' Layne but no deal came to fruition – in retrospect this was a huge let-off given what was to follow. Instead Everton paid a record British transfer fee of £85,000 to bring Fred Pickering from Blackburn to wear the number nine shirt. A defender turned centre-forward, Pickering was a 'Harry' type of striker: big and physical with a thunderous shot (which gave rise to his nickname 'Boomer'). There was consternation among the supporters who had marvelled at the goals and interplay of Vernon and Young over the previous two years. Young, seeing the writing on the wall, submitted a transfer request in April before having a change of heart in July. It is telling that the board, no doubt guided by Harry but also keen to recoup funds, accepted the transfer request. Brentford and Stoke, among others, failed to meet the £45,000 asking price so Young remained at Everton to battle for his place.

Harry recalled to Mike Langley: 'The signing of Fred Pickering, a record deal that I whizzed through in an hour, was criticised on Merseyside. I wanted height and finishing power, the fans wanted the attractive skills of Alex Young. In the end I showed that it was possible to have both.'

Despite supporters' misgivings, Pickering announced himself on the Goodison stage with a debut hat-trick against Nottingham Forest and hit nine goals in nine appearances as the season reached its conclusion. Despite the injection of Pickering's punch up front, Everton would not retain their title. The team lacked the consistency shown in the final furlong of the previous season – three consecutive away defeats consigned them to third place behind Manchester United and newly crowned champions Liverpool.

Missing from the final two fixtures of the season would be Tony Kay; he would never play professional football again. Sunday, 12 April 1964, was a day that left an indelible mark on Everton and English football as a story broke that would rock the game. Copies of the *People* landed on people's doormats carrying the sensational allegation that Sheffield Wednesday players had bet on their team to lose before a defeat to Ipswich in December 1962. David 'Bronco' Layne, Peter Swan and Tony Kay found themselves at the centre of the storm.

Everton's board met on 13 April and relieved Kay of match duties pending the outcome of the FA investigation and any potential legal action. Kay continued to train and even go on the occasional scouting trip while the investigations continued. He recalls Harry calling him into the office: 'I think you're in trouble; listen, whatever is needed we'll get it done and look after it.'

The loss of the talisman that was Kay was a crushing blow to Harry's aspirations. Alex Young recalled, in his memoirs, the impact Kay had made on the team: 'If he hadn't packed it in Tony was going to be a brilliant player. He was a terrific ferocious player – what a guy to have on your team. If he had stayed we'd have won another championship with him there. Taking the ball, winning the ball, playing the ball to everybody – to me and Vernon. He was a super player.'

Although Brian Harris was restored to the half-back position and performed with distinction for two years, the loss of Kay would be sorely felt on the pitch until the acquisition of Alan Ball two years later.

Harry Catterick was devastated by the scandal, as he recounted in 1977 to John Roberts. 'It left me bitter,' Harry said, 'as I am a disciplinarian and I would feel that a wrong-doer needs to be punished.' He continued:

> But the punishment meted out to Kay was far too severe for the offence committed. I read three newspaper reports for the match he played for Sheffield Wednesday against Ipswich, that was supposed to have been arranged, and Tony Kay had rave notices. However, subsequently it was proven that he had committed some crime of that nature but he was put out of the game even as a coach – the injustice was terrible. He had to go to jail for a few months – that in itself must have left an awful mark – and then to be kept out of the game for at least seven or eight years ruined the boy's whole life. It broke up his home life too, he really did suffer.
>
> I, as the manager, felt it was a great injustice to Everton, we had paid £60,000 and Sheffield Wednesday had benefitted from that. His crime was in the service of Wednesday yet we lost the player and the £60,000. It did badly affect the side. I had great ambitions of building up the side with Tony Kay and Ray Wilson at left-half and left-back. Signing Alan Ball

alongside Kay and Harvey would have given me that character,
steel and so much ability. He made players play, both in front of
and behind him – not many players could do that. He was an
arrogant type, not easy for players to handle, but he knew I could
handle him, as I had done at Sheffield Wednesday. He took no
chances with me and always toed the line. He was tough – but
I was tougher. I am quite sure that Tony could have handled
Bally – they would have got on like a house on fire; there'd have
been arguments but they'd have got on. Tony Kay was probably
one of the most talented players I have ever handled – I still
think Everton lost a very, very good player.

Despite low-key support from Everton, Kay, alongside
Layne and Swan, was sentenced to four months' imprisonment
in January 1965. When Kay's life ban from football was lifted in
1974 he was 34 years old and only played at amateur level. After
a brush with the law, he lived in Spain for an extended period. It
was a tragic waste of a footballing talent that was likely to have
shone on the world stage two years later.

A posthumous insult would be hurled at Harry 32 years later by the BBC when it
depicted the Kay affair in the 1997 TV production *The Fix*. In a feat of miscasting
up there with Dick Van Dyke as a cockney chimney sweep, the eloquent, immacu-
late and sophisticated Everton manager was portrayed by Colin Welland as a bluff
Yorkshireman in a sheepskin coat. As the *Daily Post*'s Len Capeling deliciously put it:

There was the elegant Harry, who prided himself on his mea-
sured words, his tidy figure, his well-groomed head, and his
expensively-tailored mohair suits being grotesquely caricatured
as some ranting, rotund Yorkshireman who sounded like a Barn-
sley barrow-boy and had the dress sense to shame even Kenneth
Clarke. Where Welland was gross and unbuttoned, Catterick was
the very model of the reserved soccer scholar in an age when there
were more rough edges on managers than spikes on a porcupine.

The involvement of the press in uncovering and reporting the betting scandal
soured, perhaps irrevocably, the already distant relationship Harry had with the
media. In Sheffield Harry had had a ghosted column in the city newspaper and he

was on reasonable terms with local sports reporters. In the Merseyside goldfish bowl he was supremely protective of both his personal life and club affairs. Much of this may be put down to the football obsession on Merseyside, the sheer size of Everton and the spectre of Littlewoods on his shoulder.

Perhaps the death-knell for Harry's trust of the media came six months after the Kay affair when the *People* printed unsubstantiated accusations under the banner headline: 'BRIBERY AND DRUGS AT EVERTON'. Albert Dunlop, a goalkeeper who had briefly played under Harry before being displaced by Gordon West, was a 'colourful' character with a difficult personal life. Falling on hard times, he had taken his revelations about life at Everton to the press, accusing the club of pushing a culture of 'Purple Heart' pep-pill popping to enhance performance. Equally damaging were suggestions of a conspiracy to encourage West Bromwich Albion players to 'go easy' against Everton in the penultimate match of the 1962/63 season. The allegations were investigated by Everton chairman E. Holland Hughes, who found them to have 'no substance'. His report was sent to the football authorities, who took no action. In his memoirs Alex Young set the record straight: 'The only substance that Alex Parker and I ever resorted to before a match was a wee dram of whisky from an old bottle of Bell's kept in the dressing room.'

Harry would continue to speak to newspaper journalists but generally only in connection with articles for which he retained some editorial oversight. Journalist James Mossop recalls: 'You rang Bellefield and spoke to his secretary and said, "I'd love to see Mr Catterick." She would come back to you and give you a time and a place. To be fair to him you could have as long as you wanted – normally half an hour or forty minutes.' Although lacking the Shankly sound-bites, Harry came across in interviews as perceptive and eloquent – revealing a deep knowledge of the game.

In 1963 Mike Ellis was appointed as the *Daily Herald*'s football reporter on Merseyside: 'The sports editor had arranged a meeting with Harry at Goodison Park. When we got there the receptionist said that Harry was expecting us and we were to take the lift to the boardroom – it was a very impressive stadium. Harry was very smart in his suit, he opened up the directors' bar and offered us drinks, stating: "I'll do anything I can to help you." Then he took us to the players' lounge. Jimmy Gabriel and Roy Vernon were playing snooker. Roy looked up and said, "Hi, Mike, what are you doing here?" Roy and I had grown up together in North Wales. Harry's face was a picture as he obviously thought: "I've got to be careful with this fella." From then on our relationship was difficult. He was always immaculately dressed and if you were meeting him for the first time he could turn on the charm but it was only when you had to deal with him that you saw the other side of him.'

During the 1960s most sports editors, at some stage, received a blast down the phone from Harry regarding perceived liberties that their reporters had taken. One such instance occurred in 1966 when Fred Pickering had injured his knee and was admitted to hospital for exploratory tests. Mike Ellis wanted to know more: 'Fred had been injured and gone to hospital for a check-up. He was in Broadgreen so I rang the matron and asked if I could visit. She asked the sister to see if he'd have visitors and he said, "Yes please." I went there and he was waiting for a cartilage operation. I asked if it was OK if I ran it in the paper and he said, "Why not? No one else from Everton has rung me." When Harry found out, he told my sports editor that he'd go to the Press Council for me breaking into Broadgreen to see an ill patient!'

The one local journalist trusted to a degree was Michael Charters of the *Liverpool Echo*. Charters regularly travelled on the team coach to away fixtures and was Harry's outlet if he wished to get his views into print.

Mike Ellis recalls: 'In those days no clubs had press offices – we had phone numbers and the direct office line at Anfield and Goodison. I became very close with Shankly; you could have rows with him. If you'd written something he didn't like he'd shout at you and say, "Right, I'm not playing ball with you for another week." But then shortly afterwards you'd get a call from Peter Robinson, the Liverpool secretary, saying, "I believe you had an upset with Bill – well, he's rung me and he said just to make sure you know what's going on news-wise." Harry Catterick wouldn't do that.'

While Bill Shankly played the media like a fiddle, his stream of sound-bites a copywriter's dream, Harry was considered dour, unhelpful and elusive. Harry would tell journalist Geoffrey Mather that the latter perception was inaccurate: 'My emotions do change – but they tell me my expression doesn't. I'm a bit of a miserable-looking beggar at the best of times.'

Len Capeling, who came across both Shankly and Harry during his time on Merseyside, compared the two managers: 'Shankly was a one-off, a person who had that relationship with the fans and said the right things. No manager in this country has ever had a closer relationship with fans; there are photos of him on the touchline and it's like a messiah has appeared before an awed crowd – whereas there was no great warmth between Harry Catterick and the fans.'

When interviewed by the BBC in 1968 Harry would accept, candidly, and with a hint of resignation, that his unpopularity with supporters went with being a manager: 'I'm not a popular fellow because I've always felt that if a decision has to be made I mustn't consider whether it's going to be a popular one or not.'

CHAPTER TWELVE
LIFE AFTER KAY

AS THE TEAM boarded a flight for a 10,000-mile journey to Australia in May 1964 – a tour that earned the club £11,000 – Harry remained in England for reasons not entirely clear. Perhaps it was the crushing sense of losing Tony Kay and the effort required to reshape the team in the absence of such a key player.

One pressing need was to identify the man to succeed Vernon as club captain. With Kay unavailable Harry would eventually plump for Brian Labone. Still only 24, Labone had been involved with the first team for seven years. Unlike his predecessor, Labone was not a great talker, preferring to lead by his actions. In an era of big, hard centre-halves, Labone was uncharacteristically gentlemanly – being booked only twice in a 534-game career with his only club. Such characteristics would lead to Harry being attributed as hailing Labone as 'The Last of the Corinthians'.

As the squad prepared for departure from London Heathrow, Mick Meagan, who along with George Thomson and Brian Harris had battled for the number three shirt since Harry's arrival, got wind of some disturbing press reports. He recalls: 'I remember we were on our way to Australia on tour, we had played West Ham United in London in the last match of the season and were on our way to Australia the next morning. the *People* had a little bit about Ray Wilson coming to Everton and me going in part-exchange. Nothing was said then, Catterick never even opened his mouth about it until we got home. When we got back it was time to sign my contract for the next year but Harry said, "We are bringing in Ray Wilson, we'd like you to go to Huddersfield Town in part-exchange." In fairness he was quite good about it and he gave me advice about what to ask for from Huddersfield so I have no grumbles.'

Wilson, the England international left-back, had been on Harry's radar when he was managing Sheffield Wednesday and a bid was lodged with the Terriers then-manager, Bill Shankly. Shankly had seen Don Megson impress in a reserve match against Wolves and was tempted by the prospect of a part-exchange deal. However, the rapid progress of Megson, when called into the Wednesday first team, saw the deal called off. Shankly had later tried to lure Wilson to Anfield but Huddersfield had refused to sell. It is a measure of the esteem in which Harry held Wilson that he was prepared to deviate from his transfer blueprint and invest £35,000, plus the exchange value of Meagan, in a player approaching veteran status. Harry's standard modus operandi was to sign players in the age range of 20 to 25 and sell them on, often at a profit, before they reached 30. Wilson, approaching his 30th birthday when he signed, defied age and an early injury problem to give four years of classy service alongside Labone and Tommy Wright. In 1977 Harry spoke in glowing terms to John Roberts of the quiet world-class defender who had spent virtually his entire career outside of the top flight:

> Ray Wilson – there's a professional through and through. You talk about dossiers but Ray didn't need anything like that. Ray came, trained and went away. He would talk other players into positions – a fantastic player to be alongside. I think he was a great asset to Brian Labone; Brian, who wasn't the noisiest of players, got great benefit from Ray's talking on the field. He was a truly great player. I took him near thirty years of age when many people said that I shouldn't. I paid a good fee for him but I have never spent money more wisely.

Wilson was in a near-unique position, alongside Johnny Morrissey, to compare the management styles of the two Mersey managers. Speaking to the Everton Former Players' Foundation in 2008, he highlighted the contrasts: 'When I look back at Shankly and Catterick they were totally different. Harry just picked coaches and players and said: "Get on with it." Shankly had to be everywhere – even playing in five-a-side matches. He would have us back in the afternoon with five Englishmen and him plus four Scots and we'd be playing until dark. Once you got to 32 or 33 Harry kicked your arse and you were out so I did well to be there at 34.'

Changes were afoot in the right-back berth also. Alex Parker, a supreme player and still only 29, found his place under threat from Tommy Wright, a home-grown talent, albeit one who had never envisaged a role on the right side of defence. 'Tommy Wright,' Harry recalled to John Roberts, 'was a typical Liverpool boy.'

> He was not good enough as apprentice material when we looked at him. We decided that we would find him a bit of a job some-

where or other and got him some time off to train at Littlewoods.
He was an inside-forward at the time and he reached the stage
where we thought, 'Alright, we'll turn him pro and give him a
year of training'. Watching him I said, 'This fellow is a yard or
two short on the turn for an inside-forward.' So I tried him in
midfield and he didn't look bad. Then in a game I stuck him at
right-back and he never looked back as he had skills and that
suited him. He was a very good full-back.

After making his debut in October 1964, Wright had displaced the Scottish international by January 1965, going on to make 373 league appearances for Everton and earning 12 England caps. However, Barry Rees would play at right-back when Everton entertained newly promoted Leeds United on 7 November, a fixture that was to become infamous as 'The Battle of Goodison'.

The match would be Bobby Collins' first league outing against his former team, but the 'Wee Barra' had already put a marker down in a FA Cup clash the previous season. The players and supporters sensed the tension in the Goodison air and the trouble began within minutes of the whistle that started the match. First Sandy Brown was dismissed for clashing with Johnny Giles, then, when Willie Bell laid out Derek Temple, all hell broke loose. The referee took the unprecedented step of calling a 'time-out' after 38 minutes and ordered the teams back to their dressing rooms. After stern words and a calming-off period they returned to complete the final seven minutes of the first period. An iconic image taken that day is of Collins and Labone – little and large – walking round the pitch pleading for calm on the seething terraces.

Collins said later in his biography: 'It was diabolical… they blamed us, yet some Everton players were going over the ball time and time again… When Sandy Brown got sent off, it was like a fuse on a bomb being lit… it really got a bit nasty and brutal. There were a lot of hard challenges that day. But you can't turn the other cheek or they'll kick you.'

Collins thrived in the battle, making a point to Harry in the process and helping Leeds to a 1–0 victory. The match, and Leeds' remarkable progression – missing out on the title by goal difference – would kick-start an intense, sometimes bitter, rivalry between Harry and Don Revie and their respective clubs. Revie was another north-easterner, just as determined as Harry to win. Whereas Harry ruled from a distance to maintain the fear factor, Revie worked hard to foster team spirit. On the field his talented team would become known as 'Dirty Leeds' as they mixed great skill with a penchant for the darker arts.

Fred Pickering had made the number nine shirt his own and notched an impressive 37 goals in 51 appearances that season, contrasting with the modest totals of Vernon and Young – the latter troubled by blisters. Despite supporters' fears that Pickering's arrival would hasten the departure of Young, it was Vernon who sought fresh pastures first. Since his carpeting on the North American tour of 1961 his relationship with Harry had been difficult. Harry had turned something of a blind eye to some of Vernon's off-field behaviour and poor training on the proviso that he delivered on the pitch. Even when elevating him to captain for the title-winning season relations had remained cool, and Vernon would later joke that it was easier to get an audience with the Pope than with his manager. By April 1965 Harry was ready to cash in and move on the brilliant, yet wayward, forward.

According to Alex Young in his memoirs, Vernon was 'outspoken and must have upset Harry too many times'. Their relationship was summed up in a scene at the function to celebrate the 1963 league title win. Young recalled that Harry was talking with Vernon and his wife, Norma, and mentioned that he was considering penning an autobiography, before adding, 'I don't want it published until after I'm dead.' Vernon replied dryly: 'I look forward to reading it.'

Mike Ellis, now of the *Sun* (which superseded the *Daily Herald* in September 1964), helped facilitate Vernon's move to the Potteries: 'Tony Waddington, the Stoke manager, called me on a Friday evening asking me where he could contact Roy Vernon. I told him that he'd probably be at the Royal Tiger nightspot. He said, "Surely he won't be there the night before a game?" So we went there and waited – it got to 9.30 pm and Tony said, "He won't be coming now." Then ten minutes later he appeared with a cigarette in his mouth. We waited until he went to the urinal and followed him in. "Would you be interested in signing for Stoke City?" asked Tony. Roy turned his head and replied: "If you sign me it will be the best bit of business you ever do."'

Everton would finish the 1964/65 season in fourth place – 12 points adrift of Leeds United and title winners Manchester United. Injuries to key players and inconsistency had cost them dearly. Despite the disappointment, Harry's spirits were lifted by a 3–2 aggregate victory over Arsenal in the two-legged FA Youth Cup final. In the team were half a dozen players that would play in Everton's first XI: Geoff Barnett (who would later play in a FA Cup final with Arsenal), Gerry Glover, Frank D'Arcy, Aiden Maher, Jimmy Husband and John Hurst. The latter two would become integral parts of the team chasing honours later in the decade.

Husband was scouted from Newcastle as a schoolboy and found the transition tough: 'I did suffer from homesickness and Everton paid for my rail ticket home every month. Within weeks of me joining at fifteen, Harry Catterick called us up to the office and said what he hoped to do with us and that he thought that I had great prospects. He knew I was very homesick as well – he was from the north-east so he had a bit of sympathy with me.' Hurst, a quiet Lancastrian who had started out as a centre-forward with Blackpool Schoolboys, would go on to become a skilful, goalscoring centre-half alongside Brian Labone.

The Everton first team matchday programme, from a fixture several days before the first leg of the Youth Cup Final, contained an editorial which encapsulated the youth set-up:

> *Our lads were hand-picked by Harry Catterick, Chief Scout Harry Cooke and their helpers, and groomed and polished by one whom we consider to be the best in the business, Ron Lewin. It was tantamount to Mr Catterick saying to Ron: "Here are the finest youngsters we can find. Now you cut and polish these young stones and turn them into diamonds".*

In the same piece, club director Fred Micklesfield added sagely: "The future of the Everton club depends largely on the young players climbing the ladder."

Many Everton players of the early to mid-60s would attest to a split in the squad between 'Pro-Catt' and 'Anti-Catt' men. The division was, nominally, between players established at the club prior to Harry's arrival and those he had either signed or developed through the youth system. Maybe Harry was aware of this split; perhaps he even fostered this tension to generate competition. Jimmy Gabriel would refer to this in an interview with Becky Tallentire for *Still Talking Blue*:

> *We got split into two dressing rooms. Harry put the good guys in one and who he thought the bad guys were in the other. I was with the bad guys along with Johnny Morrissey, Alex Young and a few others, but all the new signings got put in the good dressing room. Labby was in there with Ray Wilson, Howard [Kendall], all the nice people. It was funny, we had great fun and used to laugh about it.*

One man certainly in the 'Pro-Catt' camp was Alex Scott. Once he made the switch to Goodison 'Chico' was a virtual ever-present at outside-right. However, in an episode reminiscent of Harry's handling of Don Megson back in 1959 at Sheffield Wednesday, the Scottish winger would learn to take nothing for granted, as he recalled to authors Jon Berman and Malcolm Dome.

> *In the season we won the FA Cup, Harry made the move of dropping a few of us in November. Me, Gordon West and a couple of others were just left out, no explanations, we were just dropped. At the time I thought I was playing as well as I had ever done in my career at Everton up until then. I was astounded when I was left out. I just felt 'He can't do that! I'll show him.' I think we were left out for three games in a row before finally getting back in the team, but I was so fired up then that I played the best football of my life. I was brilliant, even if I say so myself.*
>
> *After we played Chelsea Ray Wilson said he was relieved he didn't have to mark me, which was a real compliment to Harry as well. He knew that dropping us would actually give us a bit of a jolt as when you are a first team regular it's so easy to become very blasé. Of course it can have the opposite effect and annoy you so much that you demand a transfer. That's when you have to become very careful as a manager and understand which players will react in the right way and which won't. Harry was a master at this and got the very best out of us.*

Despite the occasional jolt to the players, league form in the 1965/66 season proved erratic, with the team entrenched in mid-table. Perhaps for the first time since Harry's arrival at Goodison there were murmurings that John Moores would seek to make changes if results did not improve. By January, with any hope of challenging for the league long gone, Harry looked to the future and blooded a precocious 16-year-old centre-forward called Joe Royle.

Royle recalls how he became an Everton player: 'The first time I met Harry Catterick was at the John Moores Centre (the headquarters of Littlewoods). Harry, John Moores and Harry Cooke were there to meet my mother and father with a view to me joining Everton. They knew that Manchester United, Arsenal, Chelsea and Liverpool were interested in me; it was designed to make an impression as they wanted me to sign.'

As with Tommy Wright, Royle had seen his playing position change under the watchful eyes of Harry and his staff: 'I had joined as a centre-half who played a bit as a wing-half for Liverpool Boys, it was a fetch and carry role, up and down covering a lot of ground. Sometimes they'd throw me up front and I'd score some goals. One day Harry turned round to me and said, "You've outgrown the position, son, you're going to be a striker." It was a simple as that.'

Royle's first-team call-up came out of the blue: 'I was cleaning boots down in the boot room when I got the call from trainer Ron Lewin to tell me that the boss wanted to see me; I wondered what I'd done as you didn't see a lot of him. So I went upstairs and sat outside his office. When I was called in he said, "I have just had your father on the phone. I've told him that if conditions don't change too much you'll be playing in the first team tomorrow." I was stung to say the least.'

Making Royle Everton's youngest ever debutant at Bloomfield Road was newsworthy in itself but the bombshell that Alex Young had been dropped caused apoplexy among some supporters. The controversial team selection would unleash a chain of events resulting in what the Everton historian David France dubbed 'The Blackpool Rumble'.

The match, played on an icy pitch on which Blackpool's Alan Ball excelled, ended in a 2–0 defeat for the Blues. What happened next has become etched in Everton folklore but versions vary wildly. What is indisputable is that as Harry walked from the stadium towards the team coach he was approached by some Evertonians wishing to remonstrate with him about the team selection and performance. Within a few seconds Harry was on the ground, as he recalled to John Roberts:

> *It was a bit of an injustice to say the least. We were mid table with nothing to gain. Blackpool were in the lower regions of the league. I thought 'It can't be too tough a game, I'll give Alex a rest and put Joe in. Joe Royle had terrific potential, sixteen and nothing to lose. The young goalkeeper Barnett, who I also introduced, made two bad mistakes and we lost 2–0. I was coming out of the ground, the fans showed their disappointment and made this attack on me – it shook me a lot… They had great loyalty to Alex Young and they were displaying that; it is wrong to think bad of Everton fans as a whole.*

Everton chairman E. Holland Hughes recounted his version of events to the Merseyside press: 'Mr Catterick and I left the directors' entrance together. We were met by a hostile crowd numbering about thirty or forty shouting, "Catterick, Catterick, Catterick!" Mr Catterick was just ahead of me in the crowd when he appeared to be swept off his feet and the next thing I saw was him stagger to the coach. The attack was a brutal action which all of us in the game will condemn and deplore.'

Others present at the time, Brian Labone included, would later suggest that Harry had been berated and jostled by the irate supporters and had stumbled to the ground. Whatever the truth, Harry was shook up as he boarded the team coach and the incident did nothing to warm relations between supporters and the under-pressure manager. After recuperating with his family in Stockport over the weekend he was back at work on the Monday with what the press described as 'badly bruised legs and ankles'.

Looking back at the incident with John Roberts, Harry gave an insight into his expectations of players – harking back to his father's and his own experiences as footballers: 'My image, constantly portrayed, was of a tough disciplinarian. This may have brought out some physical resentment. It is far from the truth – players always knew where they stood with me. They also knew that they couldn't take chances, if they fooled about I'd be after them. They knew very well they'd get a good wage and I'd expect a bloody good day's work and every effort to present themselves fit for matches. I didn't ask any more, I'm not entitled to.'

In the next game Young was back in the number eight shirt, starring and scoring against Sunderland at the start of a FA Cup run that would go all the way to Wembley. As with Scott earlier in the season, the shock of being dropped had driven 'The Golden Vision' to higher levels of performance. Royle returned to the reserves, but his time would come.

Having overcome Manchester City in a marathon FA Cup quarter-final tie that required two replays, Harry incurred the wrath of the FA and a fine by fielding a second-string XI at Elland Road, a week before the semi-final at Bolton. Joe Royle recalls his second first-team appearance:

> It was a time when the reserves and first team both played at the same time on the Saturday but on this occasion the reserves had no game so we were told to report just to watch the first-team game as we thought. As we arrived in Harrogate, to have a bite to eat, the first team were coming out and getting on the same coach. We were astounded when they said, 'Good luck today, lads, you're playing!' Harry had gone through with the ruse of taking the first team away and then replacing them... I think we lost 4–1.

The scorer for Everton that day was Mike Trebilcock, a virtually unknown Cornish-man signed from Plymouth Argyle making only his fifth senior appearance. He would retain his place in the team the following Saturday for the crucial cup tie against Matt Busby's Manchester United, who were weakened by the absence of George Best. Everton's half-back line was magnificent, snuffing out the threat from Law, Herd and Charlton with ruthless efficiency. A smartly taken left-footed effort from Colin Harvey was enough to book Harry's first visit to a Wembley final on 14 May 1966.

Harry was uncharacteristically ebullient to the press afterwards, showing how much he wanted, maybe needed, another cup in the Everton trophy cabinet: 'The boys were magnificent to a man, it was exactly the way we planned it... our plan was to get them coming at us and then to strike on the break. Harvey took his goal brilliantly.'

As the visit to Wembley approached, the pressure was ratcheted up by Bill Shankly's Liverpool winning the league title for the second time in three years. From having been the poor relations of Merseyside football only six years previously, Shankly had forged a formidable team in his extrovert image. Despite Everton's superior resources, the balance of power on Merseyside appeared to be shifting – an Everton trophy win was not just desirable, it was becoming essential.

The football gods had deemed that the FA Cup final would pit Everton against Sheffield Wednesday, the team Harry had walked out on five years previously. Since his departure from the Hillsborough hot seat Wednesday had been unable to seriously challenge for the title. The managerial position had been filled by Vic Buckingham and, in the wake of the betting scandal, Alan Brown, the former Sunderland manager. Brown was highly rated for his tactical acumen and had at his disposal many of the players from Harry's Hillsborough tenure including Don Megson as captain, Johnny Fantham, Ron Springett, Johnny Quinn and Gerry Young. Everton, though, were hot favourites. Harry was proud that Everton was the first team in over 60 years to reach the final without conceding a goal, telling Mike Langley: 'British players are not always keen to adjust themselves to a system or pattern of play which is in the best interests of the team generally. Our tactics varied from match to match, according to the strengths and weaknesses of the opposition, and the most vital factor was the way in which our players disciplined themselves tactically in order to achieve victory.'

Preparation throughout the cup run had been meticulous. Ron Lewin had been posted to 'spy' on opponents and prepare dossiers and the club had scoured the London area for a pitch on which to train with similar qualities to Wembley's lush turf.

In advance of the big day, the squad decamped to Selsdon Park Hotel, Surrey, away from the public gaze. Despite the hotel boasting its own golf club, the players were banned by Harry for fear of injury. A putting competition was devised instead, with the consummate all-rounder Brian Harris winning.

The team virtually picked itself: West in goal, Wilson at left-back, Labone at centre-half with Harvey, Harris and Gabriel as half-backs. Across the front line were Temple, Young and Scott. That left two berths to fill and on the Friday morning Harry knew he had two crucial decisions to make.

In early April Fred Pickering was playing at Bramall Lane when disaster struck: 'I'd never been injured before, I felt a click against Sheffield United and I thought my leg had broken, the knee just swelled up like a balloon.' Time was limited for 'Boomer' to recover from the cartilage injury and prove his fitness before Wembley.

After missing the FA Cup semi-final he returned for the final three league games of the season but did not score. Doubts remained, unspoken, in the minds of both Harry and Pickering about the robustness of the knee. Pickering recalls: 'I wasn't fit. When we travelled down on the Thursday I wasn't going to build my hopes up because I knew my knee wasn't right. In those days cartilages and ligaments took ages to heal and the physios would have a word with Catterick. If there had been substitutes in those days I would have definitely played. The turf there was different to every football ground in the country – soft, spongy; I was only 75 per cent fit, there was a 90 per cent chance that I could have got taken off – so it wasn't worth the risk.'

Should Pickering not be deemed match-fit the options for the centre-forward berth were limited to pushing the muscular Jimmy Gabriel up-field or calling the diminutive, untested Trebilcock onto the biggest club football stage of all. The Cornishman sensed his chance and did all he could to impress: 'Fred wasn't training that well leading up to the final, because of the injury he had, and I was training my arse off.'

Decision time came the day before the match, as Mike Trebilcock recalls: 'We were all sitting around having lunch on the Friday and Tommy Eggleston came over to the table and said, "Mike, the boss wants to see you." John Hurst said, "You must be playing, Treb." I said, "No, I won't be playing." The position up for grabs was between Sandy Brown and Tommy Wright. I just felt that the boss wanted me in there to see what he told them.

'When I got in there Fred Pickering was there as well, I couldn't understand what he was doing there. Then the boss said, "At a time like this decisions have to be made. And I'm the one who has to make them. Tommy, I'm putting you back in and leaving Sandy out. Fred, I'm leaving you out and putting Mike in." I nearly fell off my stool! Then Harry said, "You two can go as these two will want to say something to me now." Tommy and I went out and hugged each other but there was a lot of bad language coming from that little room, I can tell you. Fred was very upset and he had every right to be.

Jimmy Gabriel gave a similar account to Becky Tallentire in *Still Talking Blue*: 'Harry did not want to pick someone who might not perform as well as somebody who was fully fit. It was a great move on Harry's part but Fred was devastated. We all felt for him, he'd been great for the team all the way through the championship. But, as a manager, Harry made the right decision at the right time.'

On match day, there was an unusual presence. Pathé News cameras were given unprecedented access to the changing rooms as the two teams prepared for kick-off. They recorded, in colour, a nervous-looking Gordon West, a pensive Labone, Harry in conversation with staff and a relaxed Alex Young receiving a massage from Norman Borrowdale. For a media-shy manager, secretive over tactics, on possibly the biggest day of his career, to allow the cameras in seems puzzling. When asked by Becky Tallentire for *Still Talking Blue* to speculate why the manager consented to it, Gordon West speculated, tongue only half-in-cheek: 'Harry must have got paid!'

The match kicked off on a blazing Saturday afternoon, and Everton got off to the worst possible start as Jim McCalliog put the Yorkshiremen a goal up after only four minutes. Don Megson also made a painful contribution: 'When we were playing in the cup final, I was trying to make sure I'd not have too much trouble with Alex Scott – a flying machine. He got the ball in his own half and set himself up, I got in and did my usual "shake him up" tackle and whacked Scotty. Tommy Eggleston ran on, looked up at me whilst attending to Scotty, and said, "You dirty bastard!" I said, "Mate, don't you 'dirty bastard' me – I'm just doing what you taught me!"'

Wednesday's 4–3–3 formation had surprised Everton and seen them dominating the Blues' midfield duo of Gabriel and Harvey, although Young had an equaliser controversially overruled for offside and a valid penalty claim waved away. Everton went in at the break a goal down and in need of a lift from the manager, as Harry recalled to Charles Lambert in 1978:

> *At half-time it was my task to try and rescue the situation. People think that a manager can go into a dressing room at half-time match after match and motivate the players – and that's a fal-*

lacy. If you constantly come out with the same formula people grow sick of it. This was an exception, I have never known a dressing room so quiet – the players were slumped on the benches – they couldn't believe what had happened to them. I remember saying: 'I am looking round the dressing room and I can't see many people who are going to be coming back here. This must be your last chance of a cup winner's medal at Wembley. What are you going to do about it? Go out there and roll your sleeves up. I'm not asking for more ability, you've got that. I'm just asking for a bit more determination'. I think they got the message. They had the feeling that the world was against them. But fellows like Jimmy Gabriel only needed a bit of a prod, and he had all the motivation that was necessary.

Despite Harry's urging, all seemed lost with little over half an hour of the match left as David Ford put Wednesday two goals to the good. Even Harry seemed resigned to defeat, as Fred Pickering remembers: 'I was on the bench when the game was going on, you didn't have your tracksuit as there were no subs. As we went 2–0 down Harry turned round and said to me, "I wish I'd have played you now".'

Harry asserted to Lambert that he never gave up hope: 'I can be perfectly honest and say I did not consider the game lost. I've been too long in the game ever to write a team off, particularly a side as talented as Everton.'

With the copywriters and editors already preparing headlines to acclaim Wednesday's shock victory, the following seven minutes catapulted Trebilcock into FA Cup folklore. The number eight had barely had a touch in the game and was, frankly, looking like a fish out of water – until he dispatched two glorious first-time shots past Springett to draw Everton level. Trebilcock recalls: 'It was just instinct. They dropped sweetly for me so I just kept my head down.' Suddenly, with Wednesday shell-shocked, Everton sensed victory.

After an unscheduled interlude caused by an Everton supporter, Eddie Cavanagh, invading the pitch (prompting a 'Keystone Cops' chase by police), Harvey launched a speculative ball into the centre-circle where Derek Temple was loitering with intent. Temple says: 'The first goal lifted us and then Mike got the second. I'd wandered off the wing to the inside-right position and Colin Harvey hit a ball from the right-back position. The ball went under Gerry Young's foot – I must have put him off and he mis-trapped it. Then he had his back to goal and I was away with no one between me and Springett. I got to the edge of the area and it sat up nicely so I thought that I'd hit it. It went in the right place. I thought afterwards, "Blimey, if I'd missed that and we'd lost, I wouldn't have been able to show my face on Merseyside again."' It was a sublime piece of pin-point finishing by Temple and a worthy goal to secure victory in one of the greatest FA Cup finals. Reflecting on the goal, Harry paid tribute when speaking to John Roberts: 'Temple is a beautiful mover on a running ball and takes his opportunities extremely well. As he was running through I thought, "Here is the man to stick it in the back of the net."'

As the final whistle blew Harry could breathe again – the huge gamble on Trebilcock had reaped dividends and a trophy, after a three-year drought, would silence the doubters. Brian Labone received the FA Cup from Princess Margaret and, after a lap of honour, Harry was chaired off the pitch by his players.

Harry did not forget his former team and in a genuine (if slightly ill-judged) gesture, visited a despondent Don Megson and his colleagues in their changing room: 'Harry brought the cup in, with champagne in it for us to drink out of. I said, "Hey, the time I drink out of that cup will be when we have won it." But I took that opportunity to thank him for giving me my break at Wednesday.'

The day after the final the squad returned to Merseyside for a celebratory parade and banquet. Derek Temple recalls that the FA Cup was in safe hands: 'I didn't notice this but there were a few players that didn't like him [Harry] particularly and one said to me, "Did you ever notice that Catterick never let go of the cup and no one could get it off him".' Photographic evidence lends credence to the observation; the trophy never strayed far from Harry's grasp on the train journey from London to Allerton Station on the outskirts of Liverpool, or on the ten-mile open-top parade to St George's Hall. Once on the steps of the hall, the squad were welcomed by Mayor Alderman Cowley, and Harry held the trophy aloft with each of the 11 players in turn before, finally, at the request of the crowd, inviting the unfortunate Pickering to have his turn.

By Harry's own admission to Charles Lambert: 'That was my greatest moment. The cup hadn't been to Everton for many years and it was wonderful to bring it back to Merseyside.' He continued, in a nod to his sometimes strained relationship with supporters and the media: 'Many people have criticised my lack of rapport with ordinary supporters, and probably rightly so. I am not an extrovert but no one is a bigger Evertonian than me, no matter how loudly he shouts.'

After the despondency of the worst league campaign since 1960, the season had been saved. Any thoughts John Moores might have had of hailing a taxi for Harry Catterick could be shelved.

CHAPTER THIRTEEN
THE FOOTBALL FACTORY

AS THE WORLD Cup finals approached, a vital piece in Harry's Everton master-plan was unveiled. On 12 July the Bellefield Training Complex was officially opened by Joe Richards, President of the Football League. The nine-acre site had been used for over 20 years by Everton but it was only in 1964 that work to transform it from a basic recreation ground to a modern training facility got under way. Harry and John Moores, flush from the championship success of 1963 and with a healthy cash-flow, plotted a way of cementing Everton's success. Harry recalled to John Roberts:

> *Bellefield was there when I was a youngster as a sports ground with a wooden tennis hut, the pitches were not good. We'd made a fair amount of money and John Moores said, 'What do you think we can do about this?' So I replied that I'd like to see a football factory – self-contained where people can report, bathe, eat, train and have treatment. Where, once they are in, there is no need to come out until they have finished their training.*
>
> *He asked if I had any ideas so I made a few rough sketches and discussed it with an architect associate at their organisation; it evolved that way. We had an option on the land and we bought it and developed it, by-and-large, to my design. The indoor area was something that I specifically thought was a good thing. We would develop ball players with the quick hard surface. That's why South Americans get quick and sharp – it is hard to control the ball (on the hard surface). That was the whole idea of Bellefield and I still think it is a place that, if you go there as a youngster and can't make it, there is something wrong. There is every facility there; with the vast sums spent in the game it was a sound investment.*

The newly completed, £115,000 complex was used before its official opening by the Brazilian national team who were reported to be impressed with the facilities as they trained for their upcoming World Cup fixtures at Goodison Park. Wilf Dixon, who became Everton's trainer at Bellefield a year after its opening, echoed Harry's views to the BBC in 1968: 'Training is done considerably more with the ball than ever before. Here he can train when it's wet, he can train inside – it's virtually a home from home.'

Bellefield would become the nerve centre of Harry's operations – he would refer to it as the 'Work Centre'. Appearances at Goodison Park would now be restricted to match days and board meetings. Here Harry could oversee, literally, the preparation of the first team and the development of the next generation of players. Secluded in a residential area of West Derby, Bellefield afforded privacy from the press and the outside world. One delicious irony was that Bill Shankly's home backed on to it, resulting in a rich seam of jokes from the Scotsman at Everton's expense over the years. In a further twist, Shankly, in retirement and exile from Melwood, would become a regular visitor to Bellefield for massages and camaraderie.

Bellefield developed a strict regime that some players compared to boot-camp. Players were weighed every Friday and fines issued if targets not adhered to. Gordon West would struggle to keep at his peak weight for most of his Everton career and came to dread the Friday weigh-in. He would go to desperate lengths to sweat-off before a weigh-in, training in a thick sweater, a training top and raincoat, then stripping down like a boxer trying to make the weight limit.

'Mr Success', a celebratory pamphlet published in the wake of the 1970 championship victory, outlined a typical week at Bellefield:

> The key word here is detail and Everton's success is based on limitless application to routine, the flair and artistry stay on the playing-field.
>
> Every Monday Harry Catterick first reviews his injury list and starts his week's planning with a complete dossier of all the club casualties. 'Before I begin to plan I must assess the fitness of the staff and their availability for training.'
>
> He next reads all the reports on the following Saturday's opponents, reports that have been in preparation for the previous month. 'We discuss the best way to make use of these reports in training and tactical work for the rest of the week. Any points arising from our previous matches are analysed.'

'On Tuesday we put the reports into operation – here again so much depends on the availability of players. One injured man can upset the whole schedule.'

On a day-to-day basis Everton players are assessed on their physical strengths, tactical application and ball skills. While the build-up for next Saturday continues, each player is also assessed as an individual: 'I may decide that some players require more practice or more concentration on their individual needs. In this case they will report back for extra work one or two afternoons during the week.'

By Friday, what could be called the fighting strength is known. Ground conditions are assessed but no player is finally selected until he arrives at the ground. 'We have several talks about the opposition during the week and then a match talk on Friday, if at home, on Saturday morning if away.'

He added: 'Our players have to face up to an awful lot of thought and preparation before each game – we make sure they don't go around with nothing in their minds except pop records.'

Before the upgrade players had changed at Goodison Park and travelled to Bellefield by coach – or ran if they had irked Harry. Now they made their own way to training. Harry detested tardiness so a factory-style clocking-in system was introduced. Senior pros had to sign in by 9.45am for a 10.00am start. A member of the coaching staff would be on 'register duty', and the signing-in pencil was replaced at 9.45am prompt by a red pen. The register would then be taken upstairs to the manager for inspection. Latecomers would be hauled in to explain themselves and feel Harry's wrath. Excuses were rarely entertained; John Hurst recalls his experience when a bus accident delayed Gordon West and himself: 'Roger Kenyon and I used to go home to Blackpool for the weekend. Westy still lived in Blackpool so he used to pick us up on the corner of Preston New Road on a Monday morning. Once he picked us up at the same time as normal but the road was shut due to a crash and there was a big diversion up through Kirkham so we were about an hour late getting to work. We said what had happened with the road accident and Harry said, "Well, you have had since twenty to five on Saturday night, since the game finished, to get here for nine-thirty on the Monday morning." We got a nominal fine but if I remember rightly I don't think they ever took the money off us. Harry was saying, "Don't be late again," despite there being nothing we could do about it.'

Jimmy Husband was always desperately trying to beat the clock on the journey from his home in Childwall: 'I was constantly racing against time to get to Bellefield. If you were late more than twice in a week you had to come in for training in the afternoon, like detention, so I had a couple of them.'

Harry's insistence on punctuality extended to the team coach, which would wait for no man once the designated departure time arrived. Both journalists and players experienced the sight of the coach disappearing over the horizon without them. Alan Whittle, a teenage attacking prospect who had represented England Schoolboys, was instructed to report for the journey to an away-fixture in the West Midlands – a match that would have been his debut. Sadly for Whittle things didn't work out as he had anticipated: 'I missed the team bus. I got a lift down there with Howard Kendall, who was injured at the time, and was waiting in the visitors dressing room when the team arrived. Harry came in, looked at me and said, "Son, you just come and see me on Monday morning." He then fined me a fiver.' Banished back to the reserves, Whittle's debut would be delayed by months.

James Mossop, then of the *Sunday Express*, recalls the dark humour of the Everton players regarding the Bellefield regime: 'Harry had a siege mentality thing like: "This is Bellefield, nobody gets in." Normally you had to go to Bellefield on the Friday morning for a press conference but on this occasion it was midweek as I had arranged to interview Harry Catterick. So I got through the main gates and there was a door which was locked – I was puzzled by this locked door. Then I heard a sound at the window so I stood back and it was Gordon West. I said: "Hey, how do you get in to this place?" He replied: "You should worry, we can't bloody get out!"'

A rare case of leniency from 1970, recounted by Colin Harvey, illustrates the soft spot Harry had for the midfielder: 'I got married on the Wednesday and we were in for training on the Thursday. Maureen and I used a friend's bungalow in Rhyl for a couple of days so I had to drive to Liverpool for training. When I got to the Mersey tunnel on the Thursday morning I realised I had not brought my wallet so I had no money. The man at the tunnel booth eventually let me through but I was late to Bellefield. There was a knock from Harry's window so I went upstairs and started apologising but he said: "Don't worry about it... these things happen." Then on the next day there'd been an accident in the Mersey tunnel and that's why I was late again. So I had to go and see him and explained about the accident to which he responded, "Well, what are you going to do about it?" So I said: "I'm going to stay at my mother's in Liverpool tonight." Then I had to phone Maureen to tell her I'd not be coming back to North Wales that night!'

It was not in Harry's nature to tell Harvey how valued he was but a small ritual, first noticed by right-back Tommy Wright, let players know that they had played well. Harvey recalls: 'Harry wasn't one to put his arms round you but if you had a good game he'd help you to take your shirt off at the end. He wasn't over-affectionate to you and if you had a word of praise off him you knew you'd played a blinder. It made it even more special when you did get the praise. Although he was a disciplinarian I never felt his wrath. I was with Harry for twelve years and the only time I had a telling off from him was when we lost at Coventry – I'd got an infection after a kick in a midweek European Cup game in Iceland in 1970; I was not 100 per cent fit but I said nothing. So on Monday he called me in and said – "I know you always give 100 per cent but on Saturday your 100 per cent wasn't good enough."'

Harry's office was located upstairs on the corner of the building, affording him a panoramic view of the training pitches and allowing him to survey his kingdom from the comfort of his office. The *Daily Mail* columnist J.L. Manning was granted access to this inner sanctum in 1968: 'His office has wall-to-wall blue carpeting. One window faces one practice pitch, another looks on a second.' The office window blinds have taken on a folklore of their own. Although the boss was rarely seen there was always a feeling that his eyes were upon you, as Colin Harvey attests: 'The coaches would meet him in the morning and tell him what they were going to do, and then afterwards he'd meet them again and they'd tell him how it had gone. Every now and again you'd see him twitch the blinds and the pace of the game or whatever you were doing would go up 20 per cent!'

Frank D'Arcy, a long-serving squad member, experienced the omnipresence of the manager at Bellefield: 'We weren't really smokers but me and Westy went to the toilet and were having a cigarette between us. The next thing the window opens; the boss had come down, climbed up a stepladder and caught us. He gave us a rollicking and said: "That smoke was very costly for you." He fined us ten pounds each from our next pay packets.'

As well as ensuring that the first-team squad received the best facilities, Belle-field proved to be a vital tool in attracting both young and established talent to the club. Although the Moores money would continue to be available on occasion, there was an acceptance that the sustainable route was to nurture talent in-house. In 1964 Harry set out his stall in a programme column titled, The 'Catch 'Em Young' Policy:

> *My dream has been an Everton of the future which had a continuous supply of Everton-found, Everton-educated and Everton-minded players. I have insisted that every corner of Brit-ain be combed and we have come up with more winners than*

ever anticipated. It is healthy for a club of Everton's standing to possess so many darned good players whose post-school careers began right here. Any youngster who feels his football destiny is with Everton will not fail for lack of opportunity. This is no pipe dream but an image which can and must come true.

Speaking to the *Daily Mail's* Colin Wood, a few months before Bellefield was completed, Harry set out his Everton vision: 'When I came here I thought we could do more in the way of developing youngsters. It paid off last season with the Youth Cup. Now we have a period when these players have to reach senior status. Some may fall by the wayside, others may come through, but this is a natural process.'

One player lured to Everton by Bellefield was future England international David Johnson. He recalls: 'After the 1966 World Cup I played for Liverpool Schoolboys and was offered an apprenticeship by Everton – I didn't know much about Everton, having stood on the Kop. Bellefield was the thing that swung it for me. Harry Cooke invited me to Bellefield and I was introduced to the staff and players. For a young kid of fifteen it was daunting when you first walked through those secure gates – the public could not just walk in – but it was a fantastic place. It was the School of Science: the first indoor gym and largest in the country. The pitches were magnificent, there was an A and B pitch and other areas around it that you could use. In fact the whole set-up was superb.'

Johnson remembers how, despite being rarely seen, Harry's reputation was enough to instil fear in anyone: 'You used to see Harry but he wasn't the sort of person you'd have a conversation with. After training you'd have your lunch then you'd watch the TV before going home. If Harry was angry he'd lock the TV and you'd have to go and ask him for the key if you dared. Everyone was scared of Harry, from the staff to the players to the canteen. If you saw Harry coming you looked for a door to get out of the way. That's how he ran the club and got players to perform.'

Joe Royle related in his autobiography how Harry's secretary, Jean Meredith, held not only the keys to the TV cabinet but also the table tennis balls and bats: 'Jean always knew who had them last and, therefore, who was responsible for their return. Woe betide anyone who defaulted.'

Terry Darracott, like Johnson, was a boyhood 'Red' attracted to the blue half of the city. He went on to make Everton 178 appearances: 'I was persuaded by the fact that Everton's youth policy at the time was really thriving. Harry Catterick was never afraid to put a young player in the side if he thought he warranted it. It was proved right in my case, I've no regrets and look back on it with a lot of pride. I found him a dour type of person. I thought, "Don't get in his way or do anything wrong." Looking back, it wasn't a bad thing, it did teach you not to mess about and go about your job properly.'

Darracott had first-hand experience of how the reserves could suffer when the first team had a hiccup: 'I was in the reserve team which won at Blackpool and then went in on the Monday morning for training. The coach told us we were also going to be training in the afternoon – we had to do this horrendous hurdle circuit. It was all because the first team had got beaten. Harry was angry so we were playing the price. We had battered Blackpool but we were doing this hurdle circuit! As reserves, Harry used to keep us waiting for ever and a day in the passageway for the team-sheet to go up. It could have been pinned up at 12 but he just kept us waiting, I'm not sure what he was trying to do, we used to wait until two o'clock when we could have been home.'

Darracott was another player blooded in the first team at an early age, just 17, although it would be a further four years before he became a regular: 'I made my debut appearance against Arsenal in 1968. I played left-back as Ray Wilson had a hamstring injury. We beat Arsenal 2–0, with two Joe Royle goals. Harry came up to me afterwards and said, "You didn't get enough tackles in – I put you in the team because of how you played against Burnley last week in the Youth Cup." Then I was back in the reserves, learning my trade. He wouldn't let you get carried away. Looking back, I'm glad I had him as my first manager, as he told you how to conduct yourself and how you needed to be as a player.'

Good conduct and appearance were up there with punctuality in Harry's list of expectations. According to Joe Royle in his autobiography, Harry's oft-repeated mantra was: 'It is an honour to represent Everton.' In an interview shortly after Harry's passing in 1985 Royle elaborated on how the manager instilled fear and awe, citing a meeting called after a reserves defeat: 'You could hear a pin drop as Harry stepped in to read the report. "You are supposed to be the pride of Everton," he rapped. "The opposition set off with nine players and picked up a couple of hitch-hikers on the way to make up numbers, and you let them beat you."'

Harry's daughter Joyce recalls that her father did care about the youngsters and, with his background as a player, was acutely aware that most junior players would fail to make the grade in the top flight: 'When he got in a position of influence he was keen to ensure that they were given educational opportunities. He was really proud that he made sure that those that failed to make it – and that's nine out of ten – were not adrift. I think that was because my granddad did the same for him.'

A familiar refrain barked at players in the junior ranks after poor performances was, 'Have you got another trade, son? Because if you carry on like this you'll be needing one!' There was truth in the threat, as Harry knew all too well; he had it written into the apprentice contracts that the youths would be provided with 'alternative education and training opportunities'. Some apprentices attended Childwall Hall County College every Monday to study for O levels while others trained for vocational skills such as car mechanics. Naturally, some took these studies more seriously than others.

Stan Osborne was an apprentice in the late 1960s and reported his experiences in his book *Making the Grade*: 'Harry was a really heroic figure in our household, especially for me as a ten-year-old seeing his first championship-winning team in 1963. To then be rubbing shoulders with him five years later was a surreal experience. Harry rarely used two words where one would suffice; but when he spoke people listened!'

In conversation with the author, Osborne debunks the myth that Harry spent his entire day cocooned in his office sharpening pencils: 'From the few things that he'd say I got the impression that he had the finger on the pulse of everything. Once we were trotting off to the practice ground and he pulled Ronny Goodlass over and said, "When you get down the line – don't just tip it in the middle. Have a good look up for the runs the forwards are making into the box – pick out where you are going to put it." Often as an apprentice I'd be asked to take some towels to the trainers' dressing room, downstairs at Bellefield. I'd knock on the door and they'd be sitting around, a bit like in the boot room at Anfield. Very often Harry was in there and they were obviously having a detailed discussion about tactics or whatever – so he wasn't a stranger to the trainers' dressing room.'

In his book, Osborne recounted an episode that illustrated the depth of interest the boss took in players at all levels of the club. Osborne and other new apprentices were instructed to join Harry and Mike Charters of the *Liverpool Echo* for a photo opportunity at Bellefield: 'We listened as Mr Catterick gave a brief outline of each of us new apprentices, where we were from, what our positions were and what our schoolboy records were before signing for Everton. We were all taken aback about how much he knew about us, even though we'd only been at the club for a matter of weeks.'

After the revamped Bellefield opened in 1966 no fewer than 19 home-developed players would make their first-team debuts during the remainder of Harry's managerial reign. Looking back with John Roberts in 1977 Harry said: 'To my mind many people will remember me for the two championships and two FA Cup finals but I personally would like to be remembered as the guy who had the idea about Bellefield and developing that magnificent training ground as it will make a contribution to the game forever more.'

CHAPTER FOURTEEN
REBUILDING

THE 1966/67 season kicked off with a Charity Shield encounter between FA Cup winners Everton and League Champions Liverpool. Before kick-off the Jules Rimet trophy was paraded around by the Merseyside-based England players Ray Wilson and Roger Hunt, while Brian Labone and Ron Yeats showed off the previous domestic season's silverware.

Stung by the subsequent 1–0 defeat, Harry took decisive action. Within a week Wilson found himself joined in the Everton line-up by another World Cup winner, Alan Ball, who would go on to become, perhaps, the finest Everton player since Dixie Dean and Tommy Lawton. Howard Kendall would later joke that Everton's chief scout, Harry Cooke, had spotted the diminutive redhead at the World Cup. While it's true that Ball's energetic performances on England's right flank had raised his profile, Harry Catterick had been monitoring the Bolton Wanderers reject for several years, as he recounted to Charles Lambert: 'The first time I noticed Alan Ball we were playing Blackpool and Kay was left-midfield opposite Ball who was very young. They were both carrot-heads and had a ding-dong battle. This little fellow kept going past Kay and at half-time Tony said: "I've clobbered him a couple of times but the little so-and-so keeps coming back – and he can play."'

After his man-of-the match performance in the World Cup final, it was widely expected that the 21-year-old was bound for Elland Road. In his autobiography Ball would reveal that Revie had initiated a clandestine courtship, with a secret assignation taking place on Saddleworth Moor and financial inducements in brown envelopes being delivered to his door.

Harry had downplayed any Everton interest in the diminutive half-back, as he recounted to Mike Langley in the autumn of 1966: 'There's a lot of intriguing in the transfer business, mostly undercover work to gauge opposition interest. I decided to throw Leeds off the scent by leaking it around that our interest in Ball was only luke-warm, I even went to the lengths of putting in a bid that I knew Blackpool would find too low. But at the same time I phoned Ron Suart, the Blackpool manager, to say, "Don't let anyone know, but this isn't our final word. I shall want a second chance at Ball."'

With Leeds' interest confirmed by a £105,000 bid, and the player registration deadline for European competitions fast approaching, Harry swung into action. He drove with chairman Holland Hughes to the seaside resort, calling the club from a nearby phone box and demanding to speak to Ball and Suart. Having met Blackpool's valuation of £112,000, the Everton delegation laid out their vision to Ball and pressed for a quick decision:

> *We made our bid at 11.30 in the morning, saw Ball in the afternoon and explained to him: 'You've got to sign before six o'clock because that's the transfer deadline for the European Cup Winners' Cup. If you don't sign by six then it's all off.' He signed with ten minutes to spare. I handed the forms to Harry Cooke and told him: 'Get your car out and drive to London. You've got to deliver these to the FA by midnight.'*

Revie, alerted to Everton's audacious move, and believing Harry to still be in Liverpool rather than at Bloomfield Road, jumped in his car and headed west. He was too late to intervene. The cloak-and-dagger specialist had struck again.

Ball's impact on Everton was instant; he scored the winning goal on his debut at Fulham and a brace against Liverpool the following week assured him of a place in Evertonians' affections. Over the subsequent five-and-a-half seasons Ball would be the personification of Harry on the pitch – just as Tony Kay had been. Harry would acknowledge to Mike Langley Ball's triumph in overcoming his limitations to become a legend at Goodison: 'When I think of Ball I think of a player who was decidedly right-footed, limited in terms of pace and always in trouble through his temperament – but I would still classify him as a world-class player and I don't think Britain has produced many of those.'

Looking back 11 years later with John Roberts he added: 'He had a high workrate and no mean skill. He was a wonderful character with unlimited enthusiasm. A prolific trainer – he trained hard and practised hard and no manager can ask for more. He was paid to do a job as a footballer and he did it well. He is held very high in my estimation as a player.'

The tactical and personnel changes meant that some players were becoming surplus to requirements. For Fred Pickering the previous season's mental and physi-

Early in his Everton managerial career, Harry surveys Bellefield from the old pavilion. In 1966 the revamped Bellefield would become the nerve-centre of Harry's operation. (Catterick family)

Everton director E. Holland Hughes with Harry whilst at the team hotel during the summer 1961 tournament in Canada and the USA. (Catterick family)

Upon his appointment Harry shook-up Everton's backroom structure. Veteran trainer Harry Cooke Senior was retired, to be replaced by Norman Borrowdale. Cooke was presented with a watch by John Moores and the playing squad on his final day at work in 1961. (Keith Davies)

Four of the stars Harry inherited at Everton (L-R Billy Bingham, Bobby Collins, Brian Labone, Brian Harris) pictured in Montreal in 1961. The talismanic Collins would depart for Leeds United within a year. (Catterick family)

Harry making a relatively rare appearance on the Bellefield training pitch in 1962. (Author's photo)

Everton's 1962/63 squad. With Tony Kay and Alex Scott added in mid-season, Everton secured their first league title since 1939. (Catterick family)

11 May 1963. John Moores joins Harry and the team for a champagne toast after the defeat of Fulham, which confirmed that the league trophy would return to Goodison Park. (Catterick family)

"Imagine playing here when the Gwladys Street terraces are full?" Harry showing off Goodison Park to an unidentified individual circa 1963. (Catterick family)

Despite this association with big-money player acquisitions, Harry's heart was set on developing home-grown talent. Here he holds the "Everton and You" booklet, given to 15 year-old apprentices joining the club. (Catterick family)

Harry and John Moores congratulate (L-R) Gerry Glover, Geoff Harcombe and Aiden Maher on winning England Schoolboy honours in 1961. (Catterick family)

One of Harry's proudest achievements was Everton winning the FA Youth Cup in a two-legged final over Arsenal in 1965. Future first-team regulars Jimmy Husband and John Hurst were in the team. Here he clutches the trophy. (Catterick family)

Harry relaxing in the back garden at Ainsdale in the mid-1960s, perhaps demonstrating what he thought newspapers were best used for. (Catterick family)

Harry gives a team-talk in the grounds of the team's Surrey hotel before the 1966 FA Cup Final. The thoughts of Alex Young, Brian Labone and Ray Wilson seem to be elsewhere. (Catterick family)

The normally calm Harry can't suppress his euphoria at the final whistle. Everton have completed a remarkable comeback to win the 1966 FA Cup Final. Tommy Eggleston, Fred Pickering and Sandy Brown (partially obscured) join Harry in celebrating. (Mirrorpix)

A rueful Fred Pickering, controversially dropped from the 1966 cup final team, holds aloft the trophy with Harry on the steps of St George's Hall at the homecoming parade. (Catterick family)

It all gets too much for some supporters as they get to touch the cup, which remained safely in Harry's grasp for much of the day. (Catterick family)

The Everton squad in the summer of 1967. Alex Scott, Fred Pickering and Derek Temple would soon depart but the title winning squad of 1969/70 was largely in place and just needed time to mature. Alex Young, seated far right, would depart 12 months later. (Catterick family)

The record signing of Alan Ball in August 1966, from under the nose of Don Revie, was a coup that helped the team overcome the loss of Tony Kay in 1964. Ball is pictured with Harry outside Goodison Park's main entrance shortly after joining the club. (Mirrorpix)

In the late 1960s Harry and Colin Harvey survey Bellefield – Harry's pride and joy. The indoor training hall can be seen in the background. Harvey, one of Everton's finest home-grown players was a favourite of Harry's – not that he would ever tell Harvey that. (Catterick family)

Harry receives a manager of the month award from Bells in the autumn of 1969. Despite winning the league title Harry saw the press award the manager of the season accolade to Leeds United's Don Revie. (Catterick family)

Harry, with pipe, at his football pitch-topped desk at Bellefield in the late 1960s. One twitch of the venetian window blinds was enough to get the players training even harder. (Catterick family)

1 April 1970, with the league title secured Harry embraces Alan Whittle, who scored 11 goals in the run-in. (Colorsport)

With a dazzling young team Harry was expected to lead Everton to more success in the new decade. Charles Buchan's Football Monthly featured him as "A Manager for the 70s" on its cover in September 1970. (Catterick family)

Harry strides across the pitch at Panathinaikos' Leoforos stadium in Athens before the 1971 European Cup Quarter Final second-leg. A 0-0 draw saw Everton eliminated on the away goals rule – a crushing blow compounded by an FA-Cup semi-final exit to Liverpool just four days later. (Gary Talbot)

After two years in the background at Goodison, a recuperated Harry was introduced as Preston North End Manager on 1 September 1975. (Catterick family)

Harry with Everton players including Joe Royle, Howard Kendall, Tommy Wright and John Hurst at an event organised by John Moores' Littlewoods organisation for disadvantaged Liverpool children. (Catterick family)

Taking training at Preston. Harry missed having the financial backing to operate in the transfer market but, alongside Nobby Stiles and Alan Kelly, helped to develop talented players such as Tony Morley and Mark Lawrenson. (Catterick family)

Freed from their rivalry, Harry and Bill Shankly retained cordial relations and would meet occasionally at social events and matches. They are pictured here in the late 1970s. (Frank D'Arcy)

Harry found contentment with Paula Callesen in the 1970s – they married in 1981. (Catterick family)

Harry became vice-president of Fylde FC in 1980. Mel Tottoh, who Harry gave advice to, is fourth from left on the front row. (Catterick family)

In January 1985, two months before his death, Harry joined friends for a golfing holiday in Spain. His friends found that he had lost none of his will to win. (Brian Nicholson)

Harry was posthumously inducted as an Everton Giant in 2009. A tile on the wall of the Main Stand at Goodison Park confirms his status. (Catterick family)

cal traumas had dented both his confidence and his pride, while his troublesome knee never fully recovered. The forward would only make a further eight appearances for Everton, scoring two goals, before being transferred to Birmingham City in the summer of 1967.

Alex Scott had suffered cramp in the FA Cup final and told Berman and Dome in 1997 that he felt he was never quite the same player: 'I got severe cramp which is common on the Wembley turf... but after that my calf would never stand up to hard training. Pace was always a big part of my game and this injury affected the way I could move. I was never again fit enough for top-flight footie... I kept breaking down.'

Scott had an injury-interrupted season, with Young and Temple often wearing his number seven shirt. Tactical changes, with outside-rights being expected to track back as part of a midfield unit, did not suit Scott's out-and-out attacking approach. He would join Pickering in departing the following summer. As for the FA Cup hero Trebilcock – after starting in the Charity Shield XI he would only make a further five appearances before returning to the south coast with Portsmouth; however, a five-minute burst of brilliance in May 1966 ensured his footballing immortality on Merseyside.

In September 1966 Everton travelled to Denmark to play Aalborg in the European Cup Winners' Cup. An episode on the trip gave an insight into the guard Harry kept up when on Merseyside, with its football obsession and the all-enveloping Littlewoods organisation. Mike Ellis was approached by Harry during the flight out to Scandinavia: 'On the plane Harry came and sat next to me, he hadn't spoken to me in God knows how long. He said, "Are you going out tonight? It's a really lively town, I was here last week." The other press lads didn't believe me when I told them that he wanted to come out with us that night. He took us to a club and he was a totally different person. But when we landed back at Speke it was back to square one again. It was him saying, "As long as I am away from Merseyside I can relax, this is the other side of me." But once it was back to business nothing had changed.'

Having defeated Aalborg 2-1 on aggregate Everton would, once again, falter in European competition, being knocked out by Real Zaragoza. Shortly afterwards Harry worked with Mike Langley on articles intended for the *People* – a surprising choice of publication in light of the match-fixing and pill popping allegations published in the newspaper two years earlier. In their conversations Harry demonstrated amazing foresight as to how football would develop, over 25 years before the establishment of the UEFA Champions League and the English Premier League:

How can England expect top clubs to cope with forty-two First Division games, FA Cup-ties and international calls, and at the same time complain because no English club has ever won the European Cup? If we are to have a real chance the First Division must be cut. It wants re-shaping, renaming and reducing. Sixteen city clubs with the highest crowd potential in a premier division, that's what I want to see. The league programme, this monotonous diet of domestic football is losing its appeal. Modern crowds don't want to see the same old weary round of fixtures. They want to see the top teams playing in some sort of European league and I believe the fans would pay continental prices for those games – twelve bob to stand in Italy for example. Fewer League matches, better-quality teams and regular European competition – that's my vision of modern football.

Harry also envisaged a time when top-flight referees would turn professional: 'I believe British referees are the best in the world but could be even better as professionals instead of part-timers. He's the most important man on the field and should be paid accordingly. How much? A minimum of £2,000 a year. In return referees would become full-time professionals, spending the season in physical and practical training between matches. I believe that mere daily mixing with professional footballers would improve referees by giving them a clearer insight into the average player's mind.'

That summer's World Cup had seen Goodison Park play host to five matches. Seeing talent from Brazil, Hungary, Portugal, West Germany and Russia strut the Goodison Park stage, Harry became frustrated that bureaucracy prevented Everton from acquiring the services of players from beyond the British Isles. He told Mike Langley:

I'm wondering how long it will be before the age of the £200,000 footballer. In fact, if the Football Association were not so isolationist, it could be tomorrow. If Eusebio came on the market and it were possible for an English club to sign him then Everton could be interested – even it cost £200,000. I'd be ready to advise my directors that would not be wasted on any of these three Hungarian World Cup forwards: Florian Albert, Bene or Farkas. Everton want to see foreign stars in football league teams. They would improve our own players, please the fans and help us build great international club sides to compare with Real Madrid and Inter Milan. Only the FA stands in the way. If they ever change their minds, Everton will be among the first buyers in Europe. And I'll use the same methods that have worked here – pick a man, decide a valuation, and then move fast and secretly to get him.

The first £200,000 transfer in the UK would arrive four years later when Martin Peters swapped West Ham United for Tottenham Hotspur, with Jimmy Greaves moving in the opposite direction. Everton would not field a foreign player in the first team until Stefan Rehn in 1989.

Harry's willingness to import talent, should regulations permit, reflected his views that English footballers needed to improve if they were to compete in a higher echelon. He told Mike Langley:

When English clubs go into a European league we'll need players with greater skill than we have now. I don't want to take anything away from England's World Cup win but we succeeded with players who are really below the top class. The basic skills of English players must be improved. They can't pass as accurately or control the ball as consistently as continentals. In my opinion, the answer to defensive football is better forwards. We need men who can work in confined spaces. On the edge of any penalty area today a forward is likely to be confronted by six defenders. If he can't get the ball down quickly and effectively he's got no chance of scoring.

Certain matches in the 1966/67 season gave hints of the footballing riches to come. Harry recalled to John Roberts: 'Some club games stick in my mind. I can remember when we played Sheffield United at Goodison and we beat them 4–1 but it could have been fourteen. It's not that Sheffield United were bad, it was unbelievable – almost one touch. It was so good to look at, so quick and precise, very good stuff.'

As the transfer deadline day approached in March 1967, press speculation was rife linking Howard Kendall with a move to Liverpool. Kendall, one of the country's most promising young half-backs, had made a name at Preston having moved from his native north-east. The *Sun's* Mike Ellis took a surprising call from

Harry: 'I was staying at my parents' in Rhyl when Catterick rang to say, "I've got a story for you. It's only for you, don't crack on. Liverpool are going to sign Howard Kendall from Preston tomorrow. Now you've got that on your own." So we led on it the next morning: "SHANKLY SWOOPS FOR KENDALL". I was driving back to Liverpool the next morning listening to The World at One on Radio Four and they said: "Now an item of sport: Everton have signed Howard Kendall from Preston." I nearly crashed the car, I was furious. I drove straight to Bellefield to have it out with Catt and – surprise, surprise – he wasn't available. I later found out from Shankly that he had always wanted to sign Kendall but Preston were refusing to deal with Liverpool having already sold them Peter Thompson. Catterick was doing that because he knew he'd got Kendall himself.'

After a poor debut and early injury problems, Kendall would prove to be an inspired signing. A class act both on and off the pitch, he was the last piece in Harry's midfield jigsaw. Harry told John Roberts: 'Howard was a nice guy, a really nice fellow that everyone would want to meet on or off the field. Always a good passer of the ball, perhaps always a yard or so short of pace. He made an invaluable contribution to the success in my latter years at Goodison.'

Kendall's arrival precipitated the departure of Jimmy Gabriel, still only 26, to Southampton. Gabriel told Becky Tallentire in *Still Talking Blue*: 'Harry said that if I wanted to play at the back with Brian Labone then he would move me there – John Hurst wasn't settled in yet and hadn't made the position his own, besides Harry liked me playing there. I wanted to play in midfield so decided I should move.' Although never quite fulfilling his billing as 'The New Dave Mackay', Gabriel had been a stalwart for Harry and Johnny Carey before him. His personality and physical presence were of enormous benefit to younger players breaking through and in need of a mentor-cum-minder on the pitch. The decision to allow Gabriel to move to the south coast – Harry preferred his top players not to be transferred to clubs on his doorstep – does seem surprising and emphasises the faith placed in Kendall.

After a modest sixth-place finish in the league, the sale of Gabriel saw Harry come under fire from some quarters at the club's annual general meeting in July 1967. Chris James of the *Liverpool Echo* reported Harry's speech to the assembled shareholders in which he estimated that eight teams would be in the hunt for honours in the 1967/68 season: 'I am quite confident that the policy we have adopted of recruiting schoolboy players and turning them into first-class players is the right thing. I, personally, feel that the side may be a little too young for very big things, lack of experience of the young players may have a detrimental impact at first. But to play them in the first team is the only way to give them that experience.'

CHAPTER FIFTEEN

THE DAWN OF THE HOLY TRINITY

AS A NEW season kicked off in August 1967, the project to overhaul the 1966 FA Cup winners into title contenders was still a work in progress. Harry told Alan Hoby of the *Sunday Express*: 'The average age of this Everton team is around 22–23, six of the side are 21 or under. We are the youngest side in the division and we are still immature – I am looking to the years ahead.'

One significant close-season loss was the departure of Tommy Eggleston who, wishing to test himself as a manager, had taken up the post at Mansfield Town. His replacement, Wilf Dixon, was another north-easterner whose playing career at Aldershot had been curtailed by a ligament injury. Turning to coaching, he had worked his way up the league ladder, culminating in stints at West Bromwich Albion and Blackpool. At Everton he was to be reunited with Alan Ball, who he had helped to blossom at Bloomfield Road.

Former Sports Minister Kate Hoey encountered Dixon while he was working for Arsenal in the 1970s. She recounted to the *Telegraph*: 'Wilf was an optimist who believed that most people are inherently good. He was tight on discipline but loved all the lads like they were his own.' On taking up his post at Everton he made a wish that would come true: 'Everyone's ambition in football is to get to Wembley in some capacity with a club. I have never been yet, but this year I hope to be there.' Dixon would become the principal link between Harry and the first-team players for the next four years and played a key role in the successes to come.

The season kicked off at Goodison against Manchester United. The match marked the end of Everton's self-imposed exile from television coverage. Match of the Day had been launched in 1964, showing extended highlights of one match each Saturday. Due, in large part, to Harry's belief that coverage might remove the element of tactical surprise, Goodison Park had been absent from the nation's television screens. John Keith, in *Colin Harvey's Everton Secrets*, revealed Harry's views were so strong on that matter that he lobbied his board to forge an anti-television alliance with Liverpool FC.

Due to the Moores influence at Anfield, the Liverpool hierarchy felt obliged to listen to arguments put forward by Everton's chairman, E. Holland Hughes. However, Bill Shankly and chief executive Peter Robinson appreciated the value of television in promoting Liverpool and did not accede to Everton's request. Therefore Everton would go it alone in warding off the cameras from Goodison, also proposing, unsuccessfully, that action replays of controversial incidents be banned.

The cameras at Goodison for Manchester United's visit that August Saturday afternoon recorded, for posterity, a rampant 3–1 home victory. The highlight was one of the first, and finest, goals caught on camera at Goodison. Young, playing in the wide striking role to accommodate Royle at centre-forward, instantly controlled a cross-field pass on his chest, body-swerved past two bemused defenders and hammered a shot into the roof of the net.

'Easy, easy,' went up the chant, as Colin Harvey recalls: 'I have watched a DVD of the game. We didn't just beat them, we absolutely murdered them and they won the European Cup that season.'

The advent of England's 'Wingless Wonders' in 1966 and the exposure to continental tactics in European competition had seen British teams stray from the 'W-M' formation which itself had evolved in the 1920s from the long-established 2–3–5 'pyramid' pattern by dropping the centre-half into a deeper role. Many teams would adopt a narrower 4–4–2 pattern. Everton tactics would evolve towards a fluid system based on a 4–3–3 but retaining greater width than in Ramsey's England model. Joe Royle was, despite his tender years, now established as the number nine in the Everton tradition. He was supported by two wide men – normally Johnny Morrissey and Alex Young. Young himself was coming under increasing pressure from Jimmy Husband, the pacy and unorthodox wide-forward. The season would be Young's last before finally being deemed surplus to requirements.

FA Cup hero Derek Temple, still only 28, was being edged out as Morrissey became established on the left flank: 'Harry was clever,' recalls Temple. 'He dropped Alex Young, the crowd favourite, and when they announced me in the line-up I was booed, which was not very nice. Harry knew that would happen. Not long after I was called in and he said, "I've had an enquiry from Preston, what do you think?" Now I'd played my heart out for the club and that unsettled me. I said, "I don't want to leave." He replied, "No, quite right too, and we don't want to lose you, but it might be worth having a chat with Jimmy Milne.' I thought, "Does he think I'm stupid?" but that's the way it worked. Other managers did that too, once they said "Go and have a chat" your days were numbered.'

Temple, a loyal servant who was often underrated by Everton fans, left for North End in September 1967 for £35,000. This left Young and Labone as the only first-team regulars from when Harry strode into Goodison in 1961.

Harry maintained an excellent success rate with his big-money signings until the dawn of the 1970s but one that didn't work out was the £80,000 acquisition of Ernie Hunt from Wolves in September 1967. The inside-forward, a dressing room entertainer, failed to settle on Merseyside and was unable to dislodge Young, or the emerging Husband. After leaving Harry unimpressed, he departed for Coventry six months later with Everton incurring a £10,000 loss. Hunt would have one last laugh: his infamous donkey-flick free-kick routine against Everton in 1970 earned him the 'Goal of the Season' award.

In that opening-day rout, Manchester United's legendary trio of Law, Charlton and Best were overshadowed by Kendall, Harvey and Ball. A marker had been put down: the age of the Holy Trinity was dawning. A clue as to where the template evolved for Harry's second great team, with Kendall, Harvey and Ball at its heart, could be found on his office desk. Here sat two volumes of *Soccer*, a seminal coaching manual by Arpad Csanádi, the Hungarian former footballer, coach and IOC member. Harry told Mike Langley in 1966: 'Our football is going continental but the country we should copy isn't Italy, it's Hungary. Take it from me that, technically, the Hungarians are the most advanced footballing nation in the world. Their training and coaching methods are superb.'

In the spring of 1968 Harry told the *Daily Mail's* J.L. Manning about his inspiration for the tactics and playing style he had adopted:

> *Arthur Rowe's Tottenham team of 1951 – the one in which Ramsey and Nicholson played. This was the 'push and run'. It was much more than that, there was no way of countering it. Only the Hungarian team a couple of years later played more effectively in all the years I've been in football. Everything we do here is based on ball control and acquisition of fast working techniques. That was Arthur Rowe's message after the war and that's what I'm trying to do: respond to it, keep it going.*

As Europe hurtled inexorably towards conflict in 1939, Arthur Rowe had made a trip to Budapest to lecture Hungarians on English football tactics. Rowe had been a Tottenham Hotspur player in the 1930s before a knee injury had necessitated a switch to coaching. The Spurs team of the 1930s was ahead of its time in English football – it favoured a close passing game over the more established long-ball tactics. During a stay curtailed by the outbreak of conflict, Rowe had absorbed some of the prevailing Hungarian tactical thinking and taken it home. Interestingly, much of the Hungarian approach to football could be traced back to a Lancastrian, Jimmy Hogan, who spent time coaching in Vienna and Budapest in the early years of the 20th century. The Hungarians, lacking burly, English-style centre-forwards, had devised a system of play incorporating a fluid front four and a deep-lying number nine who dropped into midfield areas. The pattern of play thus adopted flummoxed the England team at Wembley in 1953, a 6–3 scoreline shattering the illusion of English footballing superiority. In England, Manchester City adapted this tactic as 'The Revie Plan', with the future Leeds United manager dropping back into deep positions.

Four years before England's Wembley capitulation, Rowe became manager of a Spurs team languishing in the Second Division. He implemented a system based on ball retention and high-speed short passing on the ground; 'Make it simple, make it quick' was his mantra – he was never enamoured with the 'push and run' label. Promoted in his first season, he led Spurs to the First Division title a year later. Opposition teams were unable to cope with the rapid inter-play; 'push and move' had arrived and yet, in conservative England, relatively few teams adopted the model – preferring to persevere with the tried and trusted 'pyramid' formation. Two members of that great Spurs team would go on to taste management success – Bill Nicholson with the double-winning Spurs team of 1961 and Alf Ramsey at Ipswich in 1962 before leading the English national team to glory four years later. Sadly, Rowe began to suffer from stress-related illnesses in the mid-1950s, culminating in a breakdown which led to his exit from Spurs. He subsequently managed West Bromwich Albion and Crystal Palace before mental health issues once again dogged him.

Playing for Everton in a 3–0 defeat to the champions elect at White Hart Lane in March 1951, Harry had taken note of the new, exciting way of playing the game. While managing Sheffield Wednesday, he tried to instigate a version of push and run but lacked the players and facilities to develop it fully. Now that the Everton 'Football Factory' was up and running with youngsters schooled from an early age in the 'Everton Way', the time was right to emulate Spurs and the Hungarians.

Aside from the specialist positions of centre-forward, centre-back and goalkeeper, the Everton teams of the late 1960s were relatively diminutive. This was no accident; Harry envisaged a side of mobile, skilful players rather than the lumbering giants of yore. Looking back with journalist Norman Shakeshaft in 1975 he said:

'When it comes to the creation of something in tight corners, which midfield men have to do, give me the little ones: 5 feet 8 inches or 5feet 9 inches. They are sharper, better balanced, with a low centre of gravity. There's a lot of heavy traffic in a football match. It is hard driving a big Rolls-Royce through heavy traffic, you are better off in a Mini.'

Kendall, Harvey and Ball would light up the late 60s with a brand of football rarely witnessed on British soil. They would be dubbed 'The Holy Trinity', 'The Three Musketeers' and 'The Three Graces'. Talking to John Roberts, Harry classed them as midfield forwards, 'because we are an attacking side and all three of them are capable of scoring goals'. The key to their success was a natural chemistry, abundant ability and hours spent together practising ball-work together rather than receiving orthodox coaching. The trio were allowed to develop an almost telepathic under-standing through small-sided, high-speed training games. Harry almost purred as recalled what he saw at Bellefield:

> This was something we worked on particularly in the indoor area with three and five a-sides with the ball going at lightning speeds. I saw games in there that were, to me, unbelievable. They weren't very big physically so they had to be quick and skilful to get by – and by God they were! The ball would almost go one touch and that's where they developed – these three players in particular. They really worked at it; you wouldn't see them passing nonchalantly at any time – they always passed it precisely and sharply .That is why they became a really important trio and they appealed to spectators more than the front runners who normally get the glamour.

Less heralded, but integral to the system developed under Harry, was a fourth 'musketeer': Johnny Morrissey. The former Liverpudlian had not always been a first choice for the number eleven shirt since joining in 1962, but the new system was ideally suited to him. Harry told John Roberts how valued Morrissey was: 'In that set-up, the player who gets little credit was Morrissey who we called our "safety valve" player. He always got the ball when it was tight. We could give it to him and then he could play it back into the trio and start it again. He was a strong player physically, with more skill than given credit for, and a lot of courage. He was very important.'

The specialist attacking 'big gun', Joe Royle, would frequently be urged to be more assertive in order to maximise the use of his physical attributes. In his auto-biography Royle recalled an incident from 1969 which illustrated how the coaches tried to goad him: 'I was never able to banish Wilf Dixon's irritating opinion that I was not aggressive enough. When I was having treatment in the physio room one day Wilf walked in and said, "What's up with you?" I explained what the injury was and… with a little satisfaction was able to reply that I had made the full hit of forty-two league appearances (the previous season). But Wilf's response was far from complimentary: "Any striker who plays forty-two games a season is a coward!"'

Early in Royle's career, Harry conveyed his frustrations in conversation with James Mossop, as the journalist recalls: 'It was the time when Joe had just got into the team. I said, "Joe is such a big, strong lad but he doesn't put his weight about, does he?" And he said, "I have tried and tried to tell him to toughen up, be harder, to get into people and use his elbows. And do you know what he said to me? 'Would you like a sweetie boss?' – and opened up a packet of sweets." That's how Harry told it.'

Royle would break the 20 goals per season barrier for four consecutive seasons before a chronic back injury took its toll. He secured a place in the pantheon of Everton centre-forwards, alongside Dean, Lawton, Hickson and Young, gaining international honours before enjoying a successful spell at Manchester City. None-theless, Harry believed he remained an unfulfilled talent, as he told John Roberts:

> Joe has always been a frustrating player. You could not meet a nicer lad, a great lad. Tremendous skills, great shooting ability and a good header of a ball. He was always the one that you felt: 'My goodness, if he had fulfilled his potential he'd have been another John Charles.' I could not see him failing on that when I saw him as a sixteen-year-old. He subsequently got international caps but, to my mind, he has never fulfilled his potential. Joe was also a little unfortunate that, by then, I'd stopped playing with wingers as such. He would have been good in the era of Dean when wingers got to the by-line and slung balls over. Joe was very good with those but he was also a good target man – his ability to lay-on goals was remarkable.

Despite a strong run of seven consecutive league victories in March and April, the league title remained beyond reach. Poor away form, with 11 defeats, restricted Everton to a fifth-place finish. Despite disappointment in the league, the team progressed smoothly to the FA Cup semi-final at Old Trafford where the draw brought the Blues up against Leeds United. Shorn of the services of the suspended Ball, Tommy Jackson, an astute capture from Glentoran, was drafted into midfield alongside Kendall and Harvey.

Even the *Yorkshire Post* felt obliged to recognise Everton's team's effort and performance:

> *The vital play was in midfield where the Everton tackling was so quick and persistent that the Bremner–Giles link was not allowed to develop. Everton's outstanding men were West in goal, the magnificent Labone – who tackled, covered and worked unceasingly – Kenyon, who joined him as a second centre-half, helping successfully to dominate Jones, the ebullient Royle and Kendall, who harried every Leeds player with the ball. Leeds could not rid themselves of these untiring challengers who were frequently reinforced by Harvey.*

Harry himself could bask in his own contribution to victory, as Howard Kendall would recall in his first autobiography: 'It was fitting that one of our manager's more subtle schemes should ultimately have decided the outcome. The direction was that Joe Royle or Jimmy Husband should stand directly in front of Gary Sprake, the Leeds goalkeeper, whenever he had possession of the ball. Harry Catterick felt that Sprake's left foot was weak and that if he was denied the use of his powerful right boot anything could happen.'

As predicted, Sprake, under pressure from Royle, mishit a clearance straight to Husband, whose goal-bound shot was handled in the box by Jackie Charlton. The match was settled from the resultant penalty, calmly slotted home by Morrissey. Harry, not a man for hyperbole, was elated and hailed the result of one of his greatest.

The magnanimous *Yorkshire Post* would record: 'Everton without question deserved their victory and on their overall record, too, they deserve to be in the final... Kenyon worked magnificently and gave further evidence that Mr Harry Catterick's kindergarten is as rich in promise and actual fulfilment as any of its kind in the country. In a year or two Everton should be a very formidable side.'

Harry himself was elated at beating a team he had little time for. He spoke to the *Liverpool Echo*'s Mike Charters: 'I am delighted that we got through. I feel we did very well when one considers the tremendous blow of being robbed of Alan Ball,

Sandy Brown and John Hurst. I regard Hurst as the king pin of our defence. The greatest win in my years of management.'

Everton were overwhelming favourites for the final against West Bromwich Albion, having thrashed them 6–2 at the Hawthorns only two months earlier. Yet cup final day in London was muggy and drizzly – not conducive to Everton's high-tempo football on the large, heavy, Wembley playing surface. The match was flat but both teams spurned opportunities to take the lead in normal time – notably a close-range header over the bar from Jimmy Husband: 'My miss against West Brom in the 1968 cup final still haunts me to this day but I don't blame myself one hundred per cent now. The whole team were off-colour that day: Joe, Alan and I each missed a couple of half-chances and we just couldn't finish it. If it had gone to a replay you could have put your house on it that we would have won.' Harry sat helpless on the distant bench as Jeff Astle's extra-time strike arrowed into the top corner of West's net.

Having been played increasingly sparingly during the course of the season, Alex Young's omission from the FA Cup final team signalled the end of his Everton career. During the summer of 1968 he bowed out to bring to an end an uneasy, yet highly productive, seven years under Harry. Who knows how much better things might have been for Young had he not been afflicted by foot blisters, hearing loss and a dysfunctional relationship with Harry?

True to form, Harry was not keen to see a man who still had something to offer another team playing on his doorstep. After a move to the USA fell through, a deal was brokered whereby Young became player-manager at Belfast's Glentoran for £10,000. Young himself was to receive a signing-on fee of £2,000 from Glentoran plus a further £1,000 from Everton to follow a month later. In his memoirs, Young recounted to David France how he returned to Bellefield some weeks later to en-quire of Harry as to the whereabouts of the second instalment: 'He smirked at me, "Listen, there will be no more for you. Let that be a lesson to you son, get everything down in writing."'

This unsavoury episode was diametrically at odds with the glowing words Harry penned, without Young's knowledge, for the foreword to the player's 1968 autobiography *Goals at Goodison*: 'It is my privilege to introduce the first literary effort of one whom I regard as one of the most cultured players in the game. In my opinion Young's skills are unsurpassed in modern football. Not physically equipped for the hurly-burly of modern football, he still excels in delicate, subtle machina-tions which are... a source of delight for the onlookers... A masterly header of the ball, he can outwit by perfect timing in rising to a ball. I dread the day when the game loses entertainers of this mould.'

Speaking nine years later to John Roberts, Harry gave his take on his relationship with the Goodison idol:

> *Alex was a highly skilful player but a problem to me in many ways because his form was so up and down. When he was 'on' he was brilliant – and I think if he'd had protection from referees he would have been really superb all of the time – but very often he was kicked out of games, especially away from home. He became a liability away from home, at times, because all they'd do was kick him up in the air and take all his skill away, which was detrimental to the team as a whole. It was said that he and I would never get on, it wasn't true. But I was always striving, knowing full-well I wouldn't succeed, to try to get him to be a little bit more robust – to stand up to these assassins. But he always felt skill was the thing and up to a point he was right. But I wanted more competitiveness.*

Young reflects: 'He never said "well done" or "terrific" to me – maybe just once or twice. That's horrible if you're winning – you're wanting someone to say, "That was great, well done." I just kept plugging along; I didn't dislike the man but he never encouraged me to do anything, unlike many managers now. I never got a pat on my head, but I might have been thinking too much about it.'

Shortly before he left Everton, Young was the subject of *The Golden Vision*, a BBC television 'Wednesday Play', directed by Ken Loach, who had made a name for himself with the gritty *Cathy Come Home* in 1966. Written by Evertonian Neville Smith, with some input from Gordon Honeycombe, The Golden Vision mixed drama about the lives of Evertonian families with documentary segments about the players and management. John Moores was naturally wary about having what was a left-wing film-making team at Everton, but his go-between Graham Wilson was able to smooth matters over. As well as featuring the softly spoken Scot, the programme was one of the few occasions cameras got inside Bellefield to capture Harry Catterick on film. Loach recalls that it was not straightforward getting Harry to open up for the camera: 'Everton were quite suspicious of what we were trying to do and Harry Catterick was quite elusive. He wasn't an open, easy, gregarious type who would take you around. He was quite formal and didn't relax. He was quite defensive, looking for trick questions and traps, whereas we were just looking for enthusiasm for the game.'

Despite Loach's perception of Harry, he came across as eloquent and almost resigned to being unpopular: 'I'm not a popular fellow because I have always felt that if a decision has to be made, I mustn't consider whether it's going to be a popular one or not. The fellow who looks for popularity has something wrong (with him).' He went on to bemoan how skill was being suppressed by physicality: 'One of the tragedies of the modern game is that now we have quite a lot of gifted ball players which the public are not seeing, mainly because of the destructive attitude of some players with lesser ability.'

A team talk for a game with Arsenal was also featured. The scene saw Harry, in tracksuit with 'broadcasting' voice to the fore, deliver a rather staid briefing with Wilf Dixon at Bellefield. However, all was not what it seemed, as Graham Wilson recalls: 'It was staged; it actually took place on the Sunday after the game.'

Harry, not renowned for his humour, was tickled that the pet dog of a lead character was called 'Catterick'. The canine Catterick was an in-joke by Neville Smith about Harry's perceived 'bite'.

Hard though it is to conceive now, Kenny Dalglish could have replaced Young in Evertonians' affections. Harry recalled to Charles Lambert in 1978 how he had stumbled on the Scot a decade earlier:

'I went up to Glasgow to watch a reserve match between Aberdeen and Celtic. I was interested in an Aberdeen player but this youngster, about 17 or so, in the Celtic side caught my eye. It was Dalglish. I spoke to Jock Stein and asked if he would transfer him - it was obvious he had a lot of class and talent. I can well remember Jock saying that he thought Dalglish was going to be a good player and he couldn't sell him while there was a chance that he could turn out well. Celtic didn't need the money, so they could afford to wait.'

CHAPTER SIXTEEN
PURE FOOTBALL

THE PREVIOUS two seasons had seen the transitional team of 1966 revamped into a pure, flowing team capable of sublime football. Many would go as far as to argue that the style and quality of play was unsurpassed, but the hard, cold fact was that the team had failed to deliver any silverware.

By common consensus the football served up in the 1968/69 season was never bettered at Goodison, but the team sacrificed points in key league games, losing six and drawing 15 to finish in third place. Leeds on the other hand were imperious; defeated only twice, they romped to their first league title with a record haul of 67 points; Liverpool trailed in second place on 61.

As Harry plotted another assault on the league crown he knew that beauty would need to be balanced with resilience in some fixtures in order to grind out results – particularly on muddy or rutted pitches that did not lend themselves to a fluid passing game. Competition would again be fierce from Leeds, Liverpool and others, meaning that only the best would be good enough to get Everton over the finish line. Even though the average age of the team was a young 24, several key members, such as Labone and Morrissey, would soon be reaching veteran stage. Time was of the essence.

Once again, close-season transfer activity had been minimal with Harry happy to rely on a core squad of 14 players. West remained established in goal, with Wright and Sandy Brown occupying the right and left full-back berths respectively, while Labone and Hurst dovetailed in central defence. In March 1968 Labone had, sensationally, given notice of his intention to retire from the game when his contract expired in spring 1969 – saying that the pressures of the game were impairing his enjoyment and eroding his form. His reversal of this decision, with encouragement from Harry, was a huge boost to the squad before the start of the 1969/70 season. Harvey, Ball and Kendall were strung across the middle, with Joe Royle the focal point of attack, supported by Husband and Morrissey in wide areas. Although nominally a 4–3–3 formation, it could seamlessly convert to 4–4–2 if Morrissey

– the 'gunslinger winger' – was required to support the midfield trio. One significant departure was Ray Wilson; the cultured-left back was now 34 years of age and had suffered a serious knee injury 12 months earlier. He would see out his playing career at Oldham Athletic before serving as caretaker-manager of Bradford City.

Everton made an important off-pitch signing in David Exall as the club's first promotions manager, who recalls: 'I arrived at the club at such a great time as I feel there has never been a better Everton team – maybe never a better team anywhere – than the 1969/70 team.' Exall's role was multi-faceted and included fundraising for the proposed new Main Stand, revitalising the dated match-day programme and improving links between the media and the club. When meeting the Merseyside press corps for the first time he was made aware of the ongoing 'cold war' between Harry and most of the journalists. It was put to Exall by the journalists that not even Lord Beaverbrook could thaw the icy relations between them and the club.

In response to the practice started at Liverpool and copied elsewhere, Everton began hosting pre-match press conferences on Friday lunchtimes. Here the match-day squad would be announced and questions were taken from the journalists by Harry. James Mossop recalls: 'You'd ask questions like "Is so-and-so fit?" and "What do you think about the opposition?" Harry would answer the questions, always brief, but I don't think he was ever difficult. You got a line but I don't recall anything that was very dramatic, whereas every time Shankly spoke it was original.'

Colin Wood of the *Daily Mail* recalls the conferences held in Goodison Park before the relocation to Bellefield: 'We had to wait at the top of the stairs outside his Goodison office before we were finally called in by Bill Dickinson to see Harry – he'd start by reading out the team for the next day in alphabetical order. So Gordon West, the goalkeeper, would be near the end of the list. Harry claimed this wasn't to be obstructive to the media but so as not to give the opposition any clues. He had an obsession almost with not letting the opposition know about his team. Then he'd take questions but he wouldn't always answer them or he'd not give you the answers that you were seeking.'

David Exall recalls: 'Harry felt that the world was against him – maybe he was right! But he needn't have been like that because he was so brilliant at the main focus of his job which was putting together great footballing teams and finding people who could coach them. He had been able to influence the careers of most of the players to such an extent that they were great players. They might have been ordinary players but became great players because they were put in the right place, at the right age, and responded to his demands.'

One task Exall was set by the hierarchy was to introduce a regular 'From the

Manager's Chair' column to the match-day programme in line with other clubs. 'Harry didn't want to know about it. I eventually got him to agree but he wasn't very cooperative. He used to say to me: "What do you think I should say?" I tried to pick things out for him to say something about but it was like pulling teeth even to get a theme for him to talk about. He insisted that every word should be vetted – if it went to print unedited he would ring and give me a rollicking. He was most vociferous with me about Leeds United. He had a terrible dislike for Leeds and Revie. If he felt I had been over-complimentary about Leeds the draft would come back with red lines through it.'

Expectations for the season were raised with an opening-day win at Highbury, the first of four consecutive wins, including two victories over Manchester United within in the space of a week; such were the eccentricities of fixture scheduling in that era. However, the midfield axis would be disrupted for much of the season – the 'Trinity' appeared together in the league on only 20 occasions due to a mixture of injury and, in Ball's case, disciplinary problems. Around the time Harry celebrated his 50th birthday on 19 November, he received a most unwelcome piece of news: Colin Harvey had suffered inflammation of the optic nerve. The ailment, according to some of the more hysterical headlines, threatened to bring a premature end to Harvey's career; in a bid to overcome the issue he underwent a lumbar puncture procedure and a course of injections. Harry recalled to John Roberts how he learned of the problem:

> Colin's injury was one of the biggest shocks I ever had,' Harry said. 'I saw the boy walking into my office. Typical of Colin there was no hoo-ha. He said, 'They have sent me up here, Boss, I can't see out of this eye.' I asked, 'Have you been fighting or something?' He said very timidly – he was always shy in my presence – 'No, I haven't, Last night I just couldn't see out of the eye.' That was the start of it. That hurt me terribly as he was a hell of a nice fellow. He was put on massive doses of cortisone, which isn't the best of things for side-effects, and he started putting a bit of weight on. To my mind he never quite got back. He did play good games but he was never quite the Colin Harvey we knew.'

Surprisingly, Harvey was back in action by late January – just as Alan Ball missed four matches through suspension – although he continued to receive treatment until the autumn. After his third Everton dismissal, Ball had been accompanied by Harry to a FA disciplinary hearing in London but they had been unable to reduce the sanction; the player's previous record was taken into account and the FA decided to make an example of him. It is of enormous credit to Tommy Jackson and Sandy Brown that momentum was maintained in the absence of the key components of the side's engine room. Crucially, however, the trio of musketeers were reunited for the final 11 games of the title run-in.

On 4 December 1969, with Everton sitting top of the league, Harry gave a rare televised interview to ITV. Not only was it unusual for Harry to go on air but the content was remarkably candid. Firstly he laid out the philosophy of the team:

> People have used the phrase, in relation to Everton, of 'instant football'. I think it is a compliment because we believe in quick play, quick accurate passing and possession until we can see an opening and then striking as quickly as possible. Instant football means, in effect, that you have got quick control and the ability to part with the ball quickly and accurately.
>
> My philosophy of the game is that ball players are the attractive players and the players that the public want to see, they certainly please the professional. Wherever you go, talking to managers and hard-boiled coaches, they'll always acclaim the clever player, the fellow who has the mastery of the basic skills. If we can get eleven of those, we should get a great side. So eight years ago I hoped to recruit boys who had these basic skills, if we could further develop them.
>
> When you build a side, and indeed as we've built Everton, you can never run away from the fact that you should not concede goals. This is your aim, but there's a limit to this. If indeed you get too defensive-conscious your attacking flair goes. So what we've got to marry is solid defensive play but sufficient constructive ability in these defenders to build up attacks. We like, whenever possible, to keep possession right from the goalkeeper and start our moves from the back.

Harry then went on to list and describe the first team in a level of detail remarkable for someone who liked to play his cards close to his chest:

> What I expect from Gordon West is his ability to start moves. Gordon does this well, both from hand and with good goal-

kicking. Gordon's assets are numerous. I think his reflexes are absolutely fantastic, he's a very big man, he's fourteen-and-a-half stone, but the way that he can throw this around is unbelievable. I, frankly, think that he is second only to Gordon Banks. His ability to come out from crosses at times is not as good as it might be. I know he'll know I would say this, but Gordon is working hard on it and is a great character, he's a good professional, he's always striving for perfection.

We have a basic back four of Tommy Wright, John Hurst, Brian Labone and Sandy Brown. Tommy Wright has great ability to look for space up-front when it's on. This may well have come from the days when he was a forward. Of course, he has great recovery powers; his ability to get back into defensive position is quite good.

John Hurst bolts up this defence along with Brian Labone. They play this twin centre-half role so common in modern football. I think they complement one another very well. John has great defensive strengths because he's so powerful, he's very, very good in the air and he reads play exceptionally well. John, if anything, lacks belief in himself. He has far more ability than he displays at times, he has greater attacking flair and, when this situation is on for him to break from the back, he rarely does it. When he does, it usually means trouble for the opposition.

Brian Labone, of course, is our captain and a man of great character. He's a one-club man, a player who has been with the Everton side from very early days and his ability to set an example, both on and off the pitch, has been a great boon to me. Being the most senior of the professionals, his ability to talk his defence into good defensive positions is probably one of his biggest assets. This, of course, is leaning back on experience in a very young side and they look to Brian to bolt this back four up. The position as regards Labone in relation with Hurst is that we don't ask either of them to be the back player, they must read the situation as it is. This theme, whilst we're talking about the back four, is something which runs throughout the team. We have no rigid role for any player.

Sandy Brown, our left flank player in the back four, is now I think getting the benefit of a sustained run in the game.

He has very good defensive powers, he's a sound header of the ball and of course he is a little bit underestimated. In my opinion he does start a lot of our moves; he can find Joe Royle very accurately from very deep defensive positions.

I don't like to think in terms of formation where you get 4–4–2 or the 4–3–3. Once I finish with my back four, we now have six forwards and we take it from there. Basically we find three of possibly the best type of midfield forwards – because we are an attacking side – in Kendall, Ball and Harvey. All three are capable of scoring goals and indeed do. They all have a great ability to construct and create for men further forward. What I look for in a player, is his ability to implement his skills. If he can be put off by intimidation, and let's face it, the ball players are liable to get rather more of this than others, then he's going to miss out on all the hard work we've put in to make him a ball Ω

Whatever I can say about Alan Ball would indeed underestimate him because this chap has great ability on and off the ball. He's a good competitor, he trains as hard as any professional I know, or indeed have ever known. He wants to win, he has skills, he wants to win so much. Many skilful players get complimented yet you forget the time they've spent standing around. This boy never stands, and he's always competing and creating. Critics often say that Alan is right-sided and plays most of his football down the right side of the field. He is right-footed but his left foot is more than useful. Some critics have said that his combination with Joe Royle is invariably down the right side. Well, I don't mind which side it is, Joe likes it down that side at times. But, by and large, Alan's ability to play both left flank and right is undoubted. Alan's temperament possibly has been his worst enemy in some aspects. He has this great competitive spirit and most of his trouble with referees and authority have been for dissent. But I've seen this boy take some terrible punishment physically on the field, with very little protection at times.

What I expect from Howard Kendall is creating moves from longer distances than most other midfield players. He also has a sound attacking flair, he can come through from behind front men and has a great ability to shoot. Allied to all this, he's probably one of the hardest tacklers in the business.

I picked Colin Harvey as a fifteen-year-old schoolboy, a good inside-forward in the 'W' formation style. He's developed a defensive quality allied to his undoubted ability and skill on the ball. If you like skills, and you like watching fellows who have mastered the basics, watch Harvey.

Up front we basically have Husband, Royle and Morrissey. Jimmy Husband came to me as a fifteen-year-old inside-left, in this present set-up he plays more or less right flank. If you want to talk about old-type formations he's an outside-right, but you won't often find him there. He has possibly the quickest turn of speed over five or six yards, of any player I've ever known, and is capable of getting goals from nothing. His heading ability is something which disturbed us. Some couple of years ago you may remember him missing a great chance in the cup final and Jimmy has never forgotten this. He's worked on it virtually night and day and we're finding now that even the boys are saying: 'Jimmy, you're heading them again.'

On the other wing we have this greatly underestimated player John Morrissey. John came to me from Liverpool some six years ago and he has certainly never looked back as regards his football with us. He doesn't look a graceful player, he doesn't look skilful, and yet he possesses great close control. We tend to think in the Everton side of Ball and Harvey, players with great ball skill; John has greater close control possibly than any other player we've got. He is of course a two-footed player, he has ability to shoot coming across the field from the left with his right foot, he packs a terrific wallop with his right foot; of course, he has ability with his left. One of his biggest assets, of course, is his undoubted courage; courage is always suspect in modern players – particularly forwards. This is possibly to be understood because of the close marking and undoubted man-to-man marking done by some sides against key players.

Finally, we've got this great big lump of a fellow, Joe Royle. Joe possibly hates me more than anyone else, but I've kicked him around to try to make him into a fellow to believe in himself. Joe arrived at Everton at fifteen years of age and had undoubted

*ability in the air. His shooting ability is unbelievable and we still
don't see enough of it. He's now married all this to skills possibly
from playing with great players like Ball, Harvey and Kendall
– he's now developing great skills on the ground. Don't forget this
boy is just twenty years of age, and he's knocking them in the net.
But even so, he comes back afternoons, trains on days when other
players are off, and a lot of the things he's developed is due to the
coach Wilf Dixon, who's spent an awful lot of time with Joe. I've
bullied him and I think he's starting to show his real form. If we
ever do get him into the positions he can find for shooting, you're
really going to see something, he packs a wallop in both feet that's
really tremendous. We get it in training, we're not getting it on
Saturdays often enough. Joe took over penalty-taking from Alan
Ball and, of course, he's got quite a record. There's great rivalry
between these two for penalty-taking, Joe took over after Alan
missed one. Sitting in the hot seat at the moment is Joe and he's
not doing badly, he really hits these penalty kicks.*

Concluding the interview, Harry was bullish about the season as it entered the winter months: 'Looking to the future, some critics have said that we may not live through heavy grounds. If they mean that once skill goes out of the game and we play on mud heaps, Everton may suffer, well, I would agree; but on the other hand there are no real mud heaps in football. In the modern game grounds are better, they rely more on skill and this is what the British public want. Let's have this skilful football, we're trying to produce it. If in producing this highly skilled stuff we win a championship, we'll be delighted. We're not going to run away from skilful football for heavy grounds or anything else.'

Just two days after Harry threw down the gauntlet in this interview, there would have been mirth in some quarters as Everton slumped to a 0–3 home defeat against Liverpool – a match immortalised by Sandy Brown's diving header past his own goalkeeper. Within a fortnight Brown was usurped by the arrival of Ray Wilson's heir apparent, Keith Newton from Blackburn Rovers. Newton, a right-footed defender who could play on either flank, would offer more craft and guile than the stalwart, but somewhat technically limited, Brown. Newton had been keen to secure a move to a bigger club in order to improve his World Cup chances. In retrospect it is strange that Harry did not act sooner when Wilson was injured in 1968. In his 13 appearances that season Newton displayed the composure and passing ability befitting such an accomplished team, but his Goodison career would peter out after two years – Harry never appeared totally convinced about his purchase and would go public in criticising what he perceived as Newton's over-elaboration with the ball.

Further changes were forced on Harry as the season progressed. When Brian Labone succumbed to a back injury with eight matches remaining of the run-in, he once again staked his reputation on home-grown talent and selected Roger Kenyon. The 20-year-old instantly gelled with John Hurst and only four goals were conceded during this period. In 2014 Kenyon would recall to Steve Zocek the two sides to Harry: 'Harry Catterick was a very deep man. I don't think anybody ever got to the bottom of him. Some days he would literally walk past you and not acknowledge you. But for instance, when you were on the way back from London by coach, if you got a result he would allow you to have a few drinks. The players would be singing, "Harry Catterick, Harry Catterick," and he loved the attention.' Ernie Horrigan, the coach driver in that era, recalled in *Gwladys Street's Holy Trinity*: 'If we won the lads were allowed a beer or two on the way home, but on the rare occasions we didn't win it was like driving a hearse. I'd position my mirror to keep one eye on Harry Catterick.'

The loss of the club captain prompted another managerial master-stroke, as Ball, returning from disciplinary exile, was handed the armband. His promotion elevated his work-rate and drive to near-superhuman levels.

Jimmy Husband's injury against Burnley in December saw Harry turn to Alan Whittle, the striker who had been on the fringes of the team for a year. There are some, Whittle included, who argue that this enforced change won the title for Everton. He recalls: 'When Jimmy Husband got injured I got in there and that was it. I was the "new kid on the block" and no one knew how to play me. But one person did know – Harry. I always remember Harry turning round to me at West Ham and he said, "I'd like you to mark Bobby Moore." I said, "Shouldn't Bobby Moore mark me, I'm the forward, he's the defender?" but Harry said "No". So where Bobby went I went... and it was getting boring. Then Moore misplaces the ball, Moore is with me but I've got speed, one against one... I score. We won 1–0. Bobby Moore had knowledge, he could read the game, but he did not have pace. It always sticks in my mind that The Catt knew something that I didn't. I thought, "Bloody hell, he knows what he's talking about... that's clever".'

Whittle's brilliant solo goal, running half the length of the rutted pitch before dispatching the ball into the net with aplomb, was the start of a glorious glut of 11 goals from the blond bomber, including six in consecutive games. According to Harry, West Ham's manager Ron Greenwood, a lover of pure football, grabbed his arm after the final whistle and said, 'My God, this is the stuff!'

Commenting to James Mossop in 1970 on Whittle's progression to the first team, an uncharacteristically effusive Harry said: 'I said five years ago this boy would one day be a great player. He has flair and a sense of timing that is reminiscent of Jimmy Greaves.' Alluding, perhaps, to the missed-coach episode in 1968, he continued: 'Of course his development hasn't been all that smooth. Sometimes youngsters have to be kicked in the backside. Sometimes they need to be coaxed. But they understand all that at Everton.'

Whittle's elevation to the starting XI was supposed to be a closely guarded secret, so Harry's ire was raised when the local sports journalists got wind of the story. Colin Wood recalls: 'A few of us had a tip that Whittle would replace Husband and used it in the Saturday editions. How Harry lost his rag over it! A few weeks later I was summoned over to the office of the chairman of Everton, George Watts, and had a very uncomfortable time when he tried to find out from me who had leaked the story to the press.'

Perhaps it was this desire to keep the free-scoring rookie under wraps that led to a bizarre stand-off between Harry and the BBC one Saturday lunchtime after David Exall had received an unusual request. He says: 'That season we were so good, and scored lots of goals. So the BBC wanted us on Match of the Day every week. The same production team who fetched up at Goodison Park on match days would be doing Songs of Praise the following day, they weren't particularly football people. Harry called me in to say that he knew I had a reasonable relationship with the BBC producer John McGonagle. I was to tell John that Harry did not want the cameras there too often.

'So I called John to say, "We love the publicity as a club but Harry says it's exposing his tactics." John responded that Everton were to be "looked at and admired" and spent the whole week trying to get Harry on the phone – without success. When Harry learned on the Thursday that the cameras would be back that weekend he was incandescent: "I'm not allowing the cameras in – you tell them not to come in". "I don't think I can do that," I replied to Harry, and went to brief the chairman, Jack Sharp. I explained, "We can't not have the BBC here." So he said, "I'll have to speak to Mr John and we'll see." I expected to hear more but didn't.'

Things came to a head on match day: 'On the Saturday morning they pitched up with the cameras. Harry used to arrive at Goodison at 11:30am, he only came to the ground on match days. When he saw the BBC there he said to me, "You could have prevented him (McGonagle) – you are his mate!" I replied: "Boss, I did everything I could within my power." The ensuing stand-off only ended when someone "on high" insisted that the television crew be allowed in.'

On 4 February it was reported that Everton had banned the cameras from covering a forthcoming fixture against Arsenal. Jack Sharp was Everton chairman at the time, although John Moores retained the real power at the club. Sharp explained the situation to the *Liverpool Echo*: 'We were in the Football League programme for the Arsenal match to be recorded. We feel that we have been over-exposed to television this season. We turned it down and wrote to the league to tell them. We feel we have had too much of it and think other clubs should get a chance. If we were asked later in the season by the league it would be considered by the directors.'

In February 1970 the team endured their first prolonged dip of the season, failing to win in three consecutive matches. The month ended, after a 1–1 draw at Nottingham Forest, with the Blues having surrendered the lead in the title race to Leeds United. At Bellefield the following Monday morning a 'crisis summit' was convened by Messrs Catterick and Dixon. In his book *Making the Grade*, Stan Osborne, then a 16-year-old apprentice, recalled eavesdropping on the meeting:

> *I could hear the raised voices getting louder with every step. As I approached the first-team dressing room I could clearly hear Harry Catterick and Wilf Dixon remonstrating intermittently with the senior players about the recent poor results and perfor-mances, and where it left the club and their chances of lifting the league trophy at the end of the season. No individual players were singled out in what was primarily a whole squad rollick-ing… the door burst open and an incandescent Harry Catterick emerged before he rounded on his players and retorted, 'And if you think that sort of performance is going to win us the league, then you lot have got another thing coming!'*
>
> *Wilf Dixon followed silently, glowering in Mr Catter-ick's wake, leaving a stunned and chastened first-team squad to reflect on the thoughts and home truths provided for them by manager and coach. One voice could still be heard. It was that of club captain Brian Labone: 'Lads, I can't disagree with a word of that. The Boss and Wilf are right and they're doing their bit – the rest is up to us. We've got a responsibility to this club and our fans. Now do we want to win the league or not?'*

Galvanised by the dressing-room showdown, the Blues travelled to Turf Moor on

7 March and got their season back on track with a 2–1 victory – it was the start of an imperious run of six victories in 23 days. After twice beating Spurs, Everton put Liverpool to the sword at Anfield – sweet revenge for the recalled Sandy Brown after the previous December's own-goal episode. The Easter weekend saw Chelsea eviscerated 5–2 before Whittle scored the decisive goal at Stoke the following Monday. As Leeds stuttered with defeats to Southampton and Derby County, Everton were on the cusp of claiming the greatest domestic prize – just a victory in the upcoming midweek home match against West Bromwich Albion was required.

There is an added spark at Goodison Park when football is played under the floodlights. On the evening of 1 April 1970, with 58,500 shoehorned into the grand old stadium, not even the curious semi-demolition of the Archibald Leitch-designed Main Stand to make way for a triple-decker replacement could detract from the intense atmosphere. As an apprentice at the time, Stan Osborne recalls being in the privileged position of witnessing the dressing-room preparations before kick-off: 'There was a steely determination when we got up to the ground; you could sense that there was serious business at hand. It was fascinating, as a bystander, to study the team as they came into the room. The contrast was palpable: for Colin Harvey, Joe Royle and Johnny Morrissey it was just as if it was a practice game – they were so laid back with a few wise-cracks. This contrasted with Alan Ball who was full of enthusiasm and geeing people up. Then there were the likes of Sandy Brown and John Hurst who were a quiet brooding presence in the corner. Roger Kenyon was on edge as he was filling the boots of Brian Labone.

'It was interesting seeing Catterick, the way he went around the room. Having a quiet word with Alan Ball and exchanging a few words, light-heartedly, with Royle and Harvey. The he sat down and spoke quietly to Roger Kenyon and you could see it really did have a calming influence on him, as there was such a responsibility on the young player's shoulders. Likewise Gordon West, who was renowned for his nervousness before matches – again, a quiet word from Catterick steadied him. There was nothing planned, it happened very fluidly, organically – he just did his usual thing. Wilf Dixon was the main one who got them geed up and focused them on what the game-plan was. He said, "We've just got to do what we've done at home all season and that is to take the game to the opposition; our superior ability, fitness and tactical awareness will see us through." And that is what happened. Fifteen minutes or so before kick-off we were dismissed and I went up to the main stand. Goodison was just coming to the boil, the tension in the air, anticipation and then this crescendo of noise when the teams emerged.'

The match started edgily but Alan Whittle – who else? – settled nerves by pouncing on a blocked shot to give Everton a 19th-minute lead. With only a slender lead the crowd could not relax until, with 65 minutes on the clock, the ball was fed to Colin Harvey in the inside-left channel. The 'White Pele' feinted to go down the outside before twisting back onto his right foot and unleashing an unstoppable shot past John Osborne's despairing dive into the top corner of the Park End net. In that cathartic moment the Goodison faithful knew the title was returning to Liverpool 4. As the final whistle blew the grand old stadium erupted; a tidal wave of blue flooded onto the turf, sweeping up their heroes. Even Harry, usually poker-faced, was caught up in the moment, striding from the dugout to embrace each of his players.

Despite reports to the contrary before the match, the League trophy was presented to Alan Ball in the directors' box by Manchester United chairman Louis Edwards. A lap of honour followed – with the trophy remaining in the stand for safekeeping.

Afterwards the champagne flowed in the dressing room as players, management and directors toasted Everton and its affirmation of pure football. Stan Osborne recalls the scene: 'You could almost feel the euphoria along the corridor as you approached the dressing room. The great and the good were there – John Moores, Cecil Moores, members of the board and various photographers jostling for position.' The boss really was 'Happy Harry' as he soaked in the euphoria and smiled broadly.

The partying went on long into the night; in 2012 Evertonian Phil Bellis reminisced, on the Toffeeweb website, about meeting Harry in surreal circumstances after the match:

> We conga'd over to the Winslow pub and sang our hearts out. In strides Johnny Morrissey, gets himself a pint despite being overwhelmed with offers, and buys a round. After his pint, he gathers us together and marches us over to the Directors' Entrance opposite. The 'doorman' says, 'These young fellas can't go up the boardroom, John,' to which Moggsy responded, 'These young fellas pay your wages pal... and mine, so shift!' Up the stairs we went to mingle with the good and the great in the boardroom and be introduced to the likes of Labby, Alan Ball Snr, John Moores and Harry Catterick – by reputation and visage an aloof, stern man but not that night – he greeted us with a big smile, shook hands and thanked each of us, in turn, for our 'wonderful' support. We were kings that night, all of us, the extended Everton family.

Harry was ebullient as he held court to the press after the final whistle: 'They have won it by playing football, by applying their skills to the team as a whole. We have achieved our results with a freer expression of the game as opposed to method foot-ball. We don't play assassin stuff. We don't have players nobbling key players.'

Harry's point was telling. In an era where teams rejoiced in possessing hard men named 'Chopper', 'Anfield Iron' and 'Bite yer Legs', Harry's Everton provided the antidote: a cultured, slick style of football, at odds with the prevailing British mentality. That said, players such as Ball and Kendall could take care of themselves, while Morrissey could be deployed by Harry as a 'destroyer' when it was deemed expedient to do so – more often than not against Leeds.

Sportswriters, despite some antipathy towards Harry, could not deny the bril-liance of his team or the achievement of winning in such style. Colin Wood was at Goodison to see the coronation of Everton as League Champions that evening. He felt he was witnessing the dawn of a new era: 'I still rate the Everton team of 1970 as one of the best British teams I have ever seen. I remember writing in the *Daily Mail* after they had beaten West Brom that I had seen the team that would dominate football for the next ten years. It was a terrific team – very attractive and effective.'

For Harry it appeared to be the dawn of a new Everton era. Here was the realisation of a long-held plan to develop home-grown talent, blend it with a smat-tering of top-class acquisitions, and create an irrepressible and irresistible brand of football. Harvey, Kendall and Ball would rightfully receive the plaudits, but the core 14 players all played a significant role – none more so than Joe Royle, with his 23 goals, and Alan Whittle, with his galvanising impact on the second half of the season. The next day Harry told James Mossop: 'I said five years ago this boy would one day be a great player. He has flair and a sense of timing that is reminiscent of Jimmy Greaves. Look at the goal he scored against West Brom, the goalmouth was as busy as a main street but he had time to pick his spot and score.'

When asked to compare his two championship teams Harry said, 'They are two different types of side. Virtually all of the 1963 team was a side I got together by means of the transfer market and players I inherited here. The present side has been built by me through youngsters developing from school into top-class players and buys such as Kendall and Ball – great players.'

Other managers praised Harry's crowning achievement. Don Revie, on the night that Leeds were defeated by Celtic in the first leg of the European Cup semi-final, sent a telegram of congratulations. Dave Sexton, manager of Chelsea, who finished the league campaign in third position, saluted the achievement in the *Football League Book* of 1970: 'It is especially satisfying to be able to congratulate Everton... because they have exploited all the facets of the football game in which I have personally been... a great believer. Their achievement has been attained with a set of small players up front, with the exception of Joe Royle. Because of this lack of size and weight they have leaned heavily on midfield crafts supplied in crisp and snappy fashion by Alan Ball, Colin Harvey and Howard Kendall.'

In the same publication, Matt Gillies, who had succeeded Johnny Carey at Nottingham Forest, added: 'Everton last season were a smooth side, almost a pure footballing side. They have resorted to only the minimum of physical application and have injected the maximum possible offering of the delightful and sheer skills which make our game so attractive when played this way.'

The season ended with a further victory and a goalless draw, ensuring a club record Everton points haul of 66. However, there was a sting in the tail from the sportswriters. It was customary for the press to award the Bell's Manager of the Season award to the man at the helm of the league champions – but not this season. The award went to Don Revie. Bill Shankly, looking back with John Roberts in 1976, recalled being rankled by the snub to his great rival: 'I'm not saying anything against Don Revie, and Leeds United were great. But that year, though they had been involved in everything, Leeds won nothing. It must have been a terrible blow for a fellow like Harry who had just won his second championship.'

In the aftermath of the title win, Harry wrote a letter of thanks to John Moores and on 22 April John Moores sent a handwritten note in response. It reciprocated the gratitude while also putting down a marker down for future expectations:

> *Dear Mr Catterick,*
>
> *May I offer you my sincere congratulations on winning the League Championship but, more particularly, on producing one of the finest teams that has ever graced the Everton colours.*
>
> *I have watched Everton for nearly 50 years and I can't remember any team which has played so attractively and credit- ably as our present one.*
>
> *Let's hope that we will acquit ourselves well in Europe. I know if it depends on you we will be very successful.*
>
> *Yours sincerely,*
> *John Moores*

CHAPTER SEVENTEEN
THE HANGOVER

THE SPRING of 1970 was the happiest time of Harry's managerial reign. This stylish, modern team was the culmination of eight years' work at Everton Football Club. As he left Goodison that glorious April evening he could dream, with justification, of Everton – his team, with the Holy Trinity of Kendall, Harvey and Ball as the fulcrum – dominating both domestic and European football. Harry had been moved to declare, 'They have a long way to go before they reach their peak.' Chairman Jack Sharp and the directors moved to tie Harry to the club for the long-term and a new contract, worth approximately £12,000 per annum, was signed. However, unbeknown to Harry, the team had already reached its zenith.

Despite the euphoria of early April there was a nagging sense of trepidation in Harry's mind: the World Cup finals. Five Evertonians were expected to be selected for England duty 5,000 miles away in the heat of Mexico. Labone, Wright, Newton, Ball and West were all in Alf Ramsey's plans; no tears were shed by Harry when West, much like Labone had done in 1966, ruled himself out of the finals citing family reasons.

Harry's focus was always on club football and he found international fixtures an unwelcome distraction. Tony Kay had first-hand experience of Harry's priorities in 1963 as Everton closed in on the title. With two league fixtures remaining Kay was selected to make his senior England debut on 8 May against Brazil. Kay recalls: 'I was called to Harry's office. "Would you like the good news or bad news first?" he asked. "The good news is that you've been selected for England to play against Brazil; the bad news is you're injured." I asked if I had any choice in that and he said, "No, I need you for the league matches."'

Kay played in Everton's final two league fixtures; he would get to make a solitary England appearance later that year, scoring in an 8–1 victory over Switzerland. The following year Harry tasked Tommy Eggleston with dissuading Fred Pickering from going on an England tour of the Americas. Harry felt that Pickering should travel with his club team-mates on a post-season tour of Australia – ironically, Harry himself would not travel with the Everton party. Pickering ignored the advice and scored a hat-trick on his international debut.

In private, Harry would rail against the FA for 'carting no less than four of my players to the other side of the world', as David Exall recalled. 'Harry was cheesed off that four players had been chosen for England, it felt to him as if the FA was trying to strip Everton of players and bring down their level of achievement in the following season. He was actually right, if for all the wrong reasons. His fears over the effect on the quartet of long-distance travel, heat, high altitude and tough matches would prove well-founded, as the players were mentally and physically exhausted after their return.'

In spite of any misgivings, the team picked up where it had left off in April as Chelsea were defeated 2–0 in the Charity Shield curtain-raiser to the 1970/71 season. Whittle continued his scoring streak with a stunning shot when cutting in from the left flank. A second-half header from Kendall made the game safe.

As the league season started it was Alan Ball shaking hands with the referee in the centre-circle, having been handed the captaincy on a permanent basis after standing in for Labone during the title run-in. This decision was harsh on the incumbent who had led the team with distinction for six years, but Harry was keen to channel Ball's competitiveness and aggression more constructively in the hope of avoiding further brushes with the football authorities. He admitted to John Roberts that, with hindsight, the change in captaincy did not reap the desired results:

> At the time he was as good a skipper as we could get and I felt it would give him a greater sense of responsibility. I toyed with the idea as to how it would affect him. I had done it previously with Roy [Vernon] but it did not do as much good (with Alan) as I'd hoped, because he was already committed in any match. He was totally committed if playing darts or table tennis. He felt so much responsibility that he wanted to do more and maybe that affected his game a bit.

In contrast to a year earlier, the team could not get out of first gear. The terraces, having been spoiled with two years of glorious football, started to grumble as the team failed to record a victory in their first six league games. As winter approached the team found itself mid-table and Harry was unable to inspire a recovery. He recalled to John Roberts: '1970/71 was a great disappointment. Where a club has provided a number of players to a World Cup competition rarely in the following season do they do particularly well. A number of key players were involved in the World Cup and we missed out a bit on their contribution the following season; we hit the leanest spell in my time there.'

However, it was not just the World Cup quartet struggling to rediscover their footballing mojo. Whittle flattered to deceive and would only score a modest ten goals during the season. No other player, Joe Royle aside, would break into double figures. Jimmy Husband won back his place from Whittle on several occasions but suffered from hamstring injuries, the curse of pacy players. Neither Husband nor Whittle would again consistently hit their best form during the remainder of their Everton careers.

By late September Harry's patience was wearing thin. He had been tracking the progress of Preston North End's promising midfielder Archie Gemmill. Surreptitiously a gentleman's agreement was reached, and fee set, for Gemmill to move to Everton. However, the deal was to be scuppered by Brian Clough of Derby County, a young manager who loved the cut and thrust of the transfer market just as much as Harry. Clough, who Everton had sought to acquire as a player from Middlesbrough in 1958, was not a man to take 'no' for an answer. A delegation from Derby County met the Preston hierarchy, which included manager Alan Ball senior, at the Pack Horse Hotel.

Ball had the unappetising task of advising Harry that their gentleman's agreement was about to be ripped up – and it was made even more difficult by him not having Harry's home number. Late that evening *The Sun*'s Mike Ellis took a call made from the hotel by the Preston manager who whispered: 'I can't speak, Brian Clough is here for Gemmill, but I have promised him to Harry Catterick and I don't have his number.' Furnished with the number from Ellis, Ball delivered the news to a nonplussed Harry, who commented later to Charlie Lambert: 'It was an agreement between two clubs and that sort of thing is never broken.' That night Clough doorstepped Gemmill at his home, sleeping on his sofa before getting his signature on the contract over breakfast.

Foiled in his plans, Harry turned to Nottingham Forest's Henry Newton. Long before the days of squad rotation the new arrival begged the question: Which member of the 'Holy Trinity' would be making way and, by implication, leaving the club? After a brief, disastrous dalliance with playing Kendall in central defence, the regular midfield trio was restored and Newton never became fully established as a first-teamer. When not ill or injured, he often suffered the ignominy of covering at left-back – a waste of a considerable talent. He would return to East Midlands in

1973, going on to earn a League Champions medal with Derby County. The Gemmill and Newton scenarios suggested that Harry's Midas touch in the transfer market – for so long his strength – was beginning to desert him. Perhaps it was tighter budgeting by John Moores or increased competition from other clubs with money to spend and managers, like Clough, with a good line in sales patter.

In October 1970 Harry was hailed on the cover of *Charles Buchan's Football Monthly* magazine as 'A Manager for the Seventies'. Perhaps conscious that Moores might read the accompanying piece, Harry stated, perhaps with his fingers crossed behind his back: 'What can a manager do at a ground sitting behind his desk? He should be out with the players all the time because that's what he's paid for. The days of secretary-managers have gone, the two jobs are entirely separate. The manager is hired to manage the playing side – not the club.'

In reality Harry was more akin to a director of football, years before the phrase became commonplace in the British game. For Harry, his role was about having the grand vision for the team, the tactical blueprint and the facilities. Finally he would recruit the staff and players to deliver success. Harry Bennett sums the approach up: 'Harry Catterick was a brilliant organiser. He employed the best coaches he could to put across his basic ideas and then develop them. The conception was Catterick's, he wanted them to play a certain type of football which was different from the rest of the league – maybe a bit similar to Tottenham. It was a lovely way to play, a bit like the Spaniards do now. That team of Harvey, Kendall and Ball, plus Morrissey, was what Catterick wanted but the man who developed and implemented it was Wilf Dixon. Catterick was very clever, he revolutionised the training methods; every team at the club played exactly the same way from the B team to the first team, so when you reached the first team you weren't fazed. The reserves would play the first team for an hour every Thursday in the style of the next opposition – such as Liverpool, Burnley or Manchester United – so the first team would get a feel of how the opposition would have to be played.'

Perhaps by the early 1970s Harry had failed to move with the times. Howard Kendall and others felt that after the championship victory the training was becoming stale. Alan Ball would later opine that he wished Harry had employed a Malcolm Allison or a Bobby Robson-style tracksuit coach who could nurture and develop them as players. Just along the East Lancs Road, Allison had formed a partnership with Joe Mercer that would deliver domestic and European silverware. Perhaps Harry was loth to take on someone who might undermine his authority by being seen as his successor. The subsequent breakdown in the relationship between Mercer and the ambitious Allison gave credence to his reservations.

A beacon of light for Everton was the rapid progression of David Johnson, by now 19 years of age. He would make goalscoring debuts in the league, European Cup and both domestic knockout competitions. He remembers his progression to the first XI: 'Tommy Casey had been instrumental in getting me into the squad. I travelled to about six games to carry the skip and then wander onto the pitch for the big-match atmosphere experience. At Burnley I went into the changing room and the lads were starting to get changed. Harry Catterick stood there with the number nine shirt in his hand. As I was stood next to Jimmy Husband and Alan Whittle he threw it to me; I caught it and he said, "Put it on then." I had no chance to worry and scored on my debut.'

By default, rather than design, cup competitions had become the season's focus and one week in March would define not just the season but the future for the club. The European Cup trail had begun with a 9–2 aggregate win over Keflavik. Gary Talbot, the former Chester striker, had been appointed as the club photographer in 1969 and accompanied the team on their European excursions: 'I had a night out in Reykjavik with Harry, we went to quite a few bars, just him and me. As I'd played football before he thought of me as an ex-pro rather than a photographer.'

The next round brought, on paper, the sternest of tests in German champions Borussia Mönchengladbach. The away leg yielded an excellent 1–1 result, with Kendall grabbing the away goal. However, David Exall did note that on the trip Harry had complained of feeling unwell. Despite taking an early lead in the return leg, through a Morrissey cross-shot, the Germans equalised to level the tie. Extra time could not separate the teams and in the end it was an Andy Rankin save in Everton's first penalty shoot-out that secured progression to the quarter-finals. The subsequent draw appeared to be kind to Harry as Panathinaikos of Athens, managed by Ferenc Puskas, were the next opponents. A European Cup final at Wembley, and the chance to become only the third British team to lift the trophy, seemed a tantalisingly close prospect.

The FA Cup had also seen Everton smoothly progress to the quarter-final stage and a home tie against Colchester. The television cameras recorded the Blues recapturing much of their 1969 swagger, scoring five goals without reply – the perfect preparation for the first leg against the Greeks the following Tuesday. Harry knew that at least a two-goal cushion would be required to take to Athens, but Panathinaikos came to Goodison with a packed defence. Despite dominating the match Everton just could not finish, hitting the woodwork three times. Antoniadis delivered a late sucker-punch on 81 minutes with a goal at the Park End. Substitute David Johnson had come on to make his debut after Jimmy Husband had been poleaxed by a crude challenge from Domazos, and it was the European debutant who fired into the roof of the net with the last kick of the game to level the scores. Despite the relief about the equaliser the damage had been done – Panathinaikos had a precious away goal to take back to Athens.

Harry knew the magnitude of the task ahead and the 'welcome' that would await in Athens. David Exall recalls the expedition as being his worst in football: 'Athens was an absolute nightmare. The night before the Greek FA hosted an elaborate dinner in our honour at a posh, out-of-town restaurant by a marina. It was something like twelve courses; Harry didn't want to be there.'

Despite the intricate planning for the Greek expedition, which saw Everton bring their own food supplies to minimise the risk of food poisoning, the club had, inexplicably, booked the Aperghisa hotel in Kifissia on the outskirts of Athens. Exall continues: 'Bill Dickinson, the club secretary, was kept awake all night by people ringing him up. There was banging on doors, people shouting and cars hooting.'

The 25,000-capacity Leoforos stadium was packed, and thousands more watched from apartment blocks overlooking the pitch. The atmosphere was also unwelcoming to players and press corps alike, as Exall would discover: 'The generals were running Athens in those days and there was a lot of "security" around. Outside the ground I was accosted by Geoffrey Green of *The Times* – the "doyen of the British press". He and one or two other journalists had been rounded up as they were accused of not having the right credentials, which was rubbish, and they weren't going to be admitted to the press box. One guy started jabbing Green in the back with his gun. I managed to persuade this guy that they were genuine blokes and we made our way to the press box. Green never let me forget it and would always describe me as the "Angel of Athens"!'

Alan Whittle also has bitter memories of the trip: 'They were driving around the hotel all the time and when we went to the stadium beforehand there were six thousand people there just abusing us. It was rough. We battered them there, but they got away with murder.'

On the pitch things were not much better – the playing surface was dusty and uneven, far from conducive to Everton's preferred slick passing game. The wily Puskas had offered his team a hefty bonus should they win the tie. Knowing that they had the away goal the opposition did all in their power, legitimate or underhand, to stop Everton playing their natural game. Gary Talbot, pitch-side to capture photographs, offered encouragement to the team: 'I was near the goal-line and shouting to the players – stuff like "Man behind you!" – as I often did. When the crowd heard me shouting they started pelting me.'

On the bench the squad felt the ire of the home supporters. Substitute Roger Kenyon recalled in *Gwladys Street's Holy Trinity*: 'We were subjected to a torrent of Greek phlegm. From my experience on the subs bench Panathinaikos supporters were all heavy smokers who suffered from catarrh.' Fellow substitute David Johnson, sat next to Harry, recalls: 'With twenty-five minutes to go, Harry said, "Get on there and do exactly what you did at Goodison." But we drew nil-nil and we got knocked out.' In failing to score in the bear-pit, Everton went out on the away-goals rule. Harry was devastated and bitter in the immediate aftermath, stating to the press pack: 'All my players are injured because of the Greek tackling; even I was in danger sitting on the touchline. We should have had a penalty when Whittle was brought down and there were many debatable decisions.'

A number of the English contingent sensed that the refereeing of Frenchman Robert Héliès had been less than impartial. Reporting on the game for the *Liverpool Echo*, Michael Charters wrote of '…a nightmare atmosphere which revealed all the worst features of European football, with strange law interpretations by a referee which would never be countenanced in England.' No evidence of malpractice ever came to light but David Exall was one who harboured suspicions: 'Harry was very down about the whole thing. He went to his grave convinced that the referee for that game had been bought.' In the aftermath of the elimination from the cup Harry was asked by the press if Panathinaikos had played better than at Goodison. He replied: 'They had a better referee.' Regardless of the ill-feeling, there is no evidence to substantiate Catterick's suspicions and Héliès went on to have an illustrious refereeing career, and took charge of the following season's European Cup final between Ajax and Inter Milan.

After the Greek tragedy the demoralised party flew overnight into Manchester airport. During the flight, Harry was taken ill on board and the club doctor dashed down the aircraft aisle to give him an injection. The worrying episode was put down to 'a bug' but Harry would not return to the dugout for a fortnight. Some, including Royle, suspected something more significant was ailing Harry. Whatever the truth, it was a harbinger of health problems to come. In fact several of the party, including Wilf Dixon and David Johnson, were unwell with flu-like symptoms after the Athens trip. The latter had been pencilled in to play in the upcoming FA Cup tie but was declared unfit.

Rather than return home the squad stayed in Lymm and trained at Bellefield in preparation for the FA Cup semi-final against Liverpool at Old Trafford, decamping to a Blackburn hotel the night before the match – ironically because Liverpool had already booked the hotel in Lymm. Most players felt that keeping them away from their homes, where they could relax and recuperate rather than brood after Athens, was an error. The semi-final assumed much greater significance following the European exit – the FA Cup now offered Everton their only remaining route to silverware and entry into European competition the following season. Despite this Harry was nowhere to be seen in the hotel or on match day as he convalesced.

Bill Shankly most certainly was present as the Everton team headed for the dressing rooms. Joe Royle recounted in his autobiography the Liverpool manager indulging in some tasteless, yet highly effective, mind games: 'Hinting at surprise he asked, "Where's Harry?" Someone replied, "Oh, he's not very well, Bill, he isn't here." Shanks responded by saying, "Jesus! They would have to put a window in my coffin so I didn't miss this game."'

Despite Shankly's ploy and the bad omens, Everton got off to a flying start with Alan Ball striking a tenth-minute volley into the Stretford End net to put the Blues 1–0 up. The turning point was a pulled leg muscle suffered by Brian Labone – perhaps a reaction to the exertions on the bone-hard Greek pitch the previous Tuesday; a number of players including Morrissey and Whittle were carrying knocks. Substitute Sandy Brown came into central defence but struggled to cope with the height and power of John Toshack as Everton conceded two second-half goals; it would be Brown's final Everton appearance. Looking back with Charles Lambert in 1978, Harry pondered if his presence on the touchline might have tipped the tie in Everton's favour: 'Losing at Wembley (in 1968) wasn't as bad as losing in the semi-final as we did against Liverpool at Old Trafford. I am sure that, had I been there, I would have handled things differently when Brian Labone came off injured.'

In his autobiography Joe Royle described the two cup defeats within five days as 'the week the team died' and he had a point. The season petered out with a whimper – only one win in the last eight league fixtures resulted in a 14th-place finish – the lowest Harry had experienced as a manager. Before the season's curtain call against Blackpool Harry was in no mood for programme-notes platitudes and told David Exall, the editor: 'A bloody disgrace; print what you bloody like, you're having nothing from me!'

Exall had witnessed, with dismay, that season's decline at close quarters: 'Some played as many games in 1970/71 as they did in 1969/70 but they were just never able to perform at the level Harry knew they were capable of. It actually broke his heart; he failed to understand how the standards had fallen in what he felt was his greatest ever side. He never came to terms with that.'

Colin Wood concurs that Harry never recovered from the cup exits and the health scare: 'We knew he wasn't right after the Liverpool game at Old Trafford.

From then on we could tell from our dealings with him that he wasn't the same man or manager. We didn't get on with him but we still admired him as a manager – because the important thing was what happened on the football field and he produced some great teams.'

Harry, looking back with John Roberts on the season that had promised so much but delivered only disappointment, attributed the demise to the World Cup hangover and the complexity of the team structure: 'Some clubs lay down a system which you can easily duplicate each season, if you just have a big fellow up front and throw the ball up to him. But it is not easy to replicate if you build it on a highly skilful, complicated pattern as the team was then. When it disintegrates it is not easy to put back together. I felt that … we were held back by the World Cup and players had lost – albeit only temporary – their zest for the game.'

However, when interviewed in the club programme in 1971, Ball played down the impact of the Mexican exertions on his own form: 'Every footballer has a bad time occasionally, it just happened to be my turn last season. There was no question of being worn out by too much football… If there was a reason for me slipping below form it was more likely my groin injury. These things are very nagging and can put you off your game more than anything.'

Despite a summer of rest and recuperation the spark failed to return for the start of the 1971/72 season and only four wins were achieved by the end of October. The physical demands of the past decade were manifesting themselves in long-term injury problems to key players, Brian Labone, Johnny Morrissey and Tommy Wright all being afflicted. Their absence left the team bereft of much of its backbone; those seeking to fill the void were, despite their best endeavours, not of the same calibre.

Though few realised it, the break-up of the Holy Trinity was just around the corner. Colin Harvey had begun to struggle with niggling injuries linked to an undiagnosed (at the time) arthritic hip condition. He only managed 20 appearances in the entire season.

As Christmas 1971 approached, with Everton on the back of another winless streak, Harry made his boldest transfer gamble to date, dwarfing the sales of Bobby Collins and Roy Vernon. The news that Alan Ball was to be sold to Arsenal came out of the blue – even to club insiders such as David Exall: 'It was after midnight and I started to get calls from local journalists, saying that they'd got a "stringer" telling them that Alan Ball was being transferred to Arsenal. Did I know anything? The calls persisted so I didn't quite know what to do. Eventually, I rang Harry at home. He didn't say that it wasn't true but said that discussions might be starting in the morning. One or two journalists had mentioned about going to John Moores but Harry said: "I'll speak to him in the morning if I need to. Just play it dumb, say that you have no knowledge of such a thing and that if the club has anything to say it will comment in the morning."

'The phone kept ringing with people saying that they had it on good authority from London. In the morning it soon became clear that the story was true – in the main it was too late for the national papers but the air was alive with stories and phone blocked out with messages. By the middle of morning it was still not 100 per cent positive until I got confirmation from Harry's secretary, Jean, that the transfer was proceeding. The transfer was effectively without approval from on-high; maybe there was a fear of John Moores blocking it.'

The transfer bombshell had some logic. Ball's groin injury had continued to trouble him, causing him to miss matches and perhaps obliging him to play within himself for the very first time. By taking on a deeper midfield role Ball upset the equilibrium of the team and reduced his own goal output, just when it was needed more than ever. In his first four seasons at Everton he scored 12, 20, 19 and 12 goals – figures of which many forwards would have been proud. Yet in the season-and-a-half leading up to his departure he had managed just 11. In selling Ball, Harry recouped £220,000 for a player who had cost £110,000 five years previously. Ball, a perfectionist with a pathological hatred of losing, had become an increasingly frustrated figure as the team's form slumped – sometimes taking it out on colleagues.

Such was Ball's on-pitch brilliance that Harry had cut him more slack than virtually any player he had ever managed. David Exall remembers: 'Bally was always one who spoke his mind – he got away with things nobody else could. Other players, even Brian Labone, shrugged their shoulders as there was no point in arguing with Harry whereas Bally would keep niggling. Harry had made him captain – an act of appeasement which was unusual as not too many crossed him.'

Keith Newton, who would himself cross Harry due to a perception that he tarried on the ball, recalled in Jon Berman and Malcolm Dome's Everton Greats: Where Are They Now?: 'Alan was a fabulous player but by the time he left he'd driven us mad with his incessant moaning. I remember during one game at Elland Road we conceded a goal and Bally came racing back to have a right go at the defence. We just felt it was totally uncalled for and that he'd be better occupied getting back up the pitch and doing his own job. The fans obviously didn't see it that way but, with all due respect to him, Alan Ball wasn't very good for team morale.'

Howard Kendall would tell in his autobiography, Love Affairs and Marriage, of a training ground incident which may have been the catalyst for change: 'We were having a practice match that Wilf Dixon was in charge of. I'll always remember Wilf stopping the play and saying, "Alan, what's wrong with you?" He put his hands out and said, "How can I play with this lot?" Harry Catterick was standing behind the goal and I thought, "What's he doing out here?"... He went straight back to his office and I'm sure the deal was done to sell him to Arsenal that day.'

When interviewed on television some time later about Ball's exit Harry explained: 'Alan Ball had ceased to be the player he was for Everton for some reason or another. I believe the Mexico trip took an awful lot out of him there, and it may well be that only now is he starting to recover from that. This, allied to other players losing form, had a bearing on our overall performance. I had to make this decision, the form of the team had gone and Alan Ball wasn't showing signs of coming back to form. We had an offer near a quarter of a million and I felt it was good business to part with him.' Somewhat cryptically he added: 'There are other factors which I have never divulged which I can't go into here. I don't think it (the transfer) was so much a shock to the players.'

Although the players might not have been surprised by the skipper's exit, there was consternation on the terraces. As people tried to rationalise the sale of a world-class player who was still aged only 26, conspiracy theories sprung up. There were rumours, fuelled by Ball's move to Worsley for family reasons, that he'd been trying to engineer a move to Manchester United. Others speculated that the transfer was precipitated by Ball's alleged gambling debts. However, Ball would claim in his autobiography to be shocked at the turn of events:

> *I was out for two months because of a pelvic injury, for the first time I was feeling fallible. I was just getting my fitness and form back... Catterick motioned me to sit down, then he looked at me and said coldly: 'I have had an incredible bid for you, it is a British record transfer of £220,000 from a top side. Their manager is in that room down the corridor. I suggest you go and speak to him.' I was flabbergasted. 'No way' was my immediate thought. He said, 'It's business, son, I am doubling my money. I have had you for six years. I am making a profit on you and I have had an awful lot out of you. Football's business, son.'*

Harry's words, though brutally honest, should not have come as a total surprise. Interviewed by the *Sunday's Express*'s Alan Hoby in September 1967 he had stated: 'Football is a business. You've got to sell it like any other commodity. And, like any other business, there is no room for complacency.'

Looking back, David Exall agrees that the sale was a business one and not linked to anything more sinister: 'There was no sentiment in Harry – he felt we had got the best out of Ball, there was a good offer on the table and it was time to cash in. I got the impression at the time when Bally left it wasn't something that he [Ball] wished to happen. He was quite shocked that the club would sell him, I don't think he had agitated for it.'

The problem with the transaction is best summed up by Howard Kendall: 'How do you replace Alan Ball?' In the previous decade Harry had proactively bought and sold star players in order to improve the overall standard of the team – now he appeared to be reacting to circumstances. When Alan Ball walked out of Bellefield for the last time there was no superstar replacement lined up, nor was there a home-grown prodigy ready to break through as Colin Harvey had in 1963. The Bellefield production line continued to produce first-team players into the 1970s, such as Cliff Marshall, Peter Scott, Steve Seargeant and the mercurial Gary Jones. Sadly, few had the raw talent or drive of a Hurst, Royle, Husband or Wright. Mick Buckley, a slight but skilful midfielder who was highly rated by Harry, might have prospered in a more successful team but he suffered from being compared to those that had gone before him.

George Telfer was one such local lad, signed by Harry, who would break into the first team in the early 1970s. His early impressions of Bellefield life suggested that the boss had not softened with age: 'Harry signed me on as an apprentice in 1970 and as a full-time professional in 1972. I was with Mick Buckley, Ronny Goodlass, Ken McNaught and Cliff Marshall. On my first day at Bellefield it was pre-season training. I was just turned fifteen and I was just back from a school trip to Austria. I went straight into training and I was absolutely knackered. Mr Catterick called me over and said, "What's the matter with you, son?" and I said, "Errr, I don't know what you mean." "You were labouring. Do you know what that means?" he added. I was absolutely terrified.'

Telfer would soon learn of the exacting standards Harry set for players at all levels in the hierarchy: 'I remember playing in an A team game away against Fleet-wood reserves. They were a team of huge dockers and we got beaten. They kicked us off the park basically – it was a terrible game. We used to get marked out of ten by the coach, Jack Connor, and we all got given a "two".

'On the Monday morning we were summoned to the manager's office so we all had to go in individually. Harry said to me, "What was the problem on Saturday?" and I said, "It just wasn't a very good game, boss. They were big and trying to kick us off the park." "That's not really an excuse, you should be able to match these people. Do you want to make it, or would you rather become a bricklayer?" was his response. I just looked at him and thought, "Oh dear." He was very intimidating and frightening – we all came out sweating. Mr Catterick was a really intimidating gentleman.

'For our punishment, for three weeks, we had to come back every Tuesday and Thursday night to train with the amateurs. We also had to stay an extra hour every afternoon. It was a boot camp. The punishment for the extra training was what they called the Hurdle Circuit. When the Hurdle Circuit went up even the first-team players turned white. You used to have to do it in under a certain time and you were virtually vomiting at the end of it – you had to do six lots! All that after training in the morning, cleaning boots and then training in the afternoon. When I think about it now, we were still children. Now there'd be child protection policies, but we thought nothing of it in those days and just got on with it.

'I remember the only time Harry ever praised me was when I played for the youth team against Bristol City in 1971, and I destroyed them that night. Harry came up to me and said, "I thought you did really well tonight. I want to see that improvement continue." I thought, "Oh my God, that's unbelievable, I've had some praise off him."'

After the blood, sweat and tears Telfer was rewarded with a professional contract as a 17-year-old in 1972: 'Harry took me into his office. Tommy Eggleston and Harry then gave me a pep talk and told me I was being signed as a pro, which was nice. I was thrilled to bits at the time. My first time with the first-team squad was Birmingham City, away, in September 1972. I was the thirteenth man, sat on the bench next to Harry. He wasn't that vocal really – he wasn't a shouter. I made my debut in December 1973 against Arsenal after Harry had left – Alan Ball scored for them.'

Ronny Goodlass was, along with Stan Osborne and Mick Buckley, a year behind George Telfer on the apprentice scheme. He recalls the two sides of Harry: 'The Catt signed me for Everton and was a man who had a fearsome reputation, which he lived up to. He ruled Bellefield with an iron fist and even first-teamers were very wary of him. He was very intimidating and when he spoke, you listened. The other side to him was that when you played well, progressing through the Everton teams, A, B and reserves, and he said how good you were doing, it made you feel good and you wanted to do better. The Catt liked to give kids a chance. On 5 August 1970, there was the traditional game between the first team and the reserves played at Goodison Park before the season started. I was sub for the first team and went on for the second half for Johnny Morrissey. We were kicking into the Gwladys Street End and the crowd were fantastic and really supportive to me. We won 7-1; The Catt said I played really well. It was a great experience for a sixteen-year-old.'

CHAPTER EIGHTEEN
EVERTON EXIT

GUT-WRENCHING though 1971 had been, the following year would prove to be Harry's annus horribilis: Everton's downward spiral continued, he suffered a family bereavement and had severe health issues.

Talking to the *Daily Mail*'s Ronald Crowther in 1975, Harry would describe the high expectations upon him at Everton: 'I don't think that with any other club in the country there would be greater pressure than there was at Everton. They demand a very high standard. Most top clubs are demanding but Everton especially so.' On the same theme he told journalist Martin Leach in 1976: 'As a manager you're given wonderful facilities, a good stadium. You're then expected to produce results. It's certainly the test of a man's character – if anybody sticks it for ten years he's proved himself.'

Everton's woes had placed huge pressure on a man not accustomed to sharing his feelings with others. In the 1970 article 'Mr Success' Harry alluded to the pressures that he chose to shoulder alone: 'I don't have anyone sitting by my side, holding my hand. The decisions that matter are the ones that only I can make – the team selection and whether I can sign a player. I make the decisions, I carry the can.' The day after the championship was clinched in 1970 Harry gave a candid interview to James Mossop in which he touched on his personality. The conversation highlighted that whereas Bill Shankly didn't let family life get in the way of football, Harry tried to live by the opposite credo:

> *There has been pressure but I have always tried hard not to show it. I am not an emotional person. I am able to keep things bottled up and feel it is imperative that I don't show any sign of anxiety to young players. If I have to get rid of tensions somewhere I tend to take it out on the golf that I am tending to play more – at least once a week. My friends are mainly in business, they are not*

162

really interested in football, except that they are anxious to know
of the team's progress. It suits me perfectly; I would rather listen
and talk about textiles when I am away from the ground.

One person asking questions would be John Moores and it was not unheard of for Harry to receive a call on a Sunday morning from 'Mr John' requesting his presence in Freshfield to review the previous afternoon's match.

With married life becoming increasingly strained, there seemed to be no escape from the pressures of the job, which were exacerbated by the long hours and, by his own estimate, up to 40,000 miles driven around the country on business. The stress showed in his dealings with work colleagues, who found Harry increasingly distant and aloof. Speaking to Charles Lambert in 1976 he explained the strains on his health, and hinted at the effects of his estrangement from his second wife Nancy:

> *Unfortunately I didn't have a philosophy to help when the going*
> *got tough. I had other problems apart from the domestic ones,*
> *but I feel that a very happy domestic life must be a great cushion*
> *against the stresses. You can't get away from the game; if you go*
> *out on a Saturday night there are always people wanting to talk*
> *shop. As compared with a business executive a football manager*
> *presents a balance sheet every Saturday in terms of the result and*
> *the eleven selections he has made. He can get ten out of eleven*
> *and in most standards of business that is good; but in football*
> *it is bad.*

Without the safety valve of someone to share his worries the burden became intolerable. After a scouting mission to Scotland, to look at Hibernian's Alex Cropley, matters came to a head as Harry drove home from Sheffield on the wintry evening of 5 January 1972. He told John Roberts: 'I knew the routes like the back of my hand and I elected to come over Mam Tor which was the quieter route. I felt somewhat tired but that was nothing new considering my work schedule. I was pushing myself harder and harder to get Everton out of this awful run of luck.'

In 1977 Harry wrote a detailed piece about the incident for *Hope*, the magazine of the Chest, Heart and Stroke Association:

> *I was crossing the high parts of the Pennines when I suddenly*
> *began to feel hot and perspiring, then I was shivering followed by*

an acute pain across my chest and down my left arm. I decided to pull up on a desolate hillside lay-by and get in the passenger seat. Three or four minutes later, lying back in the seat, I felt a little bit better.

I was in a desperately lonely spot but knew this country-side well from my days at Sheffield Wednesday. I had a mental image of two cottages two or three miles away over the hill. I set off in the car again, still in excruciating pain. Luckily the car was automatic so I could drive just using my right hand; my left arm was quite useless. A light from one of the cottages shone through the gloom and light snow as I ran the car onto the verge. I struggled to the cottage and hammered on the door where, by the grace of God, I was greeted by a district nurse. That could have saved my life.

It was then that I realised I was having some sort of heart attack. The son of the house helped me onto the settee whilst his mother telephoned a doctor. He came within fifteen minutes and quickly made the diagnosis – a coronary. The pain was still crip-pling and the doctor gave me injections. An ambulance arrived from Sheffield in the thick of traffic from a cup-tie. I was feeling terribly cold despite the many blankets; during the journey men lay alongside me to give me body heat.

Roughly one and a half hours after the first symptoms had struck I was in the intensive care unit of the Royal Sheffield Hospital, there to stay for six days where I was treated with great efficiency and kindness. The doctors believed it was caused by the amount of driving I was doing.

Harry would spend over two months recuperating in hospital, a Liverpool nursing home and at the family home in Ainsdale. The episode was a huge knock to his confidence. Being advised to take only limited exercise was a further blow, as he recalled in *Hope*: 'Having been a trained athlete who believed in taking exercise, the world seemed to collapse around me.'

David Exall says the club went into media lock-down once journalists became aware that Harry was ill: 'The first I heard of it was in the middle of the night when Colin Wood, one of the press lads, rang me. It was absolutely hushed-up, the Little-woods machine sprang into action and the word came out that nobody was to make any statement about Mr Catterick's illness or absence but to refer any enquiries to a damage-control expert in the Littlewoods organisation. It was suggested that he was merely suffering from respiratory problems. It was some time before the truth of Harry's heart attack was formally acknowledged.'

In Harry's absence the team went into freefall; coach Tommy Casey was assigned to oversee first-team matters but his traditional training methods and tactics were anathema to the likes of Kendall, Harvey and Royle. Roger Kenyon recounted to Steve Zocek: 'Tommy Casey used to say, "If in doubt, kick it up the hey-diddle-diddle.' That was his instruction to you.' The club would only win three times from Harry's attack to the end of the season.

While Harry was convalescing the club made one of the most bizarre signings in its history. Bernie Wright, a burly striker for Walsall, had made an impression on Harry Cooke in a FA Cup encounter. Within days Wright was signed – Harry must have had a shock when he met 'Bernie the Bolt' on his return to work. Wright would only make ten appearances for Everton; his best-remembered on-field contribution was breaking an opponent's toe with his head.

By February, Harry was taking his first tentative steps to recovery back home in Ainsdale. Initially only able to walk the length of the driveway, accompanied by his pet labrador dog, he would increase the length of their walks day by day. Finally he was able to reach the seafront, a mile away – an achievement he recalled in *Hope*: 'When I reached the beach under my own steam I felt like Christopher Columbus discovering a new continent. You cannot imagine how much it meant to me.'

Despite his enforced lay-off Harry was monitoring the situation at Goodison and Bellefield. Joe Royle, suffering with fitness issues and loss of form, had found himself dislodged from the first team. Royle recalls: 'I was having a bad time. I had a call from Harry Cooke to say that Harry wanted to see me at his house. When I got there Harry asked, "What's going on, why aren't you in the team?" Harry was only sympathetic to me and very honest. Then I played in the reserve team and scored a couple against Manchester United.'

Aware, from Harry Cooke and others, of the mess unfolding at Everton, Harry steeled himself to return to his day job without further delay. One of his first acts was to accompany Harry Cooke to Carlisle on 16 March to tie up the signing of John Connolly. Perhaps the signing of St Johnstone's coveted forward came too late but, four years later, Harry affirmed his high regard for the Scot: 'John Connolly has an abundance of skill. For me he comes out of the top drawer, he was one of my best signings.' One of Connolly's early Everton duties was to join his new team-mates at Stockport's Strawberry Studios to record a Graham Gouldman-penned song called

'Forever Everton'. The song, still played at Goodison Park to this day, contained the refrain: 'Everton's the team that plays beautiful football'. Sadly, nothing could have been further from the truth at the time.

Harry returned to his Bellefield desk in late March and was greeted by well-wishing cards from around the football firmament. Bill Shankly added a personal touch, as John Keith recounted in Colin Harvey's memoirs: 'There was the sound of footsteps up the spiral staircase to Catterick's Bellefield office, a knock on the door and the arrival of Shankly with a cup of soup. "Here you are, Harry, hope you're better,' he declared. 'Now, how much do you want for Joe Royle and David Johnson?'

The return to work was premature. Harry would acknowledge to John Roberts that it took 18 months for him to feel fully recovered from the heart attack: 'I was too soon back in harness to be the power I should have been. In my absence things had got out of hand and I couldn't pick the pieces up as soon as I wanted.'

Moores, looking back with John Roberts in 1977, would admit his own error of judgement: 'After Harry was ill we were slow in reacting to the situation. The specialist told us Harry would be fine if we got him a driver and took some of the weight off his shoulders, so we let him soldier on. In retrospect we made a big mistake, because the team fell apart.'

Moores spoke in the same vein to Charles Lambert in 1976: 'Football is a harsh business. It may sound cruel but we should have moved Harry sideways and appointed a new manager right away. A man of over fifty with heart trouble just can't cope. Being a manager is a demanding job and only a person who is utterly committed twenty-four hours a day and is willing to burn himself out for the club can survive.'

Harry's return to duties could not stop the rot and the team finished the 1971/72 season in 15th place, with a meagre league goal tally of 37. The close season would see significant changes behind the scenes and in the playing staff – much of it unavoidable as age and injury decimated the title-winning squad of two years earlier. The season had seen key members of the squad succumb to career-threatening injuries. Brian Labone, the cultured centre-half and bedrock of the Catterick years, admitted defeat in a long battle with an Achilles injury – he had made only 20 league starts since the World Cup finals. Johnny Morrissey struggled with a similar complaint and was transferred to Oldham in the summer of 1972. Tommy Wright's appearances became more sporadic due to knee problems, which would end his career prematurely the following season. Colin Harvey, meanwhile, began to experience pain associated with a degenerative hip condition. He, like Joe Royle with his back complaint, was unable to withstand sustained periods of playing.

That summer £140,000 of the Alan Ball transfer money was invested in Stoke City's burly midfielder Mike Bernard – a solid if unspectacular midfielder who could not hold a candle to Ball. Replacing a legendary goalkeeper is a thankless task, as successors to the likes of Ted Sagar, Neville Southall and Peter Schmeichel have discovered. With Gordon West no longer an automatic choice, and Andy Rankin not convincing Harry that he would be more than a stop-gap, Harry turned to David Lawson. Signed from Huddersfield Town for £80,000, a record fee for a goalkeeper, Lawson would never scale the heights that West had done.

In November 1971, Wilf Dixon had been moved from the role of first-team trainer to manage the youth set-up; he left for Hull City a short time later. His eventual replacement was a familiar face. While recuperating in a Liverpool nursing home from what the club programme always referred to, euphemistically, as his 'illness', Harry received a visit from Tommy Eggleston. Eggleston, back from a spell managing abroad, told the club programme: 'Harry and I were such old pals that one of the first things I did on returning from Greece was to see him in hospital. Harry mentioned that he was looking for someone to re-organise the youth set-up. Harry asked me if I was interested and it didn't take long for me to accept.'

With Harry still fragile, and an experienced hand required on the training pitch, a decision was promptly taken to promote Eggleston to assistant manager, the first holder of the post at Everton. Eggleston commented in a 1972 Everton programme: 'I was just getting into the meat of the job when Harry came to me with a new offer: "Would I like to be assistant manager?" I was delighted; I knew that we would get on well.'

Eggleston quickly diagnosed a malaise gripping the first team: 'Football can sometimes go out of the window. The players were particularly low and it was our job to give them new motivation. They needed lifting, the lads really wanted to get back to their old style, they wanted to express themselves and that, to an Everton player, means attacking.'

In further changes Stewart Imlach, the former Scottish international left-winger, was promoted to become first-team coach in place of Tommy Casey while Eric Harrison came on board to develop the youngsters. Harrison was an inspired choice, proving that Harry, though struggling to recruit players of the highest calibre, had not completely lost his ability to source talent. Harrison would spend eight years at Everton, nurturing future stars such as Mark Higgins, Kevin Ratcliffe, Gary Stevens and Steve McMahon, before moving to Manchester United and bringing through their golden generation of the 1990s.

In late May came the news that Harry's father, such an influence on his life, had lost his long battle with cancer at the age of 74. Harry's mother Lillian would subsequently move in with Harry in Ainsdale before choosing to return to the familiar surroundings of Stockport.

Harry's capacity to surprise was illustrated when he received a wedding invitation from Alan Whittle in the summer. Whittle and his fiancée Jeanne were compiling the invite list: 'Because I thought that it was the right thing to do, with the team having done well under him, I went to Brian Labone and said, "Skip, I'm going to invite the boss." Labby turned round to me and said, "The boss won't like that… he'll refuse." Then Jeanne's mum and dad, who had sent out the invites, got a reply back which stated: "Mr and Mrs Catterick would love to come to your wedding".'

In a bid to steady the listing ship, John Moores had re-installed himself as Everton chairman prior to the start of 1972/73 season. He understood that this would be the final opportunity to turn things around under the existing managerial regime. In his programme notes for the season's opening home fixture he spelled out what was expected of the team and, by extension, Harry:

> *I have been disappointed by Everton's play in the last two years. Not so much because we tumbled from the peak of winning the Championship in 1970 but because we were no longer playing good football. There were grumblings in the Board Room… it is against this background that I agreed to become Chairman again. I was concerned about the tragic situation where Everton had departed from the days when Goodison was known as the 'School of Science'. I firmly believe that Everton can, and will, return to the style for which we are respected. There is a feeling of confidence in the air again. It stems from the happy news that Mr Catterick is able to resume full control and it is good to see Mr Tommy Eggleston back as Assistant Manager.*

The gauntlet had been thrown down – 'Improve results and improve the quality of entertainment' – two things not always compatible for a struggling team.

One forward-thinking initiative, instigated by John Moores, had been announced in the match-day programme at the end of the previous season: 'Everton have commissioned the Department of Physical Education at Liverpool Polytechnic to carry out an extensive research project aimed at providing an accurate assessment of mental and physical demands on players at all levels. It will employ methods

widely used in American ball games and in soccer, as in certain Iron Curtain coun-
ties.'

Harry was quoted in the match-day programme: 'As far as fitness, recovery
from injury etc. are concerned, a manager or coach must rely almost entirely on his
own experience in the game on making any decisions. Any advice based on truly
scientific techniques must be of irresistible value and I regard this idea as one of the
most exciting experiments in British football.'

The man heading up the project was Dr Vaughan Lancaster-Thomas. He recalls: 'I had just got my PhD as a sport scientist – sports science did not really exist
then in England but it did in East Germany. Everton were not having a good time;
I got a message to John Moores that I was the "international expert" in getting performance from sportsmen. Moores invited me to dine at his offices and was quite
intrigued. He provided a sum of money on the condition that I investigated the
Everton team, how they played the game, and came up with recommendations.

'With [my colleague] Tom Reilly on board we did a lot of physiological and
psychological testing of players in a laboratory. They monitored training sessions
and matches, and tested the players to destruction. The squad was the least fit set of
sportsmen I had ever encountered, so we gave them some pointers as to what to do.
It was general throughout soccer, so I wouldn't blame Harry Catterick. I had another
colleague join me called George Wilkinson, who was a soccer researcher, he analysed
matches.

'Everton had no idea how far anyone would run in a game or how many
sprints were made and they had no idea of the physical demands of the game. There
was no study as to where goals came from. We started to film their games, we really
did an awful lot and it had a tremendous effect – there was an immediate improvement in the team.

'We produced reports and talked directly with Stewart Imlach whose job it
was to convert the information into the delivery of training.'

The programme ended during Billy Bingham's tenure as Everton manager but
the work being pioneered would become the norm in British football 20 years later.
Reilly, a native of County Mayo, fell in love with Everton during the project. He became the UK's first ever Professor of Sports Science at Liverpool Polytechnic, which
subsequently became Liverpool John Moores University in 1992. Reilly passed away
in 2009 but his legacy is that the university remains at the forefront of sport and
exercise scientific study.

With a revamped management and coaching structure, new signings, and a
more scientific approach to preparation and analysis, it appeared that Moores' op-

timism might prove to be well-founded. Mike Beddow, who wrote for the club programme, observed: 'The pre-season build-up was perhaps the most important in many years. Apart from the usual stress on top-line fitness many hours were set aside for talks with the players and this was carried on during the important trip to Sweden.'

The 1972/73 season started as if the previous two years had not happened. After the disappointment of the injury-hit previous season in which he had managed only nine goals, Joe Royle was back in form. His six goals in the opening eight league fixtures helped an unbeaten Everton to top spot in the table. In his first full season John Connolly was making an impression as a fast, skilful, wide-striker with an eye for goal. Colin Harvey, benefitting from rest and a revised training schedule, was able to put his hip problems in abeyance and would, until Christmas, be an ever-present alongside the invaluable captain, Howard Kendall. Harry, and Evertonians, could dare to dream that, in spite of everything, the corner had been turned.

However, the team's form eroded in the early autumn and lingering hopes were dashed by a serious back injury sustained by Royle at Sheffield United in October. The debilitating ailment would end his season and threaten his career. A trip to a specialist in Glasgow failed to remedy the disc problem so the forward, still only 23 years old, was given the stark choice of undergoing risky and radical disc surgery or retiring from football. Royle opted for what he judged the lesser of the two evils but complications from the operation necessitated a follow-up procedure; it would be the summer of 1973 before Royle was fit enough to take part in any meaningful training.

Without Royle's goals and physicality the team started to splutter. The onus for scoring goals was expected to fall on Alan Whittle, yet he only made a further three appearances before being shipped out to Crystal Palace. He reflects: 'Harry wanted changes again. I got a call from him to come to the ground, Bert Head was there with him and that was it. They had done the deal beforehand, they were in control.' Sadly, the starlet had not maintained the stunning progress made between 1968 and 1970, adding only 15 goals to his tally since that heady night in April 1970. Harry would lament to John Roberts: 'Alan was probably the most talented boy I ever had at sixteen years old. He never quite did it. Everyone thought he was overconfident but he wasn't really. He was really nervous about his game but came across as cocky, sharp and probably in too much of a hurry. I felt he didn't do as well as he could have done. But in the championship season he came in and got nearly a goal a match in those last twelve games.'

More baffling to onlookers was the deal that saw David Johnson swap Merseyside for Suffolk, with journeyman Rod Belfitt and £40,000 coming in the opposite direction. Ipswich certainly got the better of the deal – while Johnson went on to gain full England honours and earn a transfer to the red side of Merseyside, Belfitt made only 19 appearances before exiting Goodison. Johnson recalls: 'Once Harry said, "You're going to Ipswich – you are no longer in my thoughts," that was it – end of. There was no option to stay and fight for my place. Football then had a big centre-forward of six-foot-one against a fifteen-stone centre-half – that's how it was. Me, at five-foot-eleven and ten-stone-four, did not fit the profile. It was quite obvious once I was at first-team level that it was a mismatch against the likes of Mike England or Ron Yeats. Maybe that's why Harry looked at Rod Belfitt being a better replacement for Joe Royle than me. Bobby Robson at Ipswich was happy to use two mobile strikers, not necessarily down the middle but using the flanks, and that was the making of me.'

A last roll of the dice, partly funded through the sale of Whittle, was the record £180,000 capture of Aberdeen forward Joe Harper. At only 5ft 6in Harper was a poacher who relied on a centre-forward alongside him to do the donkey work and create chances with aerial knock-downs. Royle's prolonged injury absence would decree that Harper's effectiveness in the team would be severely compromised. Howard Kendall was one of the few to retain the standards set three years earlier – in fact many credit him with keeping the team out of a relegation struggle during Harry's final season.

An incident in December 1972 involving Bernie Wright illustrated the sad state of affairs. David Johnson recalls: 'We all got hampers from the Moores family before Christmas. Bernie had played in the first team and got a deluxe one with wine and spirits inside. The idea was you'd take it home but Bernie must have drunk the contents. He was absolutely hammered and turned up at Bellefield in a drunken state and wanted to have it out with Harry. Gordon West tried to walk him away, but he punched Stewart Imlach. Harry's office was down a corridor from the canteen – it had a fire escape so if he wanted to avoid anybody he could disappear down it. When Bernie went to the front door Harry could be seen going down the outside staircase to his car; he wasn't having any of it.' Wright's contract was terminated after he went AWOL for a number of days following his drunken rampage. With that Wright's Everton career was terminated and he returned to the West Midlands.

A brief upturn in form over the festive period was nullified by a crushing fourth round FA Cup exit at home to Second Division Millwall. At the final whistle, as seat cushions and vitriol rained down from the stands, the writing was on the wall. Even the *Liverpool Echo*'s Michael Charters ventured in print that Harry was on borrowed time. Patience was exhausted; the silverware garnered in past years was forgotten. The supporters turned on the manager with whom they had never enjoyed a particularly close bond. In February, responding to the discontent, John Moores spelt out his own frustration to the local press: 'We should have the best team of the lot. That is what we are aiming for and that is what we mean to get.'

John Moores knew that he had a decision to make but he was loth to dispense with a man he trusted and respected. On the other hand he could see that Harry was a sick man, gaunt and increasingly remote, seemingly with the weight of the world on his shoulders. He could no longer inspire – or even scare – his players to reach the required levels of performance. Once it was decided that a change was needed the board members had to decide whether to pay Harry off with a 'golden handshake' or find a means of accommodating him in a new role for the remaining three-and-a-half years on his Everton contract. After deliberation by the directors, loyalty won out.

The decision to move Harry out of the firing line became public on 11 April 1973 as Everton prepared to travel to the Hawthorns for a midweek fixture (ironically, the previous Saturday had seen a rare victory as a Harper brace saw off Coventry). It was announced that Harry would move to another role, yet to be defined.

The *Daily Post* reported:

> At 2pm Harry Catterick himself told the players that he had ceased to be the club manager. Thirty minutes later a club statement dropped onto the desk of club spokesman David Exall and was issued to the press: 'Everton are pleased to announce that they have reached agreement with Mr Catterick under which he will continue to serve the club for the term of his present contract, but will act in a senior executive capacity not responsible for team selection and management. This will free the position of club manager and the board invites applications to fill this appointment. The directors wish to place on record their appreciation to Mr Catterick for his excellent service. We are happy that Mr Catterick can continue to make a contribution to the success of Everton.

Harry, when asked for comment, stated, 'It is a heavy blow after being a manager for more than twenty years. But I believe that this great club, with many splendid players, will continue to have success. I hope my successor is as successful in the next decade as I was in my first ten years at Everton. The decision has not been taken on health grounds, the doctors have cleared me completely.'

That evening Harry and Moores sat side by side in the stand as West Bromwich Albion hammered Everton 4–1. Tommy Eggleston became caretaker manager for the final six fixtures, with some input from Harry, but the team won only once. After an away defeat at Derby's Baseball Ground on the final day of the season David Exall noted that a weight appeared to have been lifted from Harry's shoulders: 'I can categorically state that it was a strangely relaxed Harry who travelled home from his final game.'

Tribute to Harry was paid, in a slightly back-handed fashion, by his old sparring partner Bill Shankly, speaking to John Roberts: 'Harry's record speaks for itself. He has shown shrewd judgement when it comes to assessing players. The combination of Harry and John Moores has been formidable. But opposition can be a good thing – it made me fight harder.' In their decade of going toe-to-toe neither manager had been able to deliver the knockout blow. By the end of the 1972/73 season Liverpool had secured their third league title under Shankly, compared to Harry's two, while both won an FA Cup. In league encounters they would each win eight derbies with six ending in stalemate.

Harry's record also stands comparison with his rivals. In the 1960s his Everton and Sheffield Wednesday teams accumulated more top-flight points than those managed by Revie, Busby, Clough, Nicholson, Shankly and Mercer. On a points per game basis Revie came out on top, followed by Shankly and Nicholson. But the statistics themselves don't do justice to Harry and the players who graced Goodison in that golden era. Those lucky enough to have seen the class of 1969/70 remain convinced there has been no better British footballing side since.

David Exall speaks for many when he says: 'It was just like poetry in motion. I get quite tearful even now when I think back to how good they were and how brilliantly they played.'

CHAPTER NINETEEN
'UPSTAIRS'

ONCE RELIEVED of his managerial duties there was some uncertainty as to what Harry's new role at the club would be or who might replace him. Having signed a contract extension late in 1967, Harry had intimated to J.L. Manning that, by 1974, he would be grooming a successor. This intention may have been quietly shelved when Harry signed a further extension taking him through to 1977, or perhaps the health problems of the early 1970s had disrupted his succession planning. Harry's regime at Bellefield had not nurtured a clear line of succession, in contrast to Anfield's boot room. Whereas Bill Shankly would be succeeded from within by Bob Paisley, Joe Fagan and, later, Roy Evans, Everton were obliged to cast the net wider.

Press speculation linked Brian Clough with the job but the chances of the Everton board countenancing a move for someone perceived as a maverick were extremely slim. Having failed to lure Harry's nemesis Don Revie and the avuncular Jimmy Armfield to Goodison, Moores turned to erstwhile Everton winger Billy Bingham. Understandably Bingham, who genuinely was a tracksuit manager, preferred to have Harry, his boss from his playing days, a safe distance from team affairs. The role agreed on for the deposed manager was 'consultant'; in effect this entailed attending matches and filing scouting reports. 'I was offered a form of consultancy which was a form of semi-retirement. I didn't like it, but one has to accept,' Harry told the *Lancashire Evening Post* in 1977.

Despite some rancour at being side-lined, the break from day-to-day pressures did help Harry recuperate physically and mentally. In an article penned for the Liverpool *Daily Post* in 1976 he reflected on the stresses and expectations in the Everton hot-seat:

> *I didn't find the pressure of Liverpool over-great; if anything*
> *Liverpool provided a bit of inspiration. There was never a*
> *period when I could relax, most of the pressure came from the*

directorate which was very ambitious. There is nothing wrong with ambition but there was a great desire to win everything. The directorate demanded a lot more success than any other club I had been with. The game is highly demanding, you've got four groups of people: The players, the public, the media and the directors. I never had the feeling, at Everton, that I could miss out on anything. I never felt you could say, 'We're going through a lean spell, we will live through it and come good again. I felt you had to be coming good all the time, and that was pressure from the fans too. We achieved success in 1963, 1966, 1968 and 1970 but there was always another Everest to climb.

The *Daily Mail*'s Colin Wood visited Harry in Ainsdale five months after his removal from the manager's position. He found him in reflective mood: 'I am still involved in the game; in fact I am probably watching more games now than when I was manager. Apart from looking out for new players I watch the opposition that Everton will face weeks ahead and report to Billy Bingham. In some ways I miss the day-to-day involvement but still go in two to three times a week.'

Much of the time freed up by the role change was spent on the golf links – something that had been more difficult when he was manager: 'As far as golf goes, my new life is certainly helping. While I was manager at Everton, and particularly in these last few years, I didn't have much time for the game. I didn't want to play on a Sunday because at my local club, Southport and Ainsdale, there always seemed to be an inquest on Everton's match the day before. When I started to take the game seriously again my handicap had gone up to sixteen, now it's down to ten.'

When Harry's removal from the manager's seat was made public he was asked by Michael Charters if he would seek employment as a manager elsewhere: 'I don't think so, I don't think I could get the same sort of money elsewhere. I am happy to have been asked to continue to serve the club and I will be pleased to do so in any capacity.' Despite this declaration, Charters, who perhaps knew Harry better than any other journalist, made an astute prediction: 'I don't think this strong man, so dominant in his job for many years, will be content to sit back in an obscure forgotten role.'

Despite the generous salary, and drastically improved work-life balance, Harry soon became frustrated on the fringes of the club. In *Love Affairs and Marriage* Howard Kendall recollected how Harry became a marginalised figure at the club: 'He was an unhappy figure in the shadows and not treated very well. I remember him cornering me once and telling me, "They're waiting for me to die." The club would send him money by post so that he wasn't seen at Goodison. Eventually they stopped paying him under some pretext or other.'

By late 1974 Harry was actively seeking alternative employment in the game, as he informed the *Liverpool Echo* in 1976: 'I didn't really adjust to the situation. I am quite convinced that I am just as good a manager now as I was in the days when we were winning trophies – in fact better with the experience I have had.'

Perhaps referring to his often frosty relationship with the media, he stated: 'Far too many appointments are made in management these days because of considerations of the media and public image. I think that it is ridiculous that so many experienced managers should be going out of the First Division. People like Tony Waddington, Bill Shankly, Bill Nicholson and myself have something to give the game and yet it's not being used.' Bill Shankly outlasted Harry in management by only 15 months before retiring from Liverpool. Football was Shankly's life; he would soon rue his decision but, aged 61, would not manage a football club again.

In September 1974, Terry Neill left Hull City to take up the managerial position at Tottenham. Out of the blue, Mike Ellis of the Sun received a call from Harry asking if he had any contacts at Boothferry Park. Although this came to nought, Harry was tempted to return to Sheffield Wednesday. His former club had sacked Derek Dooley on Christmas Eve 1973 and replaced him with an inexperienced manager in Steve Burtenshaw. Having narrowly avoided relegation to Division Three in the spring of 1974, Burtenshaw was powerless to prevent the team, featuring Colin Harvey in the twilight of his playing days, sliding inexorably towards relegation in the 1974/75 season.

Harry told the *Sheffield Star* in 1977: 'Wednesday seemed to be in all sorts of trouble and needed an experienced man. It went through my mind that I might be able to do a job there.' Strangely, he made no approach to the Hillsborough hierarchy, on the spurious grounds that he had never had to apply for a job previously: 'I have never applied for a job in my life and I wasn't going to start then. I took the view that people know what you are and what you have done.' Wednesday would languish in the Third Division for five seasons before experiencing a renaissance under Jack Charlton and Howard Wilkinson.

CHAPTER TWENTY

NORTH END

A REUNION with Stockport County appeared to be on the cards when Harry sat alongside County's co-chairman Freddie Pye at a League Cup tie against Southport on 20 August 1975. A return to the town where he started out in football would have had a romantic symmetry but County, struggling in the Fourth Division, were not an attractive proposition. Twelve days later Harry crossed the threshold of Preston North End's Deepdale ground, only 20 miles from his Ainsdale home. He also brought Chris Hassell, the secretary from Everton, with him.

North End had hired Bobby Charlton as player-manager in 1973. After two unfulfilling seasons, the proposed transfer of John Bird to Newcastle provided the catalyst for Charlton to walk away from football management. Charlton's assistant (and former teammate) Nobby Stiles quit the club in solidarity despite being offered the manager's post.

Harry took the reins on 1 September, signing a four-year contract worth £8,000 per annum. An interesting clause contained a dispensation which permitted Harry to continue to act as a 'consultant' for Everton, provided that it did not interfere with his Preston role or lead to a conflict of interest. Upon taking the post he told Ronald Crowther of the *Daily Mail* how his enforced sabbatical had been hard to cope with: 'It is primarily a matter of pride. The blow when Everton relieved me of my duties, after serving them for twenty-six years as a player and manager, struck hard. For me it was a humiliation. Now, after recovering, I want to prove to myself, as well as others, that I can still motivate players... that my experience can be utilised for the good of a club and for the game.'

North End were once a great club and still synonymous with the genius of Tom Finney and the playing days of Bill Shankly. Harry would eulogise about Finney in his column in the *Lancashire Evening Post*: 'Living in the past is not a good thing but you can't possibly ignore a player like Finney. I have been a great admirer of him ever since I first saw him and his skills on the field were truly wonderful. One of the best things about him was that he was so adaptable. Despite his lack of bulk he was a match for the biggest players. He proved that skill, ability and know-how is all that is needed to make a player truly effective. I put him alongside Pele, Rivera and Beckenbauer in my list of the greatest players in the world.'

The club now found itself in the Third Division and Harry was faced with constraints he had not seen since his Rochdale days. His first task was to successfully persuade Nobby Stiles to make a U-turn on his decision to leave the club. Interviewed by Neil Comer of *Football News*, Harry emphasised the magnitude of the task ahead and sent a thinly veiled message to the board about transfer funds: 'There is little money to replace weaknesses, I have to re-organise throughout the club and get them to play the way I want them to play. To progress, any manager must have means, i.e. players or money to buy players. My record in the transfer market is as good as anyone's. I know how to buy and sell, I don't often make mistakes… if you are young you make them.'

Stiles and coach Alan Kelly would soon learn that there would be no room for complacency under Harry. In his autobiography Stiles recalled how, in his first meeting with the new manager, he was instructed to draw up a written training plan within 24 hours. Having burned the midnight oil with Kelly to put it together and submit it before the deadline he was rewarded with a note of thanks and a bottle of beer. However, upon coming back into work on the Monday Stiles was shocked to be on the receiving end of a Harry blast about faults with the programme. Stiles summed up the situation: 'Harry's management policy seemed clear enough. It was to keep us on our toes, one way or another.'

Before a ball had been kicked under Harry, the deal went through which had precipitated Charlton's resignation. John Bird left for Newcastle United, to be replaced as captain by sweeper Alex Spark. Former North End striker Alex Bruce returned to Deepdale in part-exchange for Bird. He recalls: 'Bobby Charlton was on his way out of Preston. He did not want to sell John Bird and he didn't really want me, as a former player, coming back to the club. I was in the process of speaking to the directors when they informed me that Harry Catterick was coming into the club and he was quite comfortable with me coming in. So I was his first signing.'

Bruce became half of a free-scoring pairing with Mike Elwiss; they notched 30 goals between them during the 1975/76 season. Bruce says: 'I'm about five-foot-eight and Mike is about five-foot-ten. Mike was a strong all-round player and I was more of a poacher and played in the penalty box. Harry told us just to play where we wanted along the front line. We played 4–3–3 quite a bit with me, Elwiss and a winger – it gave you a chance to attack teams properly. Harry never really gave a rollicking but was always encouraging you – asking you where you wanted to play. I can remember being injured once and coming back against Wrexham and he was quite appreciative in the local newspaper, calling me "a strong boy" – not many managers give you that praise.' When it was suggested by the press to Harry that Everton might be interested in signing Elwiss he replied, deadpan, 'They can have him for £250,000 plus Bob Latchford.'

As at Everton, Harry delegated the lion's share of training activity. Bruce recalls: 'Nobby took all the training and Harry played that role which was to be a very professional man and manager. It was the same for me at Newcastle, Steve Burtenshaw took the training and you never saw Joe Harvey all week. It's nice when you have a professional with high standards, he was highly respected by the players although we didn't see a vast amount of him during the week. He was a pleasant man, he never threw tantrums. Nobby is one of the nicest people I have ever met, he really supported you and you'd play all day for him. Training was enjoyable – there was plenty of shooting practice and there was a good atmosphere at the club at the time.'

Alongside seasoned professionals, including European Cup winner David Sadler and Francis Burns (who played in several of Manchester United's European Cup ties but missed out in the final XI), Preston had been unearthing some gems, three of whom would go on to win the European Cup elsewhere: Michael Robinson, Tony Morley and Mark Lawrenson. Morley, a boyhood Evertonian, was making a name for himself as an energetic wide-man and was excited at the arrival of Harry: 'Harry was a big part of my childhood as Everton were my team. I was thrilled and a bit nervous when I heard he was coming. I once had a lift in his car, I really got the impression that he wasn't very happy about the circumstances at Everton. Harry was quite like Ron Saunders, who managed me later at Villa; he had worked that hard at Villa and then left due to politics. Ron wasn't the same manager after that, as he wanted to build on winning the league but felt it was taken away from him.'

Another player who would go on to greater things was teenage centre-back Mark Lawrenson, who recalls: 'Harry's very first game as Preston's manager was a reserve match against Burnley. We had a very young team – North End chucked you in early, and if you impressed you soon progressed to the first team. After twenty-five minutes I made a block tackle and I tweaked my knee ligaments and had to come off, straight to the treatment room. "The Catt", as we called him, came down and said, "What's your name, son?" I said, "Mark Lawrenson, boss," and he said, "As soon as you're fit you'll be in the first team." So I thought: "This bloke knows what he is doing!" True to his word, as soon as I was 100 per cent fit I was in the first team.

'Basically I was going to be taking the place of Alex Spark, the team captain, so that was a bit political. Bobby Charlton didn't want to be the manager but was such a nice bloke, then Harry came in and there was such an aura about him. I was often a lackey in the dressing room. Once Harry came in but said, "You stay here, son." So I sat in for a team talk. You could tell that this fella knew what he was doing and meant business.

'I played alongside David Sadler who had won the European Cup with Manchester United and was great with me. Training was at Willow Farm, about a mile-and-a-half from Deepdale. Nobby did most of the coaching under the supervision of Harry. Nobby was brilliant, he would go out of his way to help you. He was fiercely competitive but so different from people's perception of him from his playing days.'

Harry Catterick himself would sing the praises of Stiles, Sadler and Francis Burns to the *Lancashire Evening Post*: 'Nobby Stiles has had much to do with the dressing room spirit – he's a wonderful character. In fact, I told Sir Matt Busby that Nobby, Francis Burns and David Sadler are a great tribute to Manchester United. I do the rocketing and Nobby does the smoothing out!'

It is undeniable that some of Harry's spark had gone, as he had to cut his cloth according to the club's meagre means. In essence, the role became a holding job as his stepson Reinhard told me: 'There was no money at Preston really, it was almost flogging a dead horse. Money had been no object, to a degree, at Everton, so it was a step down for him. That said, he was happy to be back in the managerial saddle.'

The precarious financial situation faced by North End got a public airing at the Club's AGM in December 1975. Chairman Alan Jones told shareholders that the club, with an average home gate of 9,000, was losing £80,000 per season. He concluded that it would be 'suicidal and irresponsible' to enter the transfer market for new players. Harry addressed the meeting and moved to dampen expectations of progress under his management: 'There is a long, hard haul ahead as far as the playing side is concerned. The climate is such as to make it dangerous to go into the transfer market, and I can well understand the reluctance of the board.'

Certainly the adjustment to Third Division standards took some getting used to after the years of Nil Satis Nisi Optimum. Local journalist Norman Shakeshaft enjoyed recounting the occasion on which Harry purchased a first-class train ticket for himself when the team travelled to a London fixture in second class. Shakeshaft would also reveal that frustration got the better of Harry after an away defeat: 'I recall him pouring a glass of wine, given to him by one of the directors, out of the train window when asked for his verdict.'

Freed from the shackles and expectations of Everton and the Littlewoods empire, Harry's approach to the press softened and he would go on to grant lengthy interviews for articles in Merseyside, Lancashire and Yorkshire titles. Colin Wood of the *Daily Mail* recalls: 'Harry went from being obstructive at Everton to being very obliging. On Merseyside there was the pressure of Everton and John Moores. There had been times at Everton where we could see another side of him, especially away from Merseyside, but as soon as we were back there the shutters came down again. Once he left Merseyside the weight was off him. At Preston Harry was a different animal altogether, there was a different atmosphere with him and a much better relationship – he was also more sociable, you could have a drink with him.'

James Mossop concurs: 'He had changed, he had mellowed, and maybe leaving his wife had released him from something. I went to Deepdale once. At Everton you had felt like you were talking to a figurehead but at Preston it felt like you were talking to a mate. He'd greet you and ask: "How are you? Have a cup of tea," which I had not seen before.'

Shortly after taking the Preston job, Harry and Bill Shankly were interviewed by the Sunday Mirror as they had lunch together at Liverpool's Adelphi Hotel. As one might expect, Shankly's wise-cracks dominate the article, but Harry took the opportunity to bemoan the dearth of 'naturals' in the game: 'The game has become too predictable. We cram too much into young players' minds. We take them at fifteen, and, in the end, they haven't got the initiative to take a throw-in. I would like to see young players developing on their own, away from league football.'

He would often pick up on this theme as an after-dinner speaker. This new sideline came about once Harry had stood down at Everton; it came as a surprise to those that had worked with him. Graham Wilson recalls: 'I think Harry was really quite shy, that was a problem. You could never get him to speak publicly at dinners or address fans. I don't think it was him being awkward, he just was shy and didn't enjoy doing it.' From the mid-70s he would speak at functions and fundraising events, recounting stories from his playing and management days, until the time of his death. Time and again he would opine that intensive coaching could be detrimental and that players should be allowed to develop at their natural pace – often being tried in a number of positions to improve their football intelligence and also find their optimum role. He would also use the speeches to predict and welcome an increase in top-level football on Sundays.

Harry's first season at Preston started strongly before form became somewhat topsy-turvy. However, a surge in April secured an eighth-place finish – lagging eight points behind the promotion places. Harry's second and, as it transpired, final season saw a marginal improvement in form, but the 54 points accumulated only secured sixth place, five points below Crystal Palace in the third promotion spot.

Halfway through the 1976/77 season Billy Bingham, Harry's successor at

Goodison Park, was fired and Everton began the search for another manager to try to bring the glory days back. Approaches were again made to Don Revie, now England coach, and Ipswich's Bobby Robson. However, the *Daily Mail* and *Lancashire Evening Post* also reported that a Goodison return for Harry was not out of the question. The *Mail*'s Colin Wood had been led to believe by Everton insiders that Harry was on a list of contenders being considered. The dream of a remarkable comeback was ended by the recruitment of Gordon Lee from Newcastle United.

Harry had been monitoring, with concern, Everton's more physical style of play adopted by Bingham, using taller, bigger players. He recalled to John Roberts shortly after Lee's appointment: 'Many people don't like the way I manage or my public my image but I have never been noted for criticising referees or managers through the media. But I must say that in the last few years the style at Everton has disappointed me. I have seen Everton with teams near the bottom of the league previously but always attempting to play quality football. I have been upset at the style, they seem have thrown the traditional Everton pattern out of the window and there is still room for it - it's a good way to play. Everton have always been noted for a quality game, people always long for the stylish stuff. Success has to be done in the Everton tradition and that's extremely difficult in the modern game. But it is possible and that 1970 side proved it, it is hard to duplicate but it is possible. Whenever I meet Everton supporters the only thing they say is, "When are we going to get Harvey, Kendall and Ball and that type back again Harry?" I hope that Gordon Lee will be able to put that right.'

In the summer of 1977 one of Harry's last managerial acts was to sell Lawrenson to Brighton and Hove Albion as Preston sought to balance the books. Liverpool had bid £75,000 for the 19-year-old but Brighton's manager, Alan Mullery, trumped this by agreeing a £100,000 fee with the Preston board. Four years later the Irish international signed for Liverpool for £1 million. Lawrenson remembers a nice touch from Harry as the transfer to Brighton went through: 'He wrote me a really nice letter when I left, I wish I'd kept it. It contained advice. In it he stated what I'd done for him and told me to ring him up if I had any problems. Really, it was not in keeping with the manager I'd played for, and I mean that in the nicest possible way, as he was not a person you got close to as a player.'

Late in the season, Harry had been keen to bring Howard Kendall back from Birmingham City to the club where he had made his name as a teenager; there was even talk of supporters fundraising to enable the transfer fee to be met. Kendall would instead head to the Potteries with Stoke City, where he would take his first steps on the coaching path that eventually led him back to Goodison Park.

CHAPTER TWENTY ONE
NEW BEGINNINGS

A WEEK INTO pre-season training for the forthcoming 1977/78 season, Harry's managerial career came to an abrupt halt on 22 July. Preston North End's board dispensed with his services and replaced him with his number two, Nobby Stiles, alongside the long-serving Alan Kelly. In a scenario reminiscent of his Everton departure in 1973, Preston asked Harry to remain with the club in an advisory capacity for the remaining two years of his contract.

Harry was publicly gracious about his departure and told the *Lancashire Evening Post*: 'I am sorry to be leaving the club in terms of team affairs. I have been offered a consultancy and am giving it a great deal of thought. I am delighted to have had two good years with the club; my balance in terms of transfer deals during that time is around £20,000 in favour of the club.' He added: 'The club has a promising young side and I'm sorry that the sale recently of Mark Lawrenson, and Gary Williams, was found necessary but this is one of the facts of football. I would like to express my thanks to the players; I am grateful too for the able assistance given to me by Nobby Stiles, Alan Kelly and the invaluable help of chief scout Jimmie Scott.'

Norman Shakeshaft paid tribute to Harry after his dismissal, while alluding to some tensions with the board: 'Harry's ability to wheel and deal in the transfer market could never be fully exploited by Preston, because no money was available to him. An intelligent and shrewd man, his opinions were always worth considering and he had a mischievous, cynical and dry sense of humour.'

Alex Bruce recalls that the sacking was not expected by the playing staff: 'It was a surprise at the time, we weren't struggling at the bottom of the league. It is hard to always work out what goes on behind the scenes at football clubs. As a player you just carry on. We did all right, we always had the makings of a decent team, but we never had big money to bring players in; we were a bit of a selling club – just holding our own and trying to keep a fairly decent side. That's what Harry found hard after coming from the First Division. You get a bit of a shock as there is a lot more work to be done. Everton, with great players, it was more about keeping them fit and getting them on the pitch.'

Harry decided not to accept the offer of a new role at Preston and left club football for the last time. He had been finding the new economics of football increasingly hard to accept, as he told the *People*: 'Players are having it too good for their own self-interest. People have got to realise that employers can't go on paying more in wages than they are taking at the gate. The sad thing from a player's point of view is that all this affluence is often making him an inferior player. It is very difficult to have this affluence and maintain a hunger for the game. Nobody wants to go back to the old days, but a bit of poverty is no bad thing.'

Drawing on his own experiences and health problems, in 1976 Harry expressed his concerns to Charles Lambert about the impact of the 'win at all costs' mentality in the game: 'I think it would be good for football if there were less tension in it. The competitiveness, the great demand for victory all the time, is putting too much pressure on managers and players. So you are breeding players to whom the first thing to do is avoid defeat. I have always been a great believer in style, winning is important, but how you do it is also very important. That tends to be overlooked in the modern game.'

His next step was to apply for the England team manager role following the shock departure of Don Revie to the Middle East. A brief, handwritten letter of application sent to the Football Association on 29 July 1977 read:

> *I should like you to consider this letter an application for the position of England Team Manager.*
>
> *My managerial experience and character is known to most on the FA Council but, for the record, I have managed the following clubs with more than a little success: Everton 13 years, Sheffield Wednesday 3 years, Preston N.E. 2 years. I am 57 years of age and unmarried.*
>
> *Should you favour me with an interview I am sure I would convince you of my suitability for the post.*

In light of Harry's ambivalence to the international game the application may have raised a few eyebrows at the FA. In the event, Harry was not shortlisted for the post and Ron Greenwood was appointed.

Following an approach to Everton the club agreed to honour Harry's 26 years at Goodison with a tribute match on 2 May 1978. An 'Everton Eleven', in royal blue, lined up against a yellow-shirted 'All-Stars Eleven' featuring the likes of Joe Royle, Gordon West, Roger Hunt and Tony Kay, who had returned from Spain for the match. Before kick-off Harry took to the pitch one final time to receive a standing ovation. The match, on a rain-sodden night, banked a welcome £12,000 for Harry. One of the organising committee was none other than Bill Shankly.

Harry's ties with Everton were formalised again on 1 September 1978 with his appointment as 'roving scout'. Armed with a representative's pass and up to £500 per annum in travelling expenses, the role officially entailed 'submitting reports to Gordon Lee on any likely players you come across on your travels'. Everton's then manager, Gordon Lee, recalls: 'Everton was, and still is, a caring club. I think the job offer letter [club secretary] Jim Greenwood sent to Harry would have been honorary to keep him in touch in football – and if he saw any promising player he could contact the club. I can actually remember in my first job in football receiving a letter of congratulations from Harry on Port Vale's promotion to Division Three in 1970, which I appreciated very much.'

The enforced retirement from managerial roles did allow Harry to spend more time with his new family, now relocated to Lytham St Annes on the Fylde coast. Here Harry had entered the happiest period of his personal life. Having become estranged from his wife Nancy in the early 1970s, Harry had met Paula Callesen, a German who had moved to Merseyside in the early 1960s. Harry and Paula married in 1981; Paula's son Reinhard got to know Harry well: 'Harry and my mum got together when he was scouting for Everton in the mid-70s, I was about fourteen. They were good times, they were made for each other. They were going out all over the place, holding hands and laughing and joking. He'd had the massive heart attack at Everton, only given a matter of years to live, but he was a fit chap and looked after himself. He used to do his exercises in his tracksuit, doing stretches in the garden; I suspect that's what kept him going a few more years.

'I played junior rugby for Fylde Colts, and Harry mentored me and helped me keep fit. We used to drive to the beach every morning. He had me doing shuttle runs and stuff like that and if I wasn't doing well I had to run home – a real taskmaster! But he was a professional, he had high standards, I know now he was doing it for my own good but at the time I didn't see that. He was a serious man, really, but we did have a laugh because I was a young kid. He didn't really talk about football – World War Two had scuppered his career but he wasn't bitter about it – it was just a case of "wrong place, wrong time". There was no satellite television then but we'd watch Match of the Day together on Saturday night and he'd be there, "calling" people! He actually liked watching rugby as well, especially the internationals. Harry and Mum used to come and watch me playing at home games. He would cast a critical eye over everybody and sometimes give advice.'

Once settled in a flat on St Anne's Road East, Fairhaven Golf Club would become central to Harry and Paula's social life. Here they made a new circle of friends, including Brian Nicholson, who recalls: 'Harry joined the club around 1978. Every Sunday morning we were out on the golf course at eight o'clock; he was always there. On the golf course he'd look at our swings and tell us what we were doing wrong, he had the manner on him to be helpful. He was a decent golfer, I think he was on a handicap of ten or twelve in those days. Paula was very much in the social circle – she was a lovely lady and they were very happy. We had a lot of dinners with Paula and Harry, they lived in a nice little block called Silverburn. He was a quiet guy but very determined, you knew he was there and he always had to win! Harry was somebody you could always turn to – solid.'

An interest in local football came about in 1980 when Harry was appointed vice-president of Lytham FC of the Lancashire Combination League. The link-up came about as a result of Harry's friendship with Harry Thompson, club president and owner of the Clifton Arms Hotel.

Fred Willder, manager of Lytham FC at the time, recalled that Harry was modest and would rarely talk about football unless prompted. However, once he was on the subject he would wax lyrical about the wondrous Everton midfield of a decade earlier and the hours spent watching Harvey, Kendall and Ball perfecting their craft at Bellefield.

One player at Lytham upon whom Harry made a lasting impression was Mel Tottoh: 'Harry had been at the club a little while when I came. He was a real gentleman who did a lot for the club and the players themselves. I had been at Preston under Nobby Stiles and released. Fred Willder asked me to come down to Lytham and I played for a couple of seasons before Alan Kelly took me back to Preston. Harry used to come down to training and matches. He would entertain dignitaries coming to home matches – he was a real support.

'It was a challenging time for me; I was a young lad and had come out of the Merchant Navy, I'd been picked up doing football but didn't know if I wanted to pursue my engineering career and I had a very young family – because of that life was coming off the rails a bit. Harry was great and tuned into that; he took me to one side and in a very non-directive, sensitive way helped me to think about where I was going and gave me the confidence to decide – he was an absolute gentleman. He had bags of experience and thought I was a very talented player and gave me tips on my game which paid off. He had no airs and graces about him; he was just

"Harry" – a really lovely human being who would talk to you as if you were the guy next door.

'The last time I saw him was when I was out in Lytham with my wife and he was in a café with Paula. At that time my life had turned round so it was wonderful to be able to thank him for his guidance and let him know that I was doing well at British Aerospace and playing football for the reserves at Preston.'

Upon leaving Preston Harry had not kept in close touch with many involved in the professional game. One ex-player that he came to know was former Manchester United, Bolton Wanderers and Preston defender Alan Gowling: 'In the early to mid-80s I used to visit him in St Anne's as I was working for the Football League pension brokers, S.W. Taylor. He was due a pension and I went up to see him to see if I could help him, then I visited him occasionally following the initial introduction. I got on with him very well. I didn't find him a distant person, he was very sociable and knowledgeable. He just enjoyed having a chat about the football of the day, he didn't bang on about the old days.'

CHAPTER TWENTY TWO

SAINTS &
STANDARDS

ALTHOUGH HARRY'S managerial career had run its course, this period in his life was happy and fulfilling. He appeared to be at peace with himself, due in large part to his settled home life. Come the autumn of 1979, he unexpectedly found himself in the employ of Southampton FC as a northern area match assessor.

Southampton's manager at the time, Lawrie McMenemy, recalls: 'Harry was from that older group. There was a contrast with Bill Shankly although both were fantastic to be in the company of. Whereas Bill was more of an extrovert, Harry was very quiet but there was always that bit of style and class about him. Bill used to ring me and Jock Stein used to ring me every Sunday night. I think they missed the involvement, it can be a lonely job at the best of times.

'After I'd got established at Southampton and we'd won the FA Cup I realised that they didn't have a scouting network around the country, so I started networks in Newcastle, London and the West Country. I must have bumped into Harry at a game and I was delighted just to talk to him. I said to Harry that if he wanted to he could go to games and put me a report in – not necessarily looking at players but mainly looking at the opposition as we would have to play them at some stage. I honestly think that he was a proud man, I saw through the fact that he wanted to go to games but would not want to ring up asking for a ticket. So I gave Harry the opportunity to attend games. I would ring him up and ask him to go to a game and then my people would ring that club to book a ticket and parking, in that way he would be treated as he should. That was important for me, to be able to help someone who'd helped me and other young managers in their time. He wouldn't have been doing it to make money – we probably just paid expenses. It was about his dignity. He was always smartly dressed on match days. I was delighted to have ex-pro people like him and [former Cardiff manager] Jimmy Andrews.

'Once, when we were playing in the north-west, I invited Harry to come and watch us. On the Friday night we were in the hotel having dinner and we were stood in the foyer. The Southampton chairman, Alan Woodford, came by and I introduced Harry to him. He said, "Oh yes, how are you? What are you doing these days?" and Harry replied, "I'm working for you!"

'Each year I would invite all the scouts down to Southampton on a Friday before a home game and put them up in the Royal Hotel around the corner from The Dell. They'd have dinner and I'd go round with my coaching staff and we'd have a nice night together, then on the Saturday morning I'd arrange for the junior teams to be playing and I'd arrange for the scouts to watch our junior teams play so that they could have a good idea of the standard we had. On the Saturday afternoon they'd be entertained royally in the directors' box at The Dell. That was my way of making them feel valued.

'If any of them came down early, they'd come down to the ground. Harry, being a football man, was keener than any of them and came down the ground on Friday afternoon with the scout Jack Hixon. The Dell was a dump, such an old building. When you had a home game the next day the apprentices had to work their socks off, getting the changing rooms and referees room clean. When we were going down the corridor to the dressing room there was a young kid on a ladder dusting around the door edges. One of the scouts said, "What the devil are they doing that for?" I remember Harry, quietly, saying, "Standards, attention to detail." He was spot-on; he knew why I was asking apprentices to do that – it was teaching them about hard work aside from kicking a ball around. To me it was a privilege to have someone like him working for us.'

Reinhard remembers Harry's last role: 'He did quite a bit of scouting for Southampton, he was going to matches virtually every weekend, mainly in the north-west. In midweek he went round the local area, Blackpool, Preston and Blackburn, looking for up-and-coming youngsters – he could spot a good player. People probably wouldn't have recognised him on a cold winter's night with a hat on. Harry was the consummate professional; he used to keep a load of records – he'd write a full match report out every time for Lawrie. My mum would then type it up and mail it to Southampton. I went to quite a lot of matches with Harry if I wasn't playing rugby. We used to sit in the directors' boxes at Everton, Blackburn and Manchester United. We were always treated like royalty.'

Interviewed in March 1980 by the *Lancashire Evening Post*, Harry appeared disenchanted with the modern game and touched on his familiar theme of players being over-coached at an early age:

I've seen all the First Division sides this season and after I've mentioned Liam Brady and Kenny Dalglish it's difficult to know who I'd like to go and see. I am certain that standards are the lowest in thirty years. There are too many standardised players. Some clubs have more coaches than the National Bus Company. I can't think of any top-grade coaches in the country now other than Don Howe, Bobby Robson and the Liverpool coaching team. These people are all perfectionists but base their work on the fact that football is a simple game. To improve standards we've got to start way-back – to let youngsters have freedom and not let them get into a set pattern too early.

Harry would single out praise for Ron Saunders, a fellow-former Everton forward, who bore some similarities in his manner and approach to the game: 'At Aston Villa they are near to doing an exceptional job. I like the mobility Ron Saunders gets into their sides and, if you watch Villa, you'll get entertainment. Saunders is not a fashionable manager but I have great admiration for him.'

At grass-roots level Harry was instrumental in the organisation of the 1982 European Youth Five-a-side tournament in Liverpool. He had been appointed as a Vice President of the Liverpool Sunday league in 1975 and spent time visiting managers and secretaries at various clubs to give them advice on administration and tactics. This role also led to an unexpected reunion with Harry Bennett. Bennett had left Everton in 1971 and played for Aldershot under Tom McAnearney, Harry's right half-back from his Hillsborough days. Having retired from the professional game following a back injury, Bennett continued to turn out for Merseyside clubs at amateur level: 'I played amateur football for a Liverpool side called Lobster FC – a good side, they were the first north-west club to win the Sunday National Cup. One year, around 1978, Lobster won the league and cup double and the presentation was held at the Grafton in Liverpool. When I got there my friend told me that the guy presenting the trophies was Harry Catterick. I was captain but thought, "There's no way I'm going up to collect a trophy from him," so I went to the toilet and Tommy Nesbitt went up to receive it.

'When I came back out my mate said, "There's somebody who wants to talk to you." It was Harry Catterick. He was a magnificent manager, he really was, but as a player I felt he wasn't part of the human race! For all those years I said that I was going to give him a right-hook if I saw him again. So what's the first thing I do? I say, "Hello, boss, how are you?" I had a smashing little chat with him. He was a totally different man, he asked after my family and how my back was.'

In April 1981, Charlie Gee passed away in Rhos-on-Sea aged 72. Harry attended to cremation ceremony, with other Everton officials, to pay his respects to the man who had put him on the road to Goodison Park 44 years earlier. The following month the dismissal of Gordon Lee precipitated the return to Everton of Howard Kendall as manager and, on occasion, player. Kendall's first game in the dugout came at Goodison Park on 29 August, fittingly against his former team Birmingham City. With so much attention focused on Kendall's return, only the sharp-eyed would have noticed two sexagenarians sitting side by side in the Main Stand, happily discussing the game. Bill Shankly and Harry saw Kendall, the player they had both coveted in 1967, lead Everton to a hard-fought 3–1 victory. It would be one of the last games Shankly attended; a month later he passed away in Broadgreen Hospital having suffered a heart attack.

In January 1985 Harry headed to Spain for a golfing holiday with his Fairhaven golfing friends. The party included Brian Nicholson, who recalls: 'We were out every night for a meal, there'd be lots of drinking and Harry would be raising his glass with us. On the penultimate night the restaurant we visited in El Paraiso had walls covered in mirrors. We noticed, through them, that when Harry raised his wine glass he never took a drink from it. He'd spent all week getting us pissed and had never had a drink himself! So on the last night we were forcing him to drink and he said, "I've been getting away with that for years." He always had to win, he was the most determined man I have ever met.'

Harry would continue to attend Everton games when his scouting commitments allowed. He told John Roberts, 'If you've been at Everton you never change. It's a strange thing but once you're an Everton player, particularly if you start there as a youngster, you never change your allegiance deep down.' He would normally be accompanied on his trips to Goodison by Reinhard or a golfing friend, such as Brian Nicholson, who recalls: 'He'd invite us regularly to Goodison Park. We'd have a coffee and sandwich with him in the directors' lounge box before the game. He preferred to be driven, he took the view that he'd invited us so we could drive!'

By 1984 Everton's management team included two thirds of the the 'Holy Trinity' in Howard Kendall and Colin Harvey. After several barren years, the Toffees were finally emerging from the long red shadow cast across Stanley Park by their footballing neighbours. After a ground-breaking all-Merseyside League Cup Final, which Liverpool won in the replay, Everton claimed their first silverware in 14 years by winning the FA Cup in May 1984.

By the spring of 1985 the rejuvenated Blues were marching, inexorably, towards league and European success. Though lacking some of the fluid, one-touch artistry of the late 1960s vintage Everton, Kendall's team struck a brilliant balance between skill, strength and endeavour.

On 9 March Everton hosted Ipswich town, who by now had Tommy Eggleston as their physio, in the sixth round of the FA Cup. Harry had intended to take Reinhard to the match but, due to his stepson's rugby commitments, golfing friend Aubrey Shepherd took the seat next to him on the front row of the directors' box. As Everton were due to play Southampton at The Dell three weeks later, Harry was probably casting an eye over his former team for Lawrie McMenemy as well as just enjoying the spectacle.

The cup tie was an edge-of-the-seat classic, which ebbed and flowed towards a dramatic climax. Kevin Sheedy, a left-sided midfielder 'stolen' from Liverpool in similar circumstances to Johnny Morrissey 20 years earlier, had given the Blues the lead with an exquisite, twice-taken, free kick. Ipswich stunned the home crowd by countering with two quick-fire goals. As the clock ticked down in the second half Goodison was whipped into a frenzy as waves of Everton attacks rained down on the Gwladys Street goal – only to be repelled by Terry Butcher and goalkeeper Paul Cooper. With five minutes remaining, centre-back Derek Mountfield slid the ball home at the near post to induce delirium on the terraces. Most present were oblivious to the fact that, within moments of this high drama, Harry had, once again, suffered a major heart attack.

Shortly after the full-time whistle blew, the club doctor and paramedics were working frantically, yet vainly, on the flat roof of the executive boxes to try to revive Harry. Like fellow Everton legend Dixie Dean five years earlier, Harry passed away in the place he held so dear, a place where he had delivered so much pleasure to others.

His funeral took place at Lytham Parish Church, with tributes paid from across the football world. Howard Kendall and Joe Fagan represented the two Mersey footballing giants while Lawrie McMenemy attended on behalf of Southampton FC. Harry was laid to rest in the churchyard; Paula would be reunited with him in 2001. Their simple headstone was inscribed with: Love is a Durable Fire and Nil Satis Nisi Optimum.

POSTSCRIPT

ON 30 MAY 1985 the Bishop of Liverpool, Dr David Sheppard, led a memorial service of thanksgiving for Harry's life at the Church of St Luke the Evangelist. Fittingly, this place of worship is sandwiched between the Gwladys Street and Main Stands at Goodison Park. In the intervening weeks Howard Kendall's Everton team had returned to the summit of English football, winning the league title for the first time in 15 years. The club had also finally captured a hitherto elusive European trophy on a memorable night in Rotterdam. Two years later Howard Kendall would succeed Harry as the club's most successful manager by securing a second league crown.

Kendall has described Harry as a distant figure who was hard to relate to, yet acknowledges a debt to him: 'As a manager you take the ideas of previous managers that you have worked with – you take on board what you think the good points and the bad points are. From Harry, in terms of learning, there was the balance of a team and need for the right blend.'

In contrast to Harry, Kendall – reminiscent of Don Revie – advocated team-bonding and socialising within the squad. However, he could display Catterick-like clear-headedness when facing tough decisions. The replacement of the talismanic Andy Gray with the younger Gary Lineker had echoes of Harry bringing in Fred Pickering to usurp Roy Vernon. Kendall reflects, 'You learn that there are difficult decisions to make but you have got to make them. You've got to believe in what you're thinking and doing, and in that case I had a reason for doing that.' Kendall would also be capable of asserting his authority if it was challenged – winger Mickey Thomas was shipped out after only 11 Everton appearances having refused to play for the reserves.

Like Harry before him, Kendall, and his successor Colin Harvey, were ultimately unable to transform a great team into a dynasty and it was Liverpool who reasserted their dominance as the 1980s progressed. Kendall would make two returns as manager in less happy circumstances while Harvey would rejoin the youth set-up. One of his last tasks was to help develop Wayne Rooney, perhaps the most naturally gifted, home-grown, talent since Harvey himself.

Joe Royle, having bravely recuperated from his back problems of the early 1970s, retired from playing in 1981 and cut his teeth as a lower league manager. In the summer of 1982, upon being appointed to his first managerial post at Second Division Oldham Athletic, Royle received a letter from Harry offering congratulations. Royle sent a reply:

20th August 1982

Dear Boss,

Thanks for your letter of congratulations and good wishes. I was really pleased to receive it as I have never forgotten my early days at Everton and throughout a varied career they still remain the best days of the career. Although these, at times, may have seemed hard to adjust to in the early days, now that I have joined the 'other side' I see now clearly the value of discipline both on and off the park.

I will certainly take you up of your offer of advice during the season, and if you are ever in the district, or you would like to see Oldham you know your opinions would be valued highly. Thanks again for a great start to a long career and many valuable lessons.

Best regards and good health,

Joe

Royle would make a name for himself at Boundary Park, taking Oldham into the First Division and to a League Cup final before answering the call to return 'home' to Everton in 1994. In his first season back he rescued the club from probable relegation and led it to a fifth FA Cup win. Installed in the manager's office at Bellefield, Royle was confronted with Harry's old football-pitch-topped desk. One wonders if he, Kendall or Harvey were ever tempted to twitch the window blinds in order to give the players some added impetus on the training pitch.

In contrast to some of his contemporaries, who spawned a cottage industry after their passing, Harry and his achievements faded from the public's consciousness. This is due, in no small part, to his low media profile in contrast to Bill Shankly's during the halcyon years of the 1960s. The rapid demise of the 1969/70 team and the absence of a European trophy win were other factors in the lack of recognition. The flame of his memory has been kept lit by football supporters in South Yorkshire and on Merseyside who were touched by the brilliance of his teams.

Overdue recognition was finally forthcoming when Harry was posthumously recognised as an 'Everton Giant' by the club in 2009. A plaque on the wall of the Main Stand at Goodison Park serves to confirm his status. The following year Harry's daughter Joyce and grandson George were present in Manchester to see Harry inducted into the English Football Hall of Fame – taking his place alongside Matt Busby, Bill Shankly, Bob Paisley, Stan Cullis, Joe Mercer, Brian Clough, Bobby Robson, Don Revie and Alf Ramsey in the pantheon of great managers.

Goodison Park remains largely unchanged from Harry's pomp, having become a cherished, yet dated, relic of a bygone footballing age. The bricks, concrete and timber have borne witness to Dean, Lawton, Mercer, Young, Kendall, Harvey, Ball and Harry Catterick – the man linking them all.

And what of Bellefield, the 'Football Factory' that Harry wished to be remembered for? The training facility served the club with distinction for 40 years, nurturing a steady stream of talent from to Ratcliffe to Rooney. However, Everton outgrew what was once a state-of-the-art development. On 9 October 2007 Bellefield hosted a final first-team training session before the gates were locked for the last time. Everton now inhabit Finch Farm, an expansive, 55-acre facility in Halewood. Here Everton managers, present and future, can plot to emulate the league title successes of the 1960s and 1980s by winning in a style befitting the School of Science. Harry would have approved.

APPENDIX

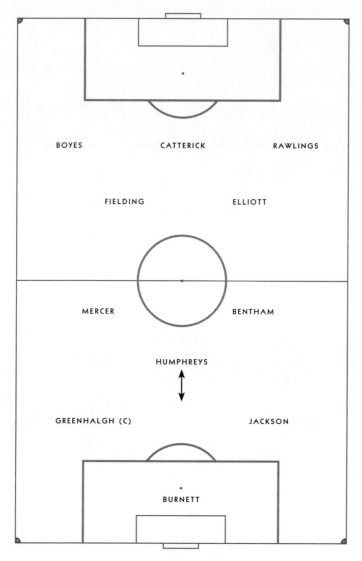

EVERTON
FA CUP TIE VS. PRESTON NORTH END – 5 JANUARY 1946
(FIRST POST-WAR COMPETITIVE FIXTURE)

Harry lined up at Deepdale as Everton's centre-forward in his first peacetime competitive fixture.

In the starting line-up only Greenhalgh, Boyes, Mercer and Bentham were regulars from the title winning team of 1939/40. Little had changed tactically from pre-war football with the 2-3-5 "WM" formation adopted. Humphreys, the centre-half "pivot" was the father of Gerry Humphreys, a member of the 1960's Everton squad under Harry.

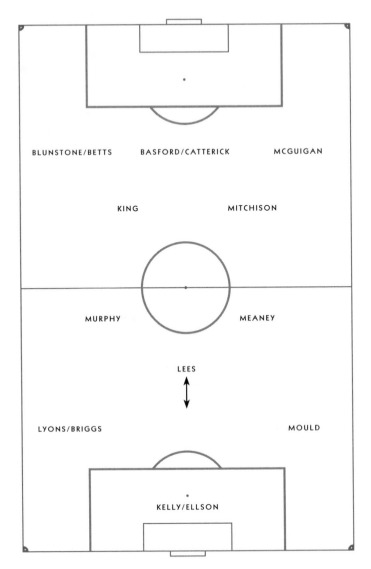

CREWE ALEXANDRA
THIRD DIVISION NORTH – 1952/53 SEASON

In Harry's first full season at Gresty Road he made only eight appearances in the forward line as Basford established himself as first-choice number nine. Blunstone had been switched to outside–left from inside-left and established a strong left-flank combination with Johnny King. Upon moving to Chelsea, Blunstone was replaced by Betts.

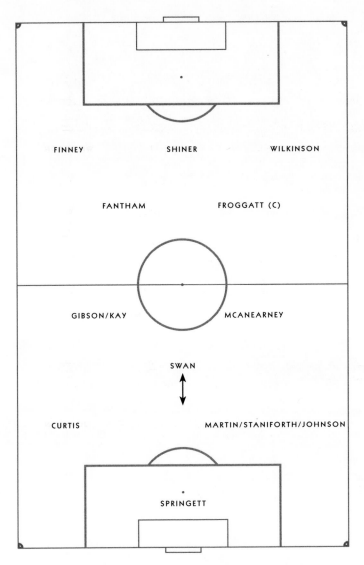

SHEFFIELD WEDNESDAY
SECOND DIVISION CHAMPIONS 1958/59

The WM formation remained popular until the mid-1960's. Centre-forward Shiner was supported in attack by Fantham, who came in for the departing Quixall, and Froggatt. Wilkinson and Finney alternated on the flanks. By mid-season Kay became first-choice left-half to complete a formidable trio alongside Swan and McAnearney.

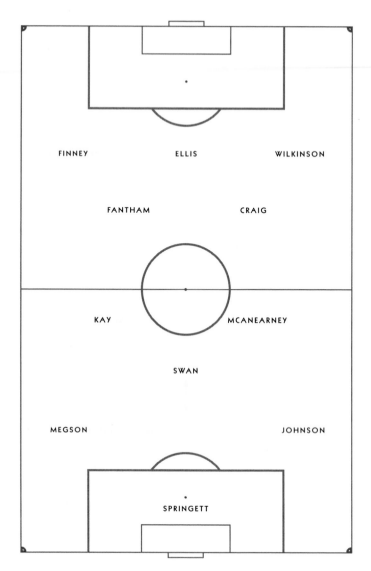

SHEFFIELD WEDNESDAY
FIRST DIVISION RUNNERS-UP 1960/61

The first-choice team was largely unchanged from the 1958/59 promotion season but veterans Curtis, Froggatt and Shiner had been superseded by Megson, Craig and Ellis respectively.

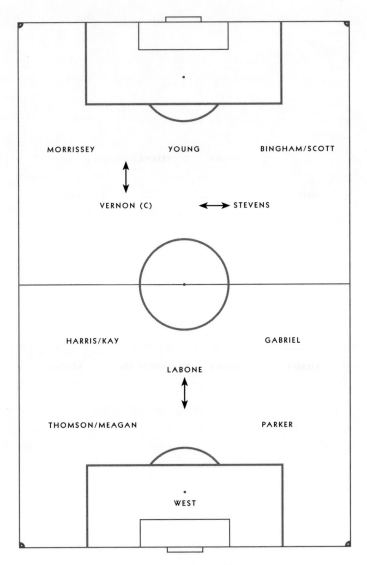

EVERTON
LEAGUE CHAMPIONS 1962/63

Although nominally a WM formation, Vernon, the inside-left forward, was allowed freedom to attack alongside Alex Young, leaving fellow Stevens to pick up his defensive duties. Kay and Scott replaced Harris and Bingham mid-season.

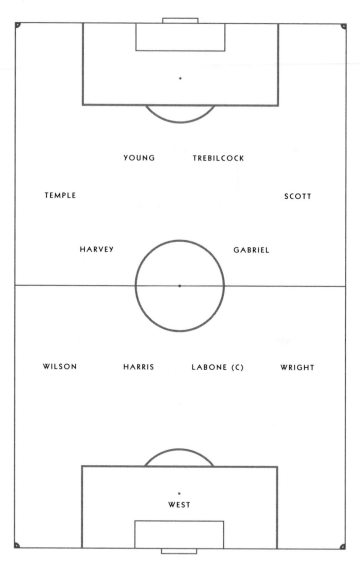

E V E R T O N
FA CUP WINNERS – MAY 1966

The cup-winning team was in transition from the squad inherited from Johnny Carey to a younger team using home-developed talent. The revised incorporated two centre halves in Harris and Labone with Gabriel and Harvey in more advanced half-back positions. A four man forward line saw surprise selection Trebilcock play off Young.

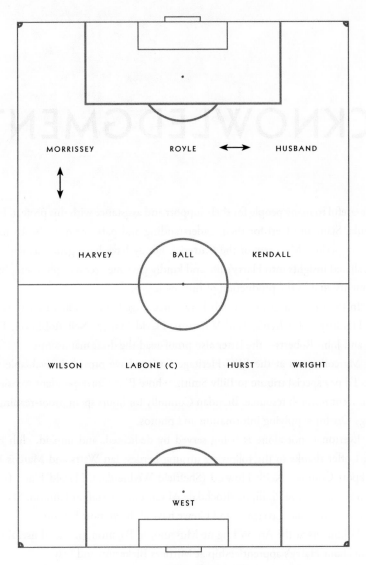

EVERTON
LEAGUE CHAMPIONS 1969/70

The culmination of Harry's project to create a fluid, attacking side inspired by the Hungarian national team of the 1950s. A fluid 4-3-3 formation, focussing on young players developed at Bellefield, A four-man defensive unit was marshalled by Labone. Harvey, Kendall and Ball formed a diminutive and mobile three-man midfield unit, bolstered by left-sided forward Morrissey dropping back to assist as required. Royle operated at centre-forward with Husband in a floating right-sided attacking role. Kendall and Wright made use of space created on right-flank by Husband's forays into the centre.

ACKNOWLEDGMENTS

I am grateful to many people for their support and assistance with this project. Firstly to Paula, Siân, and Ceri for their understanding and patience over the 18-month gestation period. Members of the Catterick family have been generous with their time, shared insights into Harry's life and kindly gave me access to photographs and documents vital to the production of this book.

In the early stages of research I was encouraged, and given wise counsel, by Don Hardisty, John Keith, Paul Wharton, David France, Neil Robinson, David Exall and John Roberts – the latter also proof-read the draft manuscript.

My colleagues at the EFC Heritage Society have provided invaluable assistance. I'd pay special tribute to Billy Smith, whose Blue Correspondent website is a magnificent research resource, Brendan Connolly for hours spent proof-reading and George Orr for supplying information and photos.

Everton is not alone is being served by dedicated, and unpaid, club historians. I offer thanks to the following unsung heroes: Ian Watts and Marcus Heap (Stockport County), Keith Howard (Sheffield Wednesday), Harold Finch (Crewe Alexandra) and Steve Phillipps (Rochdale AFC). Library staff at Chilton, Sheffield, Stockport, Rochdale, Liverpool and Crewe have all been most helpful.

Volunteers at the Anson Engine Museum, in Poynton, provided useful information about Harry's apprenticeship at Mirrlees Bickerton and Day.

Everton Former Players' Foundation, which offers valuable support to ex-players, helped with contacting some players. Steve Zocek also came to my aid on several occasions.

Thanks to the following who were happy either to be interviewed or correspond with me: Harry Bennett, Frank Blunstone, Alex Bruce, Len Capeling, John Connolly, Frank D'Arcy, Terry Darracott, Keith Ellis, Mike Ellis, David Exall, Tom Gardner, Ronny Goodlass, Alan Gowling, Billy Griffin, Eric Harrison, Colin Harvey, Chris Hassell, Gerry Humphries, John Hurst, Jimmy Husband, Gary Imlach,

Tommy Jackson, David Johnson, Hyder Jawad, Tony Kay, Howard Kendall, Dr Vaughan Lancaster-Thomas, Mark Lawrenson, James Lawton, Gordon Lee, Ken Loach, John McLaughlan, Lawrie McMenemy, Tony McNamara, David Marsh, Mick Meagan, Don Megson, Tony Morley, James Mossop, Brian Nicholson, Stan Osborne, Fred Pickering, Mark Platt, David Prentice, John Quinn, Joe Royle, Neville Smith, Gary Talbot, Becky Tallentire, George Telfer, Derek Temple, Ray Terry, Mel Tottoh, Mike Trebilcock, Ray Veall, Alan Whittle, Frank Wignall, Derek Wilkinson, Fred Willder, Graham Wilson, Colin Wood, Alex Young, Gerry Young.

Finally, heartfelt thanks to Ian Allen for his invaluable copy-editing of the final draft and James Corbett at deCoubertin Books for his guiding hand throughout this process. Thank you also to Thomas Regan of Milkyone Creative and Sabahat Muhammad for their work on design and production.

If I have omitted anyone unintentionally please accept my apologies.

BIBLIOGRAPHY

Books

The Everton Encyclopedia, James Corbett (deCoubertin, 2012)

Everton: The School of Science, James Corbett (Macmillan, 2003)

Everton, The Official Centenary History, John Roberts (Granada Publishing/ Mayflower Books, 1978)

Everton, The Official Complete Record, Steve Johnson (de Coubertin, 2010)

Colin Harvey's Everton Secrets, John Keith/Colin Harvey (Sport Media, 2005)

Only the Best is Good Enough, Howard Kendall/Ian Ross (Mainstream Publishing, 1991)

Love Affairs and Marriage, My Life in Football, Howard Kendall (de Coubertin, 2013)

Alex Young – The Golden Vision, Alex Young/David France (Skript Publishing, 2008)

Everton in the 1940s – The Lost Decade, George Orr (Blue Blood, 2013)

Everton in the Sixties: A Golden Era, George Orr (Blue Blood, 1997)

Everton in the Seventies: Singing the Blues, George Orr (Blue Blood, 1996)

Everton in the 1970s, Tim Jepson (2012)

Everton Player by Player, Ivan Ponting (Hamlyn, 1998)

Goodison Glory, Ken Rogers (Breedon Books, 2000)

The People's Club, David Prentice (Sport Media, 2007)

The Official Everton Autobiography, compiled by James Cleary (Sport Media, 2012)

Forever Everton, Stephen F. Kelly (Queen Anne Press, 1987)

Gwladys Street's Blue Book, David France (Skript, 2002)

Dr Everton's Magnificent Obsession, David France and David Prentice (Sport Media, 2008)

Everton Greats – Where are They Now?, Jon Berman and Malcolm Dome (Mainstream Publishing, 1997)

The Everton Story, Derek Hodgson (Arthur Baker, 1979)

My Father and Other Working Class Heroes, Gary Imlach (Yellow Jersey, 2005)

Making the Grade, Stan Osborne (Legends Publishing, 2012)

Bobby Collins – The Wee Barra, David Saffer/Bobby Collins (Tempus Publishing, 2004)

Joe Royle – The Autobiography, Joe Royle (BBC Books, 2007)

Playing Extra Time, Alan Ball (Sidgwick & Jackson, 2004)

Talking Blue, Becky Tallentire (Breedon Books, 2004)

Still Talking Blue, Becky Tallentire (Mainsteam Media, 2001)

Real Footballers Wives, Becky Tallentire (Mainstream Publishing, 2012)

Gwladys Street's Holy Trinity, David France and Becky Tallentire (Skript Publishing, 2001)

Brian Harris, The Authorised Biography, Chris Westcott (Tempus Publishing, 2003)

Dream, Believe, Achieve, Mike Trebilcock (Arthur H. Stockwell Ltd, 2008)

Goals at Goodison, Alex Young (Pelham Books 1968)

Bill Nicholson – Football's Perfectionist, Brian Scovell (John Blake Publishing, 2011)

Three Sides of the Mersey, Rogan Taylor, John Williams, Andrew Ward (Robson Books, 1993)

20 Legends: Sheffield Wednesday, Tom Whitworth and Chris Olewicz (Vertical Editions, 2012)

Sheffield Wednesday – Illustrating the Greats, Michael Liversidge and Gary Mackender (Pickard Communication, 2004)

Wednesday!, Keith Farnsworth (Sheffield City Libraries, 1982)

Shankly – My Story, John Roberts (Sport Media, 2009)

Joe Fagan: Reluctant Champion, Andrew Fagan and Mark Platt (Aurum Press, 2011)

After the Ball – My Autobiography, Nobby Stiles (Hodder and Stoughton, 2003)

Crewe Alexandra, Match by Match, Marco Crisp (Tony Brown, 1997)

Crewe Alexandra Football Club – 100 Greats, Harold Finch (The History Press, 2003)

Legends of Stockport County, Guy Nelson (At Heart Ltd, 2008)

Banksy – The Autobiography, Gordon Banks (Penguin, 2003)

Premier and Football League Players Records 1945–2005, Barry J. Hugman (Queen Anne Press, 2005)

Inverting the Pyramid, Jonathan Wilson (Orion, 2009)

Soccer at War 1939–1945, Jack Rollin (Willow Books, 1985)

The Man Who Made Littlewoods: The Story of John Moores, Barbara Clegg (Hodder & Stoughton, 1993)

Football League Book Number 1, Editor: Harry Brown (Football League Ltd/Arthur Baker Ltd, 1970)

BIBLIOGRAPHY

Newspapers, Periodicals and Websites

Everton FC programmes
Daily Express
Daily Mail
The People
Liverpool Echo
Liverpool Daily Post
Liverpool Evening Express
Lancashire Evening Post
Northern Echo
Crewe Chronicle
Stockport Advertiser
Rochdale Observer
Yorkshire Post
Sunday Mirror
The Star and Green 'Un (Sheffield)
Charles Buchan's Football Monthly
Blue Blood fanzine (George Orr)
When Skies are Grey
bluecorrespondent.co.uk (compiled by Billy Smith)
toffeeweb.com
gogogocounty.org
mighty.leeds.co.uk
evertoncollection.org.uk (Everton board minute books)

INDEX

INDEX